A NATIVE'S GUIDE TO NORTHWEST INDIANA

By Mark Skertic

• • • • • • • • • • • • • • • • • •

Featuring photography by John J. Watkins

First Edition

LAKE CLAREMONT PRESS

www.lakeclaremont.com
Chicago

A Native's Guide to Northwest Indiana
by Mark Skertic

Published August, 2003 by:

4650 N. Rockwell St.
Chicago, IL 60625
773/583-7800; lcp@lakeclaremont.com
LAKE CLAREMONT PRESS www.lakeclaremont.com

Publisher's Cataloging-in-Publication
(Provided by Quality Books, Inc.)

Skertic, Mark.
    A Native's guide to Northwest Indiana / Mark Skertic.
    — 1st ed.
        p. cm.
    Includes bibliographical references and index.
    LCCN: 2001099076
    ISBN: 1-893121-08-9

    1. Indiana—Guidebooks.   I. Title.

F524.3.S54 2002   917.72'904'44
                                       QBI02-200166

Printed in the United States of America by United Graphics,
an employee-owned company based in Mattoon, Illinois.

06 05 04 03   10 9 8 7 6 5 4 3 2 1

For Alison, Sarah, and Annie

Courtesy of the Lake County Convention and Visitors Bureau.

Publisher's Credits

Cover design by Timothy Kocher. Interior design by Sharon Wood-house. Principal photography by John J. Watkins. Maps by Mark Skertic. Lighthouse cover photo courtesy of the LaPorte County Convention & Visitors Bureau. Editing by Bruce Clorfene and Sharon Woodhouse. Proofreading by Karen Formanski, Sharon Woodhouse, and Ken Woodhouse. Layout by Sharon Woodhouse and Ken Woodhouse. Indexing by Ken Woodhouse and Karen Formanski.

Typography

The text of *A Native's Guide to Northwest Indiana* was set in Garamond, with headings in CAC Norm Heavy.

Notice

CONTENTS

• • • • • • • • • • • • • • •

Acknowledgments vii

Introduction 3

LaPorte County 9
  Kingsbury 13
  LaPorte...17
  Long Beach.. 23
  Michigan City 25
  Wanatah 37
  Westville.. 39

Lake County..41
  Cedar Lake.. 47
  Crown Point..51
  Dyer... 59
  East Chicago 63
  Gary...71
  Griffith 89
  Hammond 95
  Highland 109
  Hobart..115
  Lowell.. 123
  Merrillville... 127
  Munster 133
  St. John.. 143
  Schererville 147
  Schneider 149
  Whiting...151

Porter County 159
   Beverly Shores 163
   Chesterton...167
   Hebron...173
   Kouts..177
   Ogden Dunes...179
   Portage..181
   Porter 185
   Town of Pines 189
   Valparaiso...191

Recreation 205
   Antiques..207
   Boating..217
   Christmas Trees...223
   Gaming..225
   Golf Courses...235
   Lakeshore 247
   Shopping...275
   Theater..279

Other Good Stuff to Know 287
   Media..289
   Transportation..297
   Miscellaneous...305

Bibliography...309
Index 311

About the Author..324

ACKNOWLEDGMENTS

Many people are responsible for this book, even if most don't realize it: my parents, who raised me in Northwest Indiana, my wife and daughters who enjoy exploring the area, my friends and family who suggest new places to visit. My experiences with all of them convinced me it was time to tell the world that Northwest Indiana is more than a collection of belching industries jamming the lakefront.

It was Sharon Woodhouse, my publisher, who actually suggested doing a book. Her invitation came after I fired off an e-mail wondering why Northwest Indiana wasn't available in the *A Native's Guide to . . .* series. I might not have accepted her challenge if I'd known just how much work it was going to be.

I was raised in Hammond, lived there until I was eighteen, and thought I knew the city pretty well. My grandfather, Joseph Klen, was its mayor during the early 1970s. But I still learned a lot about that city and its neighbors while working on this book.

This couldn't have been done without the help and resources of the visitor centers in Lake, Porter, and LaPorte Counties. They have stacks of information and were willing to answer my questions and share some of their resources. Their help, advice, and suggestions are appreciated.

The tips in the golfing chapter wouldn't be there without the help of Doug and David Dedelow and Bob (the Godfather) Lukas. My sister, Susan Dedelow, the best cook I know, helped make sure I knew what I was talking about when I started recommending restaurants.

Thanks also to Lee Bey, former *Chicago Sun-Times* architecture critic, whose work inspired me to seek out some of Northwest Indiana's distinctive buildings and history, and to Steve Mc-Shane, curator of the Calumet Regional Archives. The resources Steve provided on earlier writing projects showed me things about the area's history I had never known.

Others who provided help include David Dabagia and Yvonne M. Clancy of the LaPorte County Convention & Visitors Bureau; Lorelei Weimer of the Porter County Convention, Recreation & Visitor Commission; Rebecca Crabb, Lake County historian; Larry Clark, Porter County historian; Katie Holderby of the Lake County Convention and Visitors Bureau, former bureau president Speros Batistatos, and former director of communications Carrie Ann Swinford; Gloria Dosen of the East Chicago Public Library's East Chicago Room; Leslie "Tutu" Hurubean; Paul Myers of Marktown; Brian Olszewski, editor of *Northwest Indiana Catholic*; Bruce Woods of the Lake County Historical Society; Bonnie Quigley of LaPorte Little Theatre; and Martha Wright, reference librarian at the Indiana State Library.

A variety of local government offices were also very helpful in providing information.

I also have to thank the people who put out the *Times* and *Post-Tribune* newspapers. For more than a year now I've been reading both each morning, clipping notices of festivals, ripping out restaurant reviews of places I had to try, learning about things at the lakeshore I never knew about. The people at those newspapers do good work.

It's because of the talent of John J. Watkins that this book captures the beauty of Northwest Indiana. His fine photography is far greater proof than anything I have written that this is a region of great wonder.

One final note: If you are familiar with Northwest Indiana, you may find as you read that I have omitted your favorite restaurant, attraction, festival, or even community. I apologize for those omissions up front. I have tried to list places and events that would not only be of interest to those from the area, but to visitors as well. If you are still not satisfied with that explanation, please make a note of whatever it is you think I should have included and pass it along to my publisher. You'll be giving me a great argument in favor of issuing a second edition.

A Native's Guide to Northwest Indiana

Photo by the author.

Indiana Dunes National Lakeshore beach at Beverly Shores.

Those dunes are to the Midwest what the Grand Canyon is to Arizona and the Yosemite to California.

—CARL SANDBURG

Courtesy of the Lake County Convention and Visitors Bureau.

A Lake County sunset.

INTRODUCTION

• • • • • • • • • • • • • • •

There is a trick question teachers in Northwest Indiana love to include in quizzes in government classes: Who is the governor of Indiana? It's a sure bet some kids are going to get it wrong because many will name the governor of Illinois.

It's not that they're not bright, but they are operating under a handicap. Children living in this corner of Indiana may never see their governor on television, because every day the dominant TV and radio news carry stories about Illinois's political leaders, about Chicago sports teams, and about Chicago's suburbs.

This is the part of Indiana where kids grow up dreaming they'll play for the Chicago Bears and Bulls, not the Indianapolis Colts and Pacers. This is that region of Greater Chicago that is not in Illinois, but is still so closely tied to Chicago that some Northwest Indiana cities continue Chicago's system of numbering streets by how many blocks they are from the Loop. Efforts to market the area by some businesses have dubbed it "Chicago's neighboring south shore."

To local residents, though, much of Northwest Indiana is simply known as the Calumet Region, or just "the Region" for short. It's a name that dates back centuries, to the time when Native Americans walked through the tall grass that covered much of the land south of the mighty dunes. When you hear people talk about "Regionites" or "Region Rats," they're talking about the local natives. As you move east, people start to refer to the area as "Duneland" or finally "Michiana" because of the closeness to southern Michigan.

Welcome to Northwest Indiana. A decade ago the area was derided as another notch on the rust belt, a relic of an industrial age that is long gone. People didn't move here, the stories said. This was a place to move from, and people left in droves.

But not any more.

The industries that founded places like Gary and Portage are still there, and people are no longer fleeing. All three of the counties featured in this book have seen population growth in recent years. The communities are growing in other ways, too—expanding their cultural offerings and embracing their history.

So who is this book for? People who already live here and are looking for something to do on the weekend? Chicagoans who turn up their noses at ever venturing down into "Hoosierville"? Vacationers from Indianapolis, Detroit, or Cleveland who will pass through Northwest Indiana en route to Chicago?

I hope all those groups find something useful in these pages.

There are some surprises here even for those who have called the Calumet Region home all their lives. There are people in Hammond who have never taken in the beauty of Valparaiso's historic Opera House, and Michigan City dwellers who don't know about Marktown, the tiny village in East Chicago that was created as a company town. In addition to a list of things to see and do, I've tried to include details about the local history, architecture, geography, and whatever else is worth knowing about this corner of Indiana.

Defining "Northwest Indiana" isn't an exact science. For purposes of this book, I've focused on the three counties that hug the southern tip of Lake Michigan—Lake, Porter, and LaPorte. Good arguments might be made for considering some of the counties south of these three, or counties that are further east. But Lake, Porter, and LaPorte are the largest; they all have beaches, good restaurants, shopping, and plenty of entertainment options.

The book includes an introduction to each, and information about what you'll find in the major communities located there. Visitors who think Indiana is only home to cows, corn, and basketball will be surprised at the range of offerings for a variety of tastes, including a symphony, museums, and one of the most popular theaters in the Midwest.

Many communities claim a part of the lakeshore, so that distinctive stretch of sand and forest gets its own chapter. As does riverboat gaming, the attraction that has brought millions of visitors to the area in recent years. There are also sections on transportation, to make getting around easier; media, so you can find out what's happening; golf courses; and antique stores.

When choosing restaurants to recommend, I've avoided the national chains. The area has its share of Applebee's, Bennigan's, Chuck E. Cheeses, and the like, and visitors already know what to expect from these. I have tried to list some of the area's most impressive restaurants, along with details on what foods they're known for and how kid-friendly they are. The area has plenty of great places to eat, and some have surely escaped my notice. So don't assume that because some place isn't mentioned it's no good.

There are also maps included with each county. Northwest Indiana is one of those urban areas so packed with cities and towns that in a 20-minute drive you can easily pass through a half-dozen of them.

Every county has its own visitors bureau. Phone numbers are included in each county's introduction. If you need help planning a weekend in the region, want details on upcoming shows, or just need to know when Whiting's next Pierogi Festival is or the date of the upcoming Oz Fest in Michigan City, give these folks a call.

Still not convinced? OK, it's time to dispel The Five Myths about Northwest Indiana:

Myth 1.
It's so far from Chicago, who has time to drive there?
It's not far from Chicago—Chicago's Southeast Side actually runs up against Hammond. There are many places in the northwest corner of Hammond where you can cross the street and be in Chicago. Via the Skyway (the eight-story toll road that runs from Hammond to the city) you can be in the heart of the Loop in 30 minutes. Contrast that with a Chicago suburb like Naperville, where the commute can run 45 minutes or more on a good day.

Myth 2.
It's all steel mills and heavy industry; who would want to go there?
The steel mills here produce more steel than any other part of the country. And it's no secret that in an earlier period their owners leveled dunes and tore up the lakeshore to establish themselves. But in recent decades, industrialists and environmentalists have worked to coexist. The mills and other industry have established natural habitats on their land and spent millions of dollars and donated time for preservation efforts.

Would the lakeshore look even better if off in the distance you couldn't see the twinkling lights at the Burns Harbor refinery? Sure. But the mills aren't going anywhere, and to stay away because of them means depriving yourself of seeing an incredible natural wonder.

Myth 3.
Aren't the big cities there scary places where gangs rule the streets?

Some of the cities have had crime problems, just like any urban area. And just like places like Chicago, New York, Cleveland, or Kansas City, there are some areas you don't wander around if you don't know where you're going. So don't just pick a neighborhood and decide to check out some architecture you've heard about at 2 A.M.! But this isn't the Old West, and people aren't walking around with guns strapped to their hips waiting to shoot it out. The crime rate in most communities here has dropped dramatically in recent years.

The bottom line: Most places in Northwest Indiana are safe, comfortable, and filled with friendly people.

Myth 4.
It's a cultural wasteland, and if you want to have fun, don't you have to go to Chicago?

Chicago is the greatest city on earth (in the author's limited experience globe hopping), and it's hard to compete with its sports, museums, and other attractions. But if you're looking for a fun evening it doesn't mean you have to head to the Loop. Some of the Chicago area's best restaurants are in Northwest Indiana, which also happens to be home to great nightspots, history, theater, casino gaming, challenging golf courses, and a rich history.

Once they get off the expressways and into the communities, first-time visitors are often surprised by the area's ethnic and racial tapestry. Fact is, you won't find a better melting pot anywhere else in the state. Immigrants were lured here in the first half of the twentieth century by the chance to earn a living in the steel mills. In the decades since, the immigrant influx has continued.

Photo by John J. Watkins.

Come back to Northwest Indiana and the dunes
for wintertime activities like cross-country skiing.

Myth 5.
OK, so maybe it's worth coming in the summer to spend a
day at the dunes and then go someplace for dinner. But
who wants to come to Northwest Indiana in the dead of
winter?
The dunes don't shut down in the winter, and there are plenty
of reasons to visit them in January—for hikes on frosty trails
and cross-country skiing. There's also ice skating, huge sledding
hills, and ice fishing. There's CBA basketball, minor league
baseball, the Gary Air Show, and the Christmas display at
Michigan City's Washington Park. And all those great restaurants, gambling boats, and theaters that you tried in the summer
are all waiting for you the rest of the year.

LAPORTE COUNTY

LaPorte County 11

Kingsbury 13
LaPorte 17
Long Beach 23
Michigan City 25
Wanatah..37
Westville 39

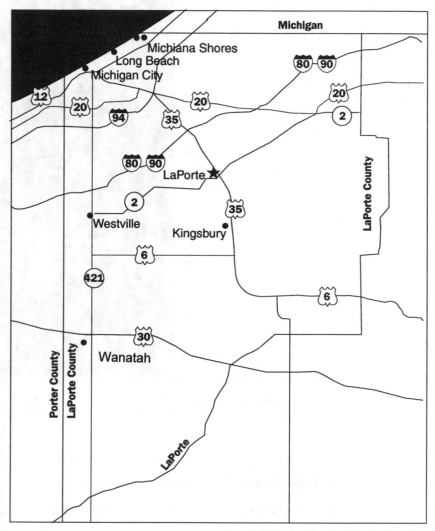

LaPorte County, Indiana

LAPORTE COUNTY

• • • • • • • • • • • • • •

Created: May 28, 1832
Named after: French word for "door"
County seat: LaPorte
Population: 110,106
Median age: 37.1
Land area: 598 square miles

French fur traders gave this county its name in the seventeenth century. LaPorte was the place where the forests began to give way to prairie. It was also the place to gain access to Lake Michigan.

Now, it's the spot in Northwest Indiana where many Chicagoans flee to escape the city. The lakeshore here is filled with summer homes and weekend getaways.

This is also the portion of Northwest Indiana where the influence of Chicago starts to give way and the region seems more like the rest of Indiana. Go just one more county east and you'll be in St. Joseph County, home to South Bend and the University of Notre Dame.

Convention and Visitors Bureau
1502 S. Meer Rd.
Michigan City
219/872-5055
800/685-7174
www.harborcountry-in.org
If you're visiting for the first time, make your first stop the LaPorte County Convention and Visitors Bureau. The office

Photo by John J. Watkins.

The Michigan City Lighthouse, a popular LaPorte County attraction.

has maps and event information and can offer suggestions about where to stay and dine. The bureau calls this area Harbor Country because of its lakefront homes and sand dunes.

County Fair
LaPorte County Fairgrounds
2581 W. State Road 2
LaPorte
219/362-2647
Each July the county fair features 4-H exhibits, livestock competition, a demolition derby, harness racing, and carnival rides. In recent years, the entertainment has included the Oak Ridge Boys.

KINGSBURY

Incorporated: 1940
Population: 229
Median age: 37.6
Size: 0.59 square miles

This tiny LaPorte County town was once home to a military instillation. The armed services depot has been replaced with a popular wildlife area that attracts a variety of nature lovers. If you've wanted to get a look at deer, muskrats, ducks, geese, and other animals, this is a great place to visit. It's isolated and far from more crowded spots such as the dunes.

Possible danger from contaminated areas and hunters keeps away many who otherwise might want to look around. But a well-planned trip to Kingsbury is a worthwhile wilderness adventure.

Kingsbury State Fish and Wildlife Area
Hupp Rd.
219/393-3612
Located about ten miles southeast of LaPorte, Kingsbury State Fish and Wildlife Area covers 5,062 acres of trails and habitats, as well as part of the great Kankakee Marsh that once dominated much of the vicinity. The area is renowned with wildlife photographers, as well and hunters and those who love sport fishing.

Visitors will quickly note that part of the property is fenced off, and there are abandoned, grass-covered bunkers. This land was used by the military during much of the twentieth century;

shells, mortar rounds, and other ammunition needed by the armed services in World War II and Korea were produced on these grounds. Those restricted areas are sometimes contaminated, and it's best to just stay away from them.

The land was given to the state in 1965 to be operated as a park. Deer, pheasant, and ducks are among the animals that call this area home. Fishing is available in the **Kankakee River** and twenty-acre **Tamarack Lake**. Canoeing and bird watching are popular here. Just northwest of the park is the **Mixsawbah Fish Hatchery**, where salmon and trout are raised.

Kingsbury has a shooting range, isolated from much of the park by the fenced-off property. Admission to the park is free, but there are fees for hunting. Fishing licenses are required. *Directions: From I–80/90 or I–94, take U.S. 421 south to U.S. 6. Go east on U.S. 6 to U.S. 35. Go north of U.S. 35 to County Road 500 South. Go east to Hupp Road. The state park entrance is on Hupp Road.*

Canoe Trip
To take a long and beautiful trip down the Kankakee River, put in at the **Kingsbury Fish and Wildlife Area** and follow it all the way to the Illinois–Indiana state line. That's nearly 50 miles of canoeing and more than most can do in a day, but the jaunt westward can be divided into smaller segments. Begin heading west and you'll go through the Kankakee State Fish and Wildlife Area, past farm fields and wooded areas, and under Dunn's Bridge. (See the section on Kouts, pp. 178–179, to find out more about this notable structure's history.)

How long a trip you make is up to you. Several spots along the way are convenient as a finish. Indiana Rte. 49 (in Porter County, just south of Kouts) is approximately 20 miles and will take about eight hours. The take-out is located where the Rte. 49 bridge goes over the Kankakee River. Parking is available.

A longer trip for more experienced canoeists runs from Kingsbury to **Grand Kankakee Marsh County Park** in Hebron (see p. 174), about 15 miles beyond Rte. 49, and could take another six or more hours.

Making the journey from Grand Kankakee Marsh County Park to the LaSalle State Fish and Wildlife Area near the state line is another 15 miles, or about six hours of paddling time.

LAPORTE

Incorporated: November 4, 1835
Population: 21,621
Median age: 35.8
Nickname: Maple City
Land area: 11.3 square miles

The first white settlers arrived here in the 1830s, drawn by the numerous small lakes, which provided LaPorte's first industry: a steady supply of ice during winters. Today, those lakes provide plenty of summertime recreation.

LaPorte is known for its historical buildings and a downtown that is home to a large number of antique stores.

Hesston Steam Museum
1201 E. 1000 North
800/933-6845 (Visitors Bureau)
Since 1957, the Hesston Steam Museum has kept alive the memory of the days when steam powered the nation. The museum is on 155 acres of rural countryside outside LaPorte. Exhibits include three steam-powered trains and a sawmill. The longest train ride is a 2.5-mile trip through the forested grounds. The LaPorte County Historical Steam Society maintains most of the collection.

The museum's season kicks off on Memorial Day weekend with the **Whistle Stop Days** festival, a celebration of steam power. If you've never heard the old locomotives roar, you'll be impressed. Labor Day weekend brings the **Hesston Steam and Power Show**.

The volunteers who staff the museum love the old equipment and have lots of stories to share. Call ahead to see whether all exhibits will be running the day you visit. *Open Sat.–Sun. noon–5 p.m., Memorial Day–Labor Day; Sun. noon–5 p.m., Labor Day–Oct. Train rides are $3 for adults, $2 for children. Directions: From I–80/90, take exit 49 and go north six miles to County Road 1000 North. Go east about two miles.*

Door Prairie Auto Museum
2405 Indiana Ave.
219/326-1337
www.dpautomuseum.com
Peter Kesling, a local orthodontist, amassed a one-of-a-kind collection of rare automobiles, now housed in this 30,000-square-foot building. Highlights include one of the only 50 Tucker automobiles ever made (this burgundy-colored one is number 12), an 1886 Benz Motor Wagon, a 1951 Studebaker convertible, 1936 Rolls Royce, and a 1912 Ford Speedster.

The museum is housed in a 30,000-square-foot building. The tour showcases antique toys, classic aircraft, one a replica of the glider air travel pioneer Octave Chanute used in some of his experiments at the dunes, and a 1932 Pientenpol Air Camper airplane. The museum's Indiana Room features a rarity: a complete set of Indiana license plates, beginning with 1913 *Open Tue.–Sat. 10 a.m.–4:30 p.m., Sun. noon–4:30 p.m. Call ahead. Admission is $5 for adults, $4 for seniors, $3 for students, and free for 9 and under. It will take at least an hour to view the cars, which are stored on three levels.*

Soldiers Memorial Park
Grangemouth and Waverly Rds.
Some say the prettiest sunsets in the area are visible in this park, which sits next to **Stone Lake**. The lake has fishing, and the park has hiking trails.

LaPorte County Public Library
904 Indiana Ave.
219/362-6156
Another library built with a gift from Andrew Carnegie, the LaPorte Library has more than tripled in size since 1916. Care has been taken to retain the architectural integrity of the original building. A 1990 addition covered up a 1961 addition that was not architecturally compatible. The original tile roof has been replicated and beautiful half-moon windows remain, as do marble stairs and limestone columns.
Open Mon.–Thu. 9 a.m.–8 p.m., Fri. 9 a.m.–6 p.m., Sat. 9 a.m.– 5 p.m.

LaPorte County Historical Museum
809 State St.
219/326-6808, ext. 276
www.lapcohistsoc.org
Ever hear of Belle Gunness, accused of killing 13 people for the insurance money in the early twentieth century? She eluded police and was never caught. You can learn more about her legend here, as well as other stories from the early days of LaPorte County.

Tucked in the LaPorte County Government complex, the museum's exhibits range from a collection of antique firearms and weapons that date back 200 years, antique toys, and family heirlooms, to scenes of a Victorian parlor and business office from the 1920s. The sports display includes the "Good-Will Bell," the prize once claimed by the winner of the annual Michigan City and LaPorte High Schools football game. The museum is next door to another historical place—the LaPorte County Courthouse, a red sandstone building erected in 1894.
Open Tue.–Sat. 10 a.m.–4:30 p.m.

Luhr County Park and Nature Center
3178 S. County Rd. 150 West
219/324-5855
www.alco.org/countyparks
A great place to take the family. The park features paved and unpaved hiking trails and a nature center with educational programs and live animals. A 2.5-acre pond is stocked with fish, and poles can be rented for $1. Bring your own bait.
The nature center is open Wed.–Sun. 12:30 p.m.–4:30 p.m. Mar. 1–Oct. 31; Sat.–Sun. 12:30 p.m.–4:30 p.m. Nov. 1–Feb. 28.

Back Road Brewery
308 Perry St.
219/362-7623
www.backroadbrewery.com
This local brewery offers free tours of its facility. Specialty brews include Belle Gunness Stout, named for the infamous killer. Also try the Midwest Indiana Pale Ale and the Back Road Ale.
Open Sat. 1 p.m.–4 p.m.

EVENTS

LaPorte County Antique Shows
LaPorte County Fairgrounds
2581 W. State Rd. 2
800/685-7174
During the several antique shows held here each year, nearly 200 dealers fill four buildings and spill over into the surrounding grounds. The shows draw collectors from Indiana and adjoining states.
Call for schedule.

Haunted Trail
Luhr County Park
3178 S. County Rd. 150 West
219/324-5855
Held in late October, a chance to hike through haunted woods!
On the trail, kids meet some scary—and some pretty funny—
characters.
Tickets go on sale more than a month before Haunted Trail weekend. Call for details. Admission is $3 per person. Children under five get in free.

DINING

Cafe L'Amour
701 Lincolnway
219/324-5683
No matter how good a meal you have at Cafe L'Amour, when you tell people about this restaurant in the old First National Bank building, the first thing you're likely to mention is the mural. The hand-painted depiction of a Paris street covers an entire wall. A bar is on the first floor, and a winding staircase leads to the upstairs dining room, where main course favorites include rack of lamb, veal, salmon, and filet mignon. Children will enjoy the pizza or some of the pasta dishes. Call for reservations.
Open for lunch, Mon.–Sat. 11 a.m.–2 p.m.; for dinner, Tue., Thu.–Sat. at 5 p.m.

Heston Bar
1000 North and Fail Rd.
219/778-2938
www.hestonbar.com
Known for its steaks and prime rib, the Heston Bar also has a nice selection of seafood. Portions are large, and this restaurant is known for making sure you leave satisfied. A children's menu

is available.
Open Mon.–Fri. 5 p.m.–10 p.m., Sat. 4:30 p.m.–10 p.m., Sun. 3 p.m.–9 p.m.

Roskoe's
1004 Lakeside
219/325-3880
www.pleastshore.com
Located next to the Blue Heron Inn, Roskoe's offers a relaxing view of Pine Lake. Their specialty is Cajun shrimp, though all the seafood here is good, and Roskoe's has some of the area's best baby back ribs. Friday and Saturday nights feature musicians who stroll through the dining room or tableside magicians.
Open Mon.–Thu. 11 a.m.–9 p.m., Fri.–Sat. 11 a.m.–10 p.m., Sun. 9:30 a.m.–9 p.m.; brunch is served 9:30 a.m.–2 p.m.

LONG BEACH

● ● ● ● ● ● ● ● ● ● ● ● ● ● ●

Incorporated: July 5, 1921
Population: 1,559
Median age: 50.5
Land area: 1.04 square miles

Long Beach, like many of its neighbors, was intended to be a summer getaway for Chicago's upper class. Local legend insists that this was one of the places mobsters like Al Capone would come to get away from business in the city. There are even stories that one of the summer cottages resembled a gun from the air. It would have been a good place to hide: houses are set amid the rolling sand dunes, providing plenty of privacy.

While Capone may or may not have sojourned here, there was one resident who did achieve a level of fame. In the early 1920s, John Lloyd Wright, the son of Frank Lloyd Wright, opened a studio in Long Beach, working here for nearly a quarter century. The younger Wright designed several homes in the area, a school, and the town hall in Long Beach.

In the 1990s there were efforts to save the Wright school and town hall buildings. The villa-like school was turned into a community center. It has been expanded over the years to keep up with a growing student population, but about one-third of the building is Wright's original design. It houses art galleries and is used regularly for reunions, receptions, and other events.

The battle over the town hall was more contentious. The building was too small and leaked, bricks were loose, and the electrical work couldn't meet modern needs, according to

Photo by John J. Watkins.

The Long Beach Town Hall, designed by John Lloyd Wright.

council president Tom Ringo. Preservationists wanted the building saved as a classic example of Wright's work. The brick building is three stories in the center, with one-story spaces on each side. *Chicago Sun-Times* architecture critic Lee Bey called it "purposeful architecture. Every bit of the superfluous is cut away from the exterior, allowing the building to speak for itself through its massing, texture and shadow." Bey's research found that the building might have been inspired by Dutch modernist Willem Dudok's design for a town hall in the Netherlands.

A final note: Even if you've never seen a John Lloyd Wright building, you've probably seen one other thing he was responsible for. He invented the popular children's toy, Lincoln Logs.

MICHIGAN CITY

• • • • • • • • • • • • • • •

Incorporated: February 8, 1836
Population: 32,900
Median age: 35.2
Size: 19.6 square miles

In early nineteenth century, proponents thought Michigan City, and not Chicago, was going to be the big city on Lake Michigan. It had everything going for it: a commercial area, industry, and popularity with travelers. But delays in building a harbor and the rapid growth of Chicago ended that dream.

Surveyors arrived in Michigan City in the 1820s, and the area was settled in the early 1830s. Major Isaac C. Elston of downstate Crawfordsville bought land, and soon a town was laid out on the low and swampy land.

Huge sand dunes, including the **Hoosier Slide**, dominated the lakefront, and sand kept nearly closing the mouth of **Trail Creek**, the tiny waterway through the area to Lake Michigan. Despite those problems, Michigan City soon developed into a port town, with goods arriving from the east and grain and other farm goods being shipped out.

The Michigan Central Railroad began running through the community in 1852 bringing more business and industry and an influx of European immigrants to work the new jobs.

In the late 1800s, workers began mining the nearly 200-foot Hoosier Slide sand dune. Its sand was used for glassmaking and as fill for Chicago's Jackson Park. By 1920 an estimated 13.5

Photo by John J. Watkins.

A view of the Michigan City marina.

million tons of sand had been moved. The dune is now completely gone, and the level site is the home of an electricity generating plant.

Today Michigan City is a city with many elements from its early days still intact. The downtown district, for instance, retains several examples of late nineteenth- and early twentieth-century architecture.

One of its famous natives is Anne Baxter, who won the 1946 Best Supporting Actress Oscar for her role in *The Razor's Edge* and was nominated for a Best Actress award for *All About Eve*. She is also the granddaughter of Frank Lloyd Wright.

Washington Park
Lakeshore Dr.
219/873-1506
Many visitors spend their whole day in this 100-acre park and on the adjoining beach. It's really several attractions in one: a jewel of a park, a great stretch of beach with a marina, the home of an historic lighthouse, and one of the best zoos in Indiana for children.

At the entrance is a huge monument honoring the soldiers and sailors who died in the Civil War. The **Winterbotham Monument** was built in 1893, thanks to the efforts of John Winterbotham, a politician, banker, and businessman.

As you pull into the park, you'll see the stunning **Naval Armory Building**. Still in use, the Art Deco structure was built in 1932. A World War I monument inside the park, a six-foot bronze doughboy on a 13-foot granite pedestal, was dedicated in 1926. Walking through the park you can't miss the bandstand, built in 1911. President Clinton spoke here in 1995.

Annual events include a summer festival and Columbia yacht race each June, the **Lakefront Art Festival** in August, and a Decem-

Photos by the author.

The limestone tower and a bear in the Michigan City Zoo.

ber **Festival of Lights**.
Directions: From I–94, exit U.S. 421 north. This becomes Franklin Street in Michigan City. Follow Franklin through the city and into the park.

Washington Park Zoo
115 Lakeshore Dr.
219/873-1510
www.emichigancity.com/cityhall/departments/zoo
Washington Park opened in 1927 when a few small animals were cared for in shelters. Today it's one of the state's oldest zoos. A six-story limestone lookout tower dominates one corner of the park. Designed by architect Fred Ahlgrim and built by the Works Progress Administration during the Depression, it was created to offer a great view of the park and lake.

Kids love **Monkey Island**, the zoo's outdoor jungle gym for primates, the Siberian tiger, the birdhouse, and the barn, where they can pet the animals. Feeding times are posted so everyone can watch handlers tossing steaks and other dinnertime treats to the big cats. Another popular stop is the **Children's Castle** that houses the reptile collection. Its design was reportedly based on the insignia of the Army Corps of Engineers. *Open daily 10:30 a.m.–4 p.m., Apr. 1–Memorial Day; 10:30 a.m.–6 p.m., Memorial Day–Labor Day; 10:30 a.m.–4 p.m. Labor Day–Oct.; closed Nov.–Mar. Admission is $4 for adults, $3 for senior citizens, $2 for children ages 3–11; those under 2 get in free. Discount membership plans are available.*

Old Lighthouse Museum
Heisman Harbor Rd.
219/872-6133
www.michigancity.com/MCHistorical/index.htm
The first lighthouse on this site was built in 1837; the current building went up in 1958 with a light that could be seen for 15 miles. John M. Clarkson was the first lighthouse keeper, followed by Harriet Colfax, who took over in 1861 and kept the job until 1904. The same year Colfax retired, the light was moved to the end of the East Pier. The old building continued to provide a home for the lighthouse keeper until 1940, when the U.S. Coast Guard took responsibility for servicing the lighthouse. After 1940, the building was used as a private home and then was abandoned. The city bought the building in 1963, and a decade later the lighthouse museum opened.

The museum houses a collection related to Great Lakes nautical history and lighthouse life in general—everything from models of ships that sailed the Great Lakes and shipbuilding tools, to the actual light from a lighthouse, the running lights from a ship, and Fresnel lenses, the rare lenses used in lighthouses.

Tour guides also have a wealth of information on shipwrecks

and life aboard a ship, along with great stories about those who tended the lighthouse. They tell of Colfax and the other lighthouse keepers who would trek out on the narrow catwalk to the lighthouse, then climb the steps inside to ensure the light was fueled and working properly. It could be dangerous work, especially in winter when the walkway was icy and strong winds were blowing. (A long, narrow catwalk leading to the current lighthouse can still get slippery, so be careful on the walk out.)

The old lighthouse building, the light tower, and catwalk are all listed on the National Register of Historic Places. The museum, which is maintained by the Michigan City Historical Society, has a library of nautical research material that is available by appointment.
Open Tue.–Sun. 1 p.m.–4 p.m. Admission is $2 for adults, $1 for high schoolers, 50 cents for those in grades 1–8.

Barker Mansion
631 Washington St.
219/873-1520
www.emichigancity.com/cityhall/departments/barkermansion
To glimpse what life was like for the rich and powerful a century ago, stop by this English manor house known as "the house that freight cars built."

In the early 1900s, millionaire industrialist John H. Barker, president of Haskell & Barker Railroad Car Co., took the modest home his father built in 1857, enlisted the help of architect Frederick Perkins, and, after a series of additions and renovations, turned it into a mansion modeled after English manors of the Victorian era.

Haskell & Barker was on the of the largest producers of railroad cars in the late nineteenth and early twentieth centuries. In 1922 the company merged with George Pullman's company and became known as Pullman–Standard.

Even by modern standards Barker was an incredibly wealthy man. When he and his wife died, they left their only daughter, Catherine, a fortune estimated at $62 million. Catherine donated the mansion to the city. The mansion has served as a community center and, for a time, was used for classes by Purdue University.

Its 32 rooms are now open to tours that spotlight the original wood floors, period furniture, a collection of books and paintings, and the third floor ballroom where the family entertained. Seasonal exhibits and events draw visitors year round. In the summer the gardens are beautiful. Many come back in winter to see the incredible holiday displays, which can include 20-plus Christmas trees. Call ahead for tour hours.
Tours available year-round Mon.–Fri., 10 a.m., 11:30 a.m., and 1 p.m., June 1–Oct. 1; additional tours Sat.–Sun. noon–2 p.m. Special tours available during the Christmas season. Suggested donation, $4 adults, $2 children ages 4–18.

The Jack & Shirley Lubeznik Center for the Arts
101 W. Second St.
219/874-4900
www.blankartcenter.org
Formerly the John G. Blank Center for the Arts, this museum was located for years in a limestone building donated by the Blank family that had served as Michigan City's first public library. The new facility is set to open in 2004 on Second Street.

In 2002, Shirley Lubeznik, a local arts patron, donated a multilevel office building to serve as the museum's new home. With that donation, the center's name was changed to honor the Lubeznik family. In the interim, the arts center left the Blank building and moved into a temporary home at 720 Franklin Square.

The Lubezniks supported the local arts for years. Shirley's late husband, a businessman who opened some of the area's first McDonald's restaurants, was a founding member of the Michigan City Center for the Arts. Plans call for a recognition at the new center for the importance of the Blank center in keeping the arts viable in Michigan City.

The collection draws heavily on the works of artists from northern Indiana, the Chicago area and southern Michigan. A competitive exhibition each spring attracts artists from those regions. The special holiday exhibits are also popular, particularly with kids.

The center has also featured exhibits featuring photography and architecture, and it sponsors art classes.
Open Tue.–Thu. 10 a.m.–4 p.m., Sat. 10 a.m.–2 p.m. Call ahead because hours can vary.

Great Lakes Museum of Military History
360 Dunes Highway Pl.
219/872-2702
800/726-5912
www.militaryhistorymuseum.org
Exhibits at the Great Lake Museum cover military history from the Revolutionary War to the present and focus on original uniforms, flags, posters, and an impressive gunroom. Among the museum's treasures are Civil War-era weaponry, a World War I uniform, and a Japanese soldier's uniform from WWII.
Open Tues.–Fri. 9 a.m.–4 p.m., Sat. 10 a.m.–4 p.m., Sun. noon–4 p.m. Memorial Day–Labor Day; Tue.–Fri. 9 a.m.–4 p.m., Sat. 10 a.m.–4 p.m. Labor Day–Memorial Day. Admission is $2 for adults, $1 for veterans and children ages 8–18. Free to those 7 and younger. Directions: I–94 to U.S. 421 north. At U.S. 20, go west. The museum will be on your right.

International Friendship Gardens
601 Marquette Trail
219/878-9885
www.friendshipgardens.org
Like the collection of futuristic homes in nearby Beverly Shores, the International Friendship Gardens have a connection with Chicago's 1933 World's Fair. Three brothers from Hammond designed a garden exhibit at the fair that caught the eye of Frank Warren, a Michigan City developer.

Warren was impressed with the Stauffer brothers' plans for an ornamental garden that would represent all people. He offered them a $1, 99-year lease on a 50 acre site in a development he was doing. In a short time, the international garden drew attention worldwide. According to the not-for-profit corporation that now maintains it, England's King George sent his personal gardener to view the garden, and Queen Wilhelmina of the Netherlands contributed 200,000 tulips.

Today the gardens are spread over more than 100 acres. Visitors enjoy the sculptured trees and bushes, the rare flowers, and productions at the two outdoor theaters. The **Little Symphony Theater** mounts small shows; the **Theater of Nations** sits on an island in a small lake while the audience sits on shore listening to its chorale and orchestra concerts.
Open Sat.–Sun. 10 a.m.–4 p.m., May.–Oct. Directions: From I–80/90 or U.S. 20, take U.S. 421 north to U.S. 12. Go east to the main entrance. Free parking.

EVENTS

In-Water Sail and Power Boat Show
www.boatindiana.com
Held each August on the waterfront, this is Indiana's largest

in-water boat show. More than 500 boats are on display, along with accessories, clothing, and other items for water use. And here's something you won't find at most boat shows: Twiggy, the water-skiing squirrel. Wearing a tiny, squirrel-size life preserver, Twiggy shows off her skills in a 25-foot pool. *Tickets are needed and can be purchased ahead of time.*

DINING

Galveston Steakhouse
10 Commerce Square
219/879-5555
This family-owned steakhouse is the perfect stop after a long day at the beach or shopping. The wooden floors and framed pictures of John Wayne on the walls give the place a rustic feel, but the Galveston Steakhouse has more going for it than an inviting atmosphere. Start off with an appetizer—the barbecued meatballs are recommended—then move on to a thick steak. Save room for dessert, especially the cheesecake.

There's live music in a separate are on weekends, and Tuesday is "Drink and Jam" night. Don't be fooled by the Western-style décor; the music is Chicago Blues.
Open Sun.–Thu. 4 p.m.–10 p.m., Fri.–Sat. 4 p.m.–11 p.m.

The Ferns at Creekwood Inn
5727 N. 600 West (Rte. 20–35 at I–94)
219/872-5323
800/400-1981
www.creekwoodinn.com/ferns.htm
The Ferns usually serves the guests of the Creekwood Inn, a beautiful bed and breakfast located just outside of Michigan City. It opens briefly to the public, however, on weekends when all can enjoy its creative menu. Try such favorites as curried

shrimp and crab cakes, grilled salmon, and pesto-crusted sea bass.

Open Fri.–Sat. 6 p.m.–9 p.m.

WANATAH

• • • • • • • • • • • • • • • • • •

Incorporated: 1968
Population: 1,013
Median age: 37.2
Land area: one square mile

This tiny community on the western edge of LaPorte County was first settled in the mid-nineteenth century when railroads passed through and it became a trading center. It has never grown much, remaining a mostly agricultural community surrounded by corn and soybean fields.

The town's name comes from a Native American phrase meaning "knee-deep-in-the-mud," according to the *Encyclopedia of Indiana*. The Potawatomi were referring to **Hog Creek**, a small stream that would sometimes overflow its banks.

Scarecrow Festival
219/733-2183
www.scarecrowfest.org
Held every September, the Scarecrow Festival is a good, old-fashioned small-town celebration. Special events include a hay-bale rolling contest, a scarecrow dress-up competition, and a toy and collectible show, with the headlining five-kilometer Scarecrow Stampede race. Plus, there's always live music, good food, and, of course, plenty of bingo.

WESTVILLE

Incorporated: September 1864
Population: 5,694
Median age: 35.5
Land area: 3.03 square miles

Some who have lived in Westville hope they never have to return, but that's because they spent their time here at the state prison. For others, Westville is a pleasant community best known as the site of **Purdue University's North Central** campus.

Heron Rookery
Indiana Dunes National Lakeshore
Part of the National Lakeshore, the Heron Rookery is the home of the blue heron. Unlike most species, herons reuse their nests each year, many of which are visible in many of the trees. The forest around here is dense, and in the summer the mosquitoes can be intense. The 1.6-mile trail, however, is worth walking, as it provides a view of a rookery available in few others places. *Directions: From I-80/94, take U.S. 20 to LaPorte County Road 500 East. Go south to County Road 1400 North. To get to the east side of the rookery, turn east on 1400 North to CR 600 East. Go south to the trailhead. To get to the rookery's west side, turn west on CR 1400 North to CR 450 East. Go south to the trailhead.*

Pinhook Bog
Indiana Dunes National Lakeshore
This may sound like an uninviting place—who wants to visit a *bog?* But from an environmental standpoint, you won't find another place like it in the state. The bog is a link to the days

when glaciers covered northern Indiana. About 140 centuries ago, a chunk of a retreating glacier broke off, creating three basins lined with waterproof clay holding water fed by rain and snow. The only way liquid escapes the bog is through evaporation or by what plants take up.

A bog's water is stagnant and highly acidic. The bog has insect-eating plants and beautiful orchids, not the kind of things you'll find on most nature walks in northern Indiana. There is a 145-acre floating mat of thick, spongy moss. Pick some up and you'll see the underside is peat. Pinhook Bog is not only filled with rare examples of plant life, it's also extremely fragile. The National Lakeshore limits access to trips with a park ranger (219/926-7561).

Westville–New Durham Township Library
153 Main St.
219/785-2015
This is one of the few Carnegie libraries still standing in Northwest Indiana. It was built in 1913 and added to in the 1990s, but care was taken to incorporate the original design. Much of the early woodwork is still in place. The original fireplace remains, although that area is now part of the librarian's office. Decorative molding between the windows was replicated in the newer section of the library.
Open Mon.–Thu. 1 p.m.–6 p.m., Sat. 10 a.m.–3 p.m.

LAKE
COUNTY

Lake County...................................43

Cedar Lake 47
Crown Point 51
Dyer...59
East Chicago 63
Gary.. 71
Griffith...89
Hammond 95
Highland 109
Hobart...115
Lowell.. 123
Merrillville 127
Munster.......................................133
Schererville 143
Schneider 147
St. John....................................... 149
Whiting 151

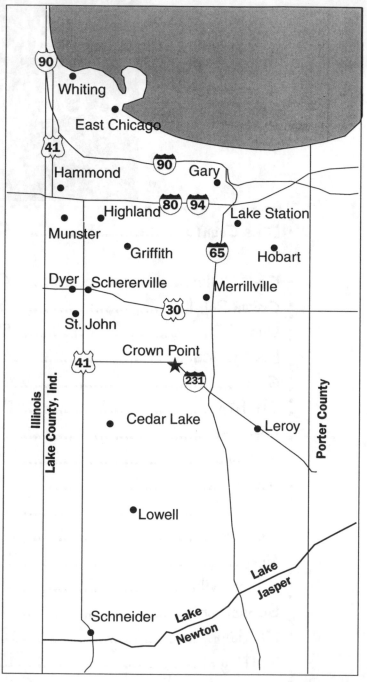

Map by the author.

Lake County, Indiana

LAKE COUNTY

● ● ● ● ● ● ● ● ● ● ● ● ● ● ● ● ●

Created: January 28, 1836
Named after: Lake Michigan
County Seat: Crown Point
Population: 484,564
Median Age: 35.9
Land area: 497.03 square miles

Thousands of people each year drive through Lake County to or from Chicago. Unfortunately, most never leave the expressways, so their impression of Lake County is a place packed with industry and little else.

Well, you can't see most of the lakeshore from the expressways. You won't see any of the small towns and big city neighborhoods that have preserved historic architecture. If you never leave the highway or toll road, you're not visiting nationally-recognized restaurants or meeting new friends at an ethnic festival. You can't climb up a sand dune from the front seat of a car.

It's time to pull off the expressway and visit.

Lake County Convention and Visitors Bureau
7770 Corinne Dr.
Hammond
219/989-7770
800/ALL-LAKE (255-5253)
www.alllake.org
Make your first stop the Lake County Convention and Visitors Bureau. When you drive up to the building you're going to stop

for a minute and wonder just what the architect was thinking. The building's look grows on you; architect Charles Bone wanted it to invoke two of the area's strongest images: sand and steel. It's designed to resemble the waves along the shoreline "crashing" into the office area, which is intended to resemble the steel mills. There's even a fountain "stream" outside and real dune grass planted near the entrance.

Inside, the center's auditorium offers video programs on attractions to look for in Northwest Indiana, along with a gift shop with books, posters, t-shirts, and other souvenirs, and plenty of information available on tourist attractions locally and throughout the state.

The **John Dillinger Museum** is also here, with a fascinating history lesson on the days when guys toting tommy guns captured the nation's attention. Among the museum's highlights is the gun carved from wood that Dillinger used to break out of the Lake County Jail.

Photo by John J. Watkins.

The Lake County Convention and Visitors Bureau.

The center's exhibition hall hosts a variety of historical programs, such as the recent display of automobiles made in Indiana through the years.

Open daily 8 a.m.–8 p.m. Directions: From I–80/94, exit Kennedy Avenue south. The entrance to the center will be on your right almost immediately.

Lake County Fair
Lake Street and 121st Ave.
Crown Point
219/663-3617
An annual event since Civil War days. The focus is agriculture, but there's plenty to do even if you don't know a barrow from a geld. The August fair always features live entertainment, great food, and a huge carnival midway. When you're on the fair grounds stop and visit **Fancher Lake**, a popular summer spot. The grounds are also home to the only covered bridge in Lake County.

Call for dates and a list of performers. Directions: From I 65, take U.S. 231 east to Indiana 55. Indiana 55 south to South Street (113th Avenue). West on South to Lake Street. South on Lake.

A day at the Lake County Fair in Crown Point.

Photo by John J. Watkins.

Photo by John J. Watkins.

Boaters on Cedar Lake.

CEDAR LAKE

● ● ● ● ● ● ● ● ● ● ● ● ● ● ● ● ● ●

Incorporated: October 1967
Population: 9,279
Median age: 33.6
Land area: 6.71 square miles

Centuries ago, the land near **Cedar Lake** was a Potawatomi burial ground. The area became much more lively in the late nineteenth and early twentieth centuries when it developed a reputation as a summer getaway spot. Well-to-do families from Chicago would make the journey to Cedar Lake to spend their days in the water and their evenings enjoying concerts. Later, during Prohibition, it was one of the secluded Indiana towns where illegal booze could be found.

Hoosiers and Chicagoans still flock to Cedar Lake for warm weather fun. The lake is not deep—about 16 feet at its deepest and about nine feet in most spots. But its size, about two miles long by one mile across, makes it perfect for boating, jet skiing, and sailing. Several fishing tournaments are held here each summer; fishing and skiing equipment can be rented.

One item of historical trivia: Cedar Lake is where famous foot doctor Dr. Scholl got his start as an apprentice.

Lake of the Red Cedars Museum
7408 W. 138th Pl.
219/374-6157
http://town-of-cedar-lake.in.totalwebgov.com/7175.html
The prominent exhibits at the Lake of the Red Cedars Museum detail the ice industry that was the town's first big business,

depict life in the Roaring '20s, and showcase its huge fashion collection.

Just as interesting is the history of the structure that houses the museum. The oldest part went up in 1895 across the lake from its present location. It was a boarding house for Armour Bros. workers. In those days before electric refrigerators, employees cut ice from the lake that was then sold to homes and businesses.

In 1919 the brothers sold their business to John G. Shedd—the same man Chicago's famous aquarium is named for. Resort owner Christopher Lassen bought the boarding house from Armour and during the winter when the lake was frozen over moved it to the east shore. He expanded and remodeled the building and reopened it as the Lassen Hotel, which became famous for its restaurant, music, and, when liquor sales were illegal, a good place to get a drink.

The Lake Region Christian Assembly bought the hotel after World War II, and in the 1970s the town bought it. The Cedar Lake Historical Association formed to save it from the wrecking ball, and today, the former hotel is on the National Register of Historic Places.

Next to the museum is a small park with a gazebo and picnic tables for those who want to spend some time enjoying the view of the lake after viewing the exhibits.

Museum hours vary depending on the time of year, so call ahead. Parking is free. Directions: From I–80/94, take U.S. 41 Calumet Avenue south. At 133rd Street, go east; it will become Lakeshore Drive as it goes around the northern part of the lake. At Morse Street, turn south.

Lemon Lake
6322 W. 133rd
219/663-7627
www.lakecountyparks.com/lemonlake.html
Lemon Lake is one of the most modern of the Lake County parks, with tennis and basketball courts, and the only arboretum in the system, as well as the only county-maintained softball diamonds. The 450-acre site has trails that skirt the lake and take hikers to the nearby **Lemon Lake Marsh**.

Seven miles of trails that wind through the prairie and hills make Lemon Lake also popular with cross country skiers. Even advanced skiers will find a challenge here, and ski rentals are available.

The lake itself is stocked with channel cat and panfish, large-mouth bass, carp, and northern pike. For Lake County residents, fishing is $7 for adults, $5 for seniors, and $3 for children. For non-residents, $9 for adults, $7 for seniors, and $3 for children. Paddle boats can be rented for $3 for half an hour. Concession stands are available.

If you're looking for a Halloween treat, visit **Lemon Lake's Forbidden Forest**. A little intense for younger children, the older ones will enjoy a romp through the woods filled with ghosts and goblins. During the winter the park hosts the **Frozen Tundra Ice Bowl Disc Golf Tournament** (another name for Frisbee golf).
Open daily 7 a.m.–10 p.m. Memorial Day–Labor Day; 7 a.m.–dusk Labor Day–Memorial Day. Parking is $2 for Lake County residents, $5 for all others. Directions: From I–65, take U.S. 231 west toward Crown Point. At Indiana 55, go south to 133rd Avenue. Take 133rd Avenue west about three miles to the park entrance.

EVENTS

Summerfest Celebration
The town grounds on the lakefront
219/374-7000
Held annually around the Fourth of July, Summerfest provides carnival rides, a beer garden, plenty of food, and lots of music. What sets this celebration apart from other community festivals are the events that happen on the lake. The **Great Cedar Lake Cardboard Boat Race** is always good for a laugh (unless you're on a boat that is slowly sinking), and watching the fireworks show from a boat on the lake can't be beat.
Festival dates vary. Call the town for a schedule.

DINING

Tobe's Restaurant
13801 Lake Shore Dr.
219/374-9805
Located right on Cedar Lake, Tobe's has good steaks and a menu varied enough to bring diners back because there's so much more they want to try. Ask about the daily specials, which include slow-cooked prime rib on the weekend, basil chicken, and more. A menu is available for the younger set.
Open Sun.–Fri. 5 p.m.–9 p.m.; Sat. 3 p.m.–10 p.m.

CROWN POINT

• • • • • • • • • • • • • • • •

Incorporated: 1868 (town), 1911 (city)
Population: 19,806
Median Age: 40.5
Motto/Nickname: Hub City (Crown Point is the county seat.)
Land area: 7.89 square miles

Nowhere in Lake County are the area's nineteenth century roots more visible than Crown Point. While the larger industrial cities to the north are children of the twentieth century, this city still has plenty of the charm of Northwest Indiana's earliest history.

Solon Robinson, who became known as the "Squatter King" because he organized local farmers to protect their land from speculators, founded the city. He purchased property in 1834, and in 1836 he named the post office on his property Lake Court House. (He was extremely confident about the area's future.) It took another year before the Indiana legislature actually created Lake County, and the city was laid out on a plat map in 1840. Robinson was almost wrong about how important the community he helped found would be. In 1839 the county commissioners chose the tiny community of Liverpool, near present-day Lake Station, as the county seat. The decision to have the center of government in the county's northeast corner angered those in the south and central parts of the county. A courthouse and other county buildings were never built in Liverpool. Instead, in 1840, a new set of county commissioners agreed to base county business at the site favored by Robinson and other Crown Point supporters. Liverpool was ultimately abandoned.

Crown Point has since become a bedroom community with many historic homes and an old-fashioned downtown square that attracts shoppers and antique hunters from around the area. It remains the center of Lake County government and home to the sprawling **Lake County Government Center**.

Yet, you're probably not coming here to watch the county commissioners spend a morning reviewing zoning appeals. If you're visiting Crown Point, the best place to start your trip is at the courthouse—the *old* one.

Old Lake County Courthouse
103 W. Joliet
219/663-0660
Want to see where silent screen legend Rudolph Valentino came for a license before tying the knot? Visit the **"Grand Old Lady of Lake County,"** as the courthouse is known.

Through the 1930s, the lack of a waiting period made Crown Point a popular destination for couples who couldn't wait to get married. Couples would get their licenses at the courthouse, then stop at a justice of the peace on the city square for a quick ceremony. Football legend Harold "Red" Grange and cowboy movie star Tom Mix are among those who came to exchange vows with their brides. In later years, famed boxing champ Muhammad Ali—then known as Cassius Clay—got his license here. Local legend often adds Ronald Reagan and Joe DiMaggio to the list of those married in Crown Point, but there are no records to verify those stories.

The building is famous for more than being a marriage mill. On the courthouse steps in October 1896, Democratic presidential candidate William Jennings Bryan addressed thousands who crowded the square to hear the legendary populist.

Today, only shoppers or diners visit the square. Many are

Photo by John J. Watkins.

The "Grand Old Lady of Lake County,"
Crown Point's historic courthouse.

headed to the nearly two dozen shops that now fill it. If you go, be sure to stop by Valentino's, the popular ice cream parlor in the basement of the old courthouse, named, of course, for old Rudy himself. Upstairs, the old council chambers have been turned into a seasonal theater.

The courthouse is also home to **Lake County Historical Museum**, a place to get a look at the clothes, tools, toys, and other artifacts of an earlier time. The museum isn't open every day, so call ahead (219/662-3975). Donations of $1 for adults and 50 cents for children are requested.

Inside, you'll find a room devoted to the history of the region's steel industry. Other displays detail the agricultural history of the area and list the names of local veterans who served in the nation's wars. Stop in the old county recorder's office and you can see the rolltop desk where the city of Gary was mapped out in 1906. Not everything on display is decades old. One exhibit focuses on the accomplishments of NASA astronaut Lt. Col. Jerry Ross, veteran of numerous shuttle missions, a Crown Point native and graduate of Crown Point High School.

The courthouse, a mix of Romanesque and Gregorian architecture, was built in 1878 and designed by architect J.C. Cochran of Chicago. By the time it was dedicated in 1880 it had cost $50,000. In 1907, work began on the north and south towers. And in 1928, additions were built on the north and south ends. In the early 1970s plans were underway to demolish the old structure because a new county building was being built. Residents, outraged that such a precious building was going to be replaced with a parking lot, fought to save the courthouse. It was placed on the National Register of Historic Places in May 1973 and remains a community treasure.

Directions: From I–80/94, take U.S. 41 south to U.S. 231. Go east on 231, which will take you to the heart of downtown Crown Point.

Old Jail
232 S. Main

This may be one of the more infamous buildings in northwest Indiana. In 1934, John Dillinger, the FBI's public enemy No. 1, busted out of the Lake County Jail armed with a gun carved from wood. The jail still stands on South Main, just a few blocks from the old courthouse.

How did Dillinger manage to escape armed only with a fake gun? That's been a mystery for decades. Some believe he had inside help, but no one was ever charged with helping him make his getaway. After he broke out of his cell, Dillinger locked the guards in cells and escaped in Sheriff Lillian Holley's car across the state line to Illinois. That may have been the mistake that ultimately cost him his life. When he fled there he committed a federal offense by taking a stolen car across state lines (at that time bank robbing wasn't a federal crime!). From then on, the FBI was on his tail. (For more on Dillinger, see the section on East Chicago, p. 66–67.)

The Old Sheriff's House Foundation has rescued the jail and sheriff's residence next door and is restoring the buildings. Both were built in 1882.

Cobe Cup
219/663-1800
219/696-0231
Indiana is famous for that race it holds every Memorial Day weekend in Indianapolis. But to really appreciate the state's ties to auto racing history, you've got to come to Crown Point.

In 1909 this little community was home to one of the nation's first major automobile races. The winner of the Cobe Cup was an engineer named Louis Chevrolet, a fellow who went on to have a pretty successful career building cars.

The race was run just once. Now, every May a celebration is held to commemorate that contest. It begins at the Lake County Fairgrounds in Crown Point, and a parade of classic cars heads to American Legion Post 101 in Lowell.

Stoney Run Park
Union St. and 142nd
219/996-6500
Located in an unincorporated area east of Crown Point known as Leroy, this county-run, 296-acre park has nearly seven miles of trails, a play area for children, and fishing for channel cat and largemouth bass in **Bramletts Pond**. The park also has a bridle path and a primitive campground.

Visit Stoney Run in the summer for the annual **Bluegrass Festival**. Terrific music and food make this a special weekend. Call the County Park Department for details: 219/769-7275 or

219/945-0543. Come in the fall for the popular for tractor-drawn hayrides. In the winter, cross-country skiers try the paths and the pond fills with ice skaters.

The **Lake County Vietnam Veterans Memorial** and the **All Veterans Monument**, a black granite slab inscribed *Thank You* reside here. The park is a link in a proposed military memorial pathway that would eventually run along U.S. 231. Plans for a Korean War Memorial just outside Stoney Run Park are underway along with the development of a World War II monument in Crown Point.

Open daily 7 a.m.–dusk. Directions: From I–65, exit U.S. 231 east about seven miles. Follow the signs into the park.

Crown Point Community Library
214 S. Court St.
219/663-0270
www.icongrp.com/~refcpcl
Many who use the Crown Point Public Library don't realize it is one of the libraries built with a donation from philanthropist Andrew Carnegie. To see the Carnegie portion, built in 1906, you need to walk around to the back of the library. In the early 1970s an addition was tacked on and the front of the library switched to Court Street. The old part of the building faces Main Street.

Most of the older structure is now used for offices in a section of the library called the Carnegie Center. The original oak trim and leaded windows remain, and one office has the fireplace that was part of the original library. The library's board and periodical rooms are also here.

Open Mon.–Tue., Thu. 9 a.m.–8 p.m.; Wed., Fri. 9 a.m.–5 p.m., Sat. 10 a.m.–noon.

Crown Point Motor Speedway

10300 Madison
219/662-4007
www.crownpointspeedway.com
The Crown Point Motor Speedway is an oval, three-eighths-of-a-mile clay track. Formerly known as Southlake Speedway, it's a popular spot on Saturday nights for local racing fans. Super streets, street stocks, and mini-stocks are among the types of cars that race here. Promotions include autograph nights, senior citizen nights, and fireworks shows.
Call for a schedule of events. Directions: From I–65, exit U.S. 30 west. Go south on Broadway (Indiana 53) to Madison, and west on Madison to the speedway.

EVENTS

Hometown Festival Days

Old Courthouse Square
219/663-1800
Hometown Days is a summer tradition presenting a variety of events lasting over two weeks and culminating in a **Fourth of July parade** and festivities. Attractions include a corn roast, **Taste of Crown Point**, arts and crafts shows, a gospel fest, and the **Dollie Parade**, a favorite with kids. The festival takes place downtown, providing a great opportunity to visit some of Crown Point's one-of-a-kind stores.

Midwest Waterfowl Expo

Lake County Fairgrounds
Lake St. and 121st Ave.
219/769-7275
Unlike many shows for hunters, this one deals especially with waterfowl and is a good event to attend in preparation for duck-hunting season. Besides the variety of decoys and calls for

sale and the information on clothing and kennels available, there's a duck- and goose-calling contest.

DINING

Louis' Bon Appetit
302 S. Main St.
219/663-6363
www.219.com/louis/
As you can guess from the name, this is French cuisine, prepared by chef Louis Retailleau himself, in a historic mansion deemed "very romantic" by the Zagat's Survey. The dining is intimate and perfect for couples or small groups, so parents will want to think twice about bringing little ones here. Everything on the menu is excellent, especially the fresh fish selections and steaks. Reservations are recommended.

Bon Appetit is the driving force behind Crown Point's annual three-day **Bastille Day Celebration**. During the event, Chef Retailleau always puts out a public feast that features a wide variety of very low-cost items. The party features dancing, games, and food, food, food!
Open Tue.–Sat. at 5:30 p.m.

DYER

Incorporated: January 24, 1910
Population: 13,895
Median age: 38.4
Size: 5.59 square miles

Dyer began both as a farming community and as a transportation hub for neighboring farmers who brought their crops here for access to the railroads that crisscrossed the small town.

Dyer received the maiden name of Martha Hart, whose husband, Aaron, was a land speculator. Hart, who made his money in publishing in Philadelphia, bought huge tracts of land in Lake County. In 1861 he and his family moved to the Hartsdale Farm, an 800-acre estate.

Hart improved much of his land by building a series of drainage ditches to clear the swamps. The operation grew until it employed 40 men, 14 yoke of oxen, two teams of horses, and three teams of mules. He died on January 12, 1882 when the banks of a ditch he was working in collapsed on him.

His work lives on. **Hart Ditch** still runs from Dyer, through Munster, and to the **Little Calumet River** in Highland.

Meyer's Castle
1370 Joliet St. (U.S. 30)
219/865-8452
www.meyerscastle.com
Joseph Ernest Meyer, one of Hammond's first millionaires, began building this mansion in 1929, the year of the great stock

market crash. Seven decades later, it is still an impressive site. Hidden from U.S. 30 by a thick grove of trees, the castle stands on a hill above the highway. Cars pulling into the lot pass through a large gate with gargoyles perched on the top glaring at the intruders.

According to a history compiled by the current owners, the three-story castle, secluded and completed in 1931, enabled Meyer to pursue his interest in botany. He had learned about plants while growing up in a Kenosha, Wisconsin, orphanage, and amassed a fortune selling and promoting herbal medicine.

Meyer's Castle is an example of Jacobean Revival architecture and has cut Indiana limestone staircases, a red-clay slab tile roof, and carved black walnut and oak trim and paneling. *Directions: From I–80/94, exit at Indianapolis Boulevard south. At U.S. 30, turn right (west).*

Experimental Highway
You might not be able to tell today, but a stretch of **U.S. 30** through Dyer was once the most modern piece of roadway in the world. After Congress passed a road construction bill in 1921, an Indianapolis businessman, Carl Fisher, convinced the U.S. Rubber Co. to aid in the construction of part of the Lincoln Highway using then-modern techniques. U.S. 30, or the Lincoln Highway, is in fine shape today, but, of course, it's no longer the marvel it was in the '20s. A marker now commemorates this experiment in road construction.

Dyer Historical Society Museum
Dyer Town Hall
One Town Square
219/865-6108
www.dyeronline.com/history/index.htm
Located in the town hall, this historical museum has a nice collection of items from the town's early days. In addition to

the usual photos, newspaper clippings, and yearbooks, you will find an assortment of vintage postcards depicting local scenes, and several old banking machines that date back to the 1920s and '30s.

Usually open Mon.–Fri. 8 a.m.–3 p.m.; Thurs. 6 p.m.–8 p.m. Call to confirm. Tours by appointment.

DINING

Rodizio's
Meyer's Castle
1370 Joliet St. (U.S. 30)
219/865-8452

For years, few people saw the interior of **Meyer's Castle**. At times it was rented for private parties, but most couldn't get inside without an invitation. The opening of Rodizio's changed that and brought thousands of diners for a peek inside this community jewel.

But people aren't coming here just to gawk at the dramatic ambiance. Rodizio's is one of the best restaurants in the area. The menu has a heavy Argentinean influence, but the dining experience is what makes this special. Diners don't just sit and order from a menu. There is a huge buffet that lines two ends of the room, spilling over with tapas, spit-roasted entrees, seafood delicacies, exotic salads, and fresh pasta made to order. Reservations are almost always needed. The set price of $23.50 does not include wine, dessert, tax, or tip.

Open Wed.–Sat. 5 p.m.–10 p.m.

A view of Marktown, an East Chicago "company town" built in 1917 by industrialist Clayton Mark, Sr.

EAST CHICAGO

• • • • • • • • • • • • • • • • • •

Incorporated: 1889 (as a town), 1893 (as a city)
Population: 32,414
Median age: 30.8
Motto/Nickname: Twin City
Land area: 11.98 square miles

The nickname Twin City comes from the two distinct areas of East Chicago—the portion known as East Chicago and neighboring Indiana Harbor. For years travel between the two was difficult because they were separated by railroad tracks and a ship canal. They wound up with their own neighborhoods, business districts, and high schools. East Chicago was a city with two identities.

The separation has lessened in recent decades. For many, it ended in 1985 with the closing of Roosevelt High School in East Chicago and the Harbor's Washington High. Instead of two fiercely competitive high schools, all students go to the new Central High. Yet, even today residents identify themselves as being from East Chicago or the Harbor.

The first settlers came to East Chicago in the 1850s. In November 1881, 8,000 acres were sold to the East Chicago Improvement Company, a New Jersey concern backed by a London banking house speculating that the land here would soon be snapped up by industry. They were right. The land changed hands several times, rail lines were extended here, and in 1887 the Standard Steel and Iron Company laid out the town that would soon be named East Chicago, according to historian Powell A. Moore's *The Calumet Region*.

Although the community is still packed with and dominated by heavy industry, including steel mills and part of the BP oil refinery, attractions for visitors do exist.

Marktown
405 Prospect St.
219/397-2239 (Call preservationist Paul Myers for tours.)
www.marktown.org
"Someone once said we're like Brigadoon, coming out of the mist of the mills," says Paul Myers, longtime Marktown resident and its official historian.

Pullman, on Chicago's south side, where Pullman railroad cars were made, is probably the Midwest's best-known example of a company-built town. But for another look at a place built by industry for its workers, stop in Marktown, the 1917 creation of industrialist Clayton Mark, Sr.

About 200 stucco homes designed by architect Howard Van Doren Shaw are still here and still occupied. Chicagoan Shaw also designed Mark's mansion in Lake Forest, Illinois, as well as downtown Chicago's original Goodman Theater and several buildings on the Northwestern University campus in Evanston, Illinois.

In Marktown, Mark hoped to create a cozy English country-style village of Tudor Revival homes. With the beginning of World War I, his plans for a company town collapsed. But Marktown remains. Today the community is boxed in on all sides by industry, but the neighborhood has some families that have lived there for generations. Its placement on the National Register of Historic Places has helped ensure Marktown's future.

If you visit, residents will likely know you don't live there as soon as you park your car. The streets in Marktown are so narrow, just 16 feet across, that most homeowners park on the sidewalks next to their homes and use the streets for foot traffic. That unconventional arrangement earned Marktown a mention in *Ripley's Believe It or Not* as the place where people walked in the street and left their cars on the sidewalk. *Directions: From I–90 or I–80/94, exit at Cline Avenue. At Riley Road go east.*

Pastrick Library
1008 W. Chicago Ave.
219/397-5505
Renamed in 1986 for Mayor Robert Pastrick, who has served for generations, the Pastrick Library building is one of two completed in 1913 with a gift from Andrew Carnegie. The Pastrick branch remains in constant use nearly a century after it was built. Although a large addition was annexed to the red

Photo by the author.

A portion of *Gift of the Book to Mankind,* the mural in
East Chicago's Pastrick Library, painted by local artist
Ernest Kasas as part of the Public Works Art Project in 1930.

brick building with a barrel tile roof, it retains some features of the original library, including twin fireplaces in the main reading room. The library's most striking feature is a large mural painted on the wall opposite the fireplaces. It's called *Gift of the Book to Mankind* and is a mixture of modern and classical styles. Painted by local artist Ernest Kasas as part of the Public Works Art Project in 1930, the work shows goddesses and average people, along with symbols of the arts, music, and sciences. He used family and friends as the models and included a self-portrait of himself as a radio broadcaster.

Open Mon.–Thu. 9 a.m.–8 p.m.; Fri.–Sat. 9 a.m.–5:30 p.m. Directions: From I–90, exit at Calumet Avenue. Go south to Chicago Avenue and turn left (east).

East Chicago Room
East Chicago Library
2401 E. Columbus Dr.
219/397-2453
www.ecpl.org
Located in the East Chicago Library—the name of the newer, main library building on the Harbor side of town—the EC Room is home to thousands of pieces of local history, from footballs used in championship games and old sports trophies, to newspaper clippings and pictures of the city in the 1930s.

Open Mon.–Fri. 9 a.m.–5 p.m. Directions: From I–80/94, take Cline Avenue north to Columbus Drive (U.S. 12). Go west.

First National Bank building
720 W. Chicago Ave.
Now called National City Bank, this building holds an infamous distinction in local history. On January 15, 1934, John Dillinger and one of his men walked into the bank at Indianapolis Boulevard and Chicago Avenue and announced, "This is a holdup." A third man waited outside in their getaway car.

Dillinger carried a Thompson submachine gun in a saxophone

case, according to a history compiled by the East Chicago Public Library. Caught in a shootout as he tried to leave, Dillinger fatally shot East Chicago police officer Walter Patrick O'Malley. Dillinger escaped and hid out in Tucson, Arizona. He was captured there in late January and brought back to the Lake County Jail in Crown Point. (For more on what happened, see the entry on the jail in the Crown Point section, p. 54–55.)

The First National Bank was built in 1929 and was considered a sign of the community's growth and prominence. It has been renovated extensively over the years, but a section of the grillwork that covered the tellers' cages in 1934 has been saved in the public library's East Chicago Room (see above). The bank remains an architecturally imposing site; it still has its original vaulted ceiling and elaborate marble work.

You won't find any memorials to Dillinger's robbery, though. After all, a holdup isn't the kind of thing any bank wants to pay tribute to! An interesting historical detail: When Dillinger was gunned down on July 22, 1934, outside Chicago's Biograph movie theater, five East Chicago police officers joined the 20-plus FBI men who waited for him to emerge. The FBI and East Chicago police both claimed credit for fatally shooting Dillinger that day.

EVENTS

Puerto Rican Festival
Block Stadium
144th St. and Parrish Ave.
219/391-8206 (East Chicago public affairs office)
800/255-5253 (Lake County Convention and Visitors Bureau)
This annual July weekend celebration begins with a parade and culminates in a huge festival, attracting 25,000 people, both

those of Puerto Rican heritage and those who just come to share in the food and music. If you've never had green bananas and plantains, this is your chance to try them.

Mexican Independence Celebration
219/391-8206 (East Chicago public affairs office)
219/397-1872 (Union Benefica Mexicana)
Drawing about 15,000 visitors, this annual September event is one of the state's largest ethnic celebrations. Many come for the food, which is as authentic as you'll find anywhere, but there's also a parade and all-round carnival atmosphere. The streets fill with food vendors, and live entertainment has the streets ringing with the sounds of mariachi bands.

DINING

Casa Blanca
4616 Indianapolis Blvd.
219/397-4151
The first thing you'll notice when you walk in is the fountain that dominates this large, excellent Mexican restaurant. The last thing you'll remember as you leave is the meal. The carne asada, a skirt steak marinated and then grilled, brings customers back. You won't find better in the entire Chicago area. The chile relleno and shrimp dishes are also terrific. East Chicago is a city with a large Hispanic population. Immigrants who grew up with authentic Mexican food will tell you that Casa Blanca gets it right. Casa Blanca also has a bar and banquet rooms.
Open Sun.–Thu. 9 a.m.–9 p.m., Fri.–Sat. 9 a.m.–10 p.m. Directions: From I–80/94, take Indianapolis Boulevard north. From the Chicago Skyway, exit Indianapolis Boulevard south.

El Ranchero
3809 Main St.
219/398-1508
Not very large, but a good place to get authentic Mexican food at a reasonable price. The steak tacos, rice, and beans are first rate. For a treat, try the *posole*, a tomato broth with pork and hominy. *Open Mon.–Sat. 7 a.m.–9 p.m., Sun. 7 a.m.–8 p.m. Directions: From I–90, exit Cline Avenue north to Columbus Drive. Take Columbus Drive west to Main Street in the Indiana Harbor neighborhood, north on Main. From I–80/94, go north on Indianapolis Boulevard to Columbus Drive; take Columbus Drive east to Main, and go north.*

A statue of Elbert Gary, the longtime chairman of
U.S. Steel who founded the city of Gary in 1906,
stands outside of Gary's City Hall.

GARY

● ● ● ● ● ● ● ● ● ● ● ● ● ● ● ●

Incorporated: 1906 (town), 1909 (city)
Population: 102,746
Median age: 33.6
Motto/Nickname: The Magic City, The Steel City
Land area: 50.24 square miles

Founded nearly a century ago, Gary has gone from being known worldwide as the Steel City to its more dubious reputation as a place people fled. In the 1950s it was immortalized in song in the Broadway hit, *Music Man*, but in the years since it has had to contend with a decaying downtown district and a host of other urban problems.

There are signs, however, that Gary has turned the corner. It has always had a rich history that was worth visiting, but a series of successes are giving people reasons to take a renewed look at the town that once earned the nickname "The Magic City" because it rose from bare sand dunes and swamp to a vibrant city of national renown in less than a generation. Millions have been invested to once again make Gary a visitors' destination.

It is named for Elbert H. Gary, the longtime chairman of U.S. Steel and one of the town's major benefactors in its early years. A statute of Gary stands in front of **City Hall**. For decades this was a company town, and the residents either worked in a steel mill or provided services to those who did. When the steel industry took a downturn in the late 1970s, Gary was among the cities hardest hit.

Working to rebuild Gary's image, city leaders realized they

GARY FACTOID

Vee-Jay Records
This label is long gone, but it holds a special place in rock 'n' roll history. Vee-Jay was the first U.S. label to release a Beatles record: *Please Please Me* and *From Me to You.* The Spaniels, a local doo wop group, also had a big hit with Vee-Jay, *Goodnight Sweetheart, Goodnight.*

needed to give people who haven't visited Gary in decades a reason to return. A renewed emphasis on community activities such as the **Gary Airshow** (pp. 80–81), and minor league baseball and basketball are some of the ways they are hoping to get the region's attention.

Gary Steelheads
Genesis Convention Center
One Genesis Center Plaza
Fifth Ave. and Broadway
219/882-4222
www.steelheadshoops.com
Want to see powerful dunks, in-your-face defense, and some of the finest ball-handling this side of the NBA? Then make plans to be courtside for a Gary Steelheads game.

The Steelheads are part of the rejuvenated Continental Basketball Association that began play in 2001. The league is among the destinations that players who don't make an NBA roster head. Here, they're still playing professional basketball, and they've got a chance to work on their game and try to impress some NBA scouts.

For fans, it's just a lot of fun. In addition to the game, there's plenty going on to keep everyone entertained. Come to a game and you might be one of the fans pulled out of the seats for a free-throw contest. Or sit back at halftime and watch Steelie, the team mascot, or the Steelhearts, the cheerleaders.

Few teams have had to survive the tribulations the Gary team faced its first year in the league. And the problems had nothing to do with what was happening on the court. In February 2001, a few months after Gary joined the league, the CBA collapsed because of financial problems that had plagued the 55-year-old league for some time.

Gary and a handful of other teams jumped to the rival International Basketball League in midseason. Then the IBL went out of business when the season ended.

In mid-2001, a group of investors reformed the CBA with Gary as a charter member. Gary plays in the league's American Division along with the Grand Rapids (Michigan) Hoops, the Sioux Falls (South Dakota) Skyforce, and the Rockford (Illinois) Lightning.
Tickets are $50/$25 for a courtside seat, $12/$10 for the lower level, and $5 for the upper level. Ticket packages are available. Call for details and a schedule.

Gary Southshore RailCats
210 E. Fifth Ave.
219/882-2255
www.railcatsbaseball.com
The name of Northwest Indiana's minor league baseball team pays tribute to the nearby South Shore commuter line. The ball club said the name was chosen because, like the South Shore in the 1920s and '30s, the team is an example of the area's "progress and success."

The team began play in 2002. In the summer of 2003 they moved into **U.S. Steel Yard**—an intimate, state-of-the art, $45-million stadium downtown. The park is among the finest minor league ballparks in the country, with seats close to what's happening on the field. Among the amenities: even every bleachers seat is just that—a seat. In most parks bleacher seats are rows of benches. The ballpark also features a year-round restaurant. On game days it offers a great view of the action.

The Class A minor league ball club plays in the same league with teams that include the Schaumburg Flyers and Joliet Jackhammers, both teams from Chicago's suburbs. Other Northwest League teams come from as far away as Lincoln, Nebraska, and Winnipeg, Canada.
Directions: From I–90, exit Broadway south. From I–80/94 take Broadway north. At Fifth Street, go east two blocks.

Marquette Park
Just east of Lake St. and Grand Blvd.
Marquette Park has a beautiful collection of large oak and maple trees set amid rolling sand dunes and lakefront beaches. A statue of Father Jacques Marquette holding a cross greets visitors to this local gem, known as Lake Front Park when it opened in 1919. In 1932 it was renamed to honor the Jesuit priest who was among the first to explore the area. Henry Hering, a New York sculptor, created the bronze likeness.

Visible from the statue is the **Marquette Park Pavilion**, built on the **Marquette Lagoon** that is fed by the Grand Calumet River. There are two bridges over the lagoon, one leading to a small island. Architect George W. Maher designed the pavilion, a popular place for receptions and parties.
Directions: From I–80/94, take I–65 north to U.S. 12. From I–90, exit at U.S. 12. Follow U.S. 12 east to Grand Boulevard. Take Grand Boulevard north into the park. Once there, follow Grand through the park and to the beach.

Marquette Park Aquatorium and Aviation Museum
Marquette Park
Just east of Lake St. and Grand Blvd.
219/938-8081
Past generations knew this simply as "the bathhouse." It got the
new name as part of an aggressive effort to save the distinctive
building, which was built in the 1920s and designed by architect
George Maher. It served its intended purpose for generations,
giving families a place to change before hitting the beach along
Lake Michigan. But a lack of upkeep and the vandalism that
followed allowed the structure to fall into disrepair. It hasn't
been used as a bathhouse since 1970, and for years remained
vacant.

Not anymore. In recent years the **Aquatorium Society** has
taken on the formidable task of restoring the building, which
the group calls the world's first example of modular block
architectural design. About $2 million was raised to restore the
east end. It now has a banquet room and houses exhibits
dedicated to the Tuskegee Airmen, the famed World War II
flying unit made up of African-Americans. Efforts to raise
money and restore the west end are now underway. The society
plans to also rehabilitate the center of the Aquatorium with a
museum and eventually to add statues commemorating the
Tuskegee Airmen and Octave Chanute. Chanute, one of the
pioneers of air flight, conducted some of his glider experiments
in the dunes where the Aquatorium now stands.

Frank Lloyd Wright Homes
669 Van Buren (Ingwald Moe House)
600 Fillmore (Wilburt and Etta Wynant House)
Frank Lloyd Wright has been called the nation's greatest architect, a man whose work influenced generations and changed the
way builders think about home design.

His work has been saved and preserved across the nation. Two of his homes in Northwest Indiana might have been lost if not for Christopher Meyers, a graduate student who identified the buildings and worked to save them. Until he realized their significance, the homes had fallen into disrepair. The information here is taken from research done by Meyers:

The Ingwald Moe House was built between 1909 and 1910 for Moe, a successful Gary-area contractor. Located at 669 Van Buren, it is a two-story stucco building with overhanging eaves

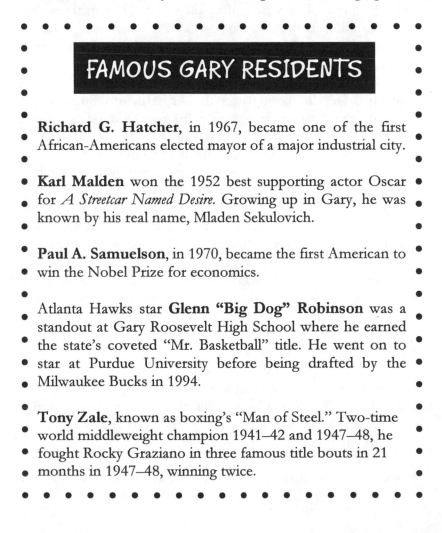

FAMOUS GARY RESIDENTS

Richard G. Hatcher, in 1967, became one of the first African-Americans elected mayor of a major industrial city.

Karl Malden won the 1952 best supporting actor Oscar for *A Streetcar Named Desire*. Growing up in Gary, he was known by his real name, Mladen Sekulovich.

Paul A. Samuelson, in 1970, became the first American to win the Nobel Prize for economics.

Atlanta Hawks star **Glenn "Big Dog" Robinson** was a standout at Gary Roosevelt High School where he earned the state's coveted "Mr. Basketball" title. He went on to star at Purdue University before being drafted by the Milwaukee Bucks in 1994.

Tony Zale, known as boxing's "Man of Steel." Two-time world middleweight champion 1941–42 and 1947–48, he fought Rocky Graziano in three famous title bouts in 21 months in 1947–48, winning twice.

and a front veranda. The interior includes extensive use of natural materials and a Roman brick fireplace.

The Wilburt and Etta Wynant House was the result of a short partnership between Wright and the Richards Company, a Wisconsin builder. Built between 1915 and 1916, it was an early experiment in modular architecture. The material was pre-cut and designed to be put together on the spot. The house at 600 Fillmore has a flat roof, projecting eaves, and a front veranda. It was sold to the American Heritage Trust in 2000, which announced plans to use it as a tourist attraction.

Thomas Edison Homes
Polk St. between Fourth and Fifth Sts.
Frank Lloyd Wright wasn't the only famous person to design homes in Gary. Thomas Alva Edison, who invented the light bulb among other marvels, built a series of rowhouses that still stand.

Photo by the author.

Inventor Thomas Edison built a series of rowhouses in Gary, originally for U.S. Steel workers; they were the first pre-fab homes of the early twentieth century.

These were the first pre-fab homes of the early twentieth century. Cement was poured into molds with steel-reinforcement bars used to add support. Edison designed the homes to go up quickly, and an entire stretch of houses could be built within days. They were originally intended for U.S. Steel workers and were built at a time when the mill's labor force was rapidly expanding.

Several of the buildings, called terrace homes, still stand on Polk Street between Fourth and Fifth Streets. After decades the homes fell in disrepair and were empty, but in the 1990s an effort was made to save them and help rejuvenate the neighborhood. The Horace Mann–Ambridge Neighborhood Improvement Organization began rehabbing the homes and offered them for sale. Today they are painted light blue and are again home to families.

Lake Etta County Park
4801 W. 29th Ave.
219/944-7461
This 105-acre park has a small lake for fishing, paddle boats, and water slides; hiking trails; and shelters and barbecue facilities that make it a popular spot for family picnics. An annual fishing contest offers a prize for the biggest catfish. Water slides are $2 per person; paddle boat rentals are $3 for half an hour; and parking is $2 for Lake County residents, $5 for everyone else. Annual passes are available.
Open daily 7 a.m–dusk year-round; the lake is open daily Memorial Day–Labor Day 10 a.m.–6 p.m. Directions: From I–80/94, exit Burr Street south to 29th Avenue. Take 29th west to the park entrance.

Indiana University Northwest
3400 Broadway
219/980-6500
www.iun.edu
Indiana University's local campus offers a variety of degree

programs. Even if you're not a student, you can visit the 33-acre campus, home to art galleries, theatrical productions, and the **Calumet Regional Archives**. Housed in offices on the third flood of the campus Library and Conference Center, the archives are a treasure trove for researchers digging into the area's history. The collection includes the personal papers of past community leaders, including former congressman Ray Madden, documents from labor unions and environmental groups, and engrossing memorabilia, such as a set of posters once used to promote the South Shore Line railroad.

Check out the two galleries that feature student artwork. **The Gallery for Contemporary Art** is located on the main floor of the Savannah Center. **Gallery Northwest** is in Tamarack Hall.

Some may prefer visiting to see the IUN RedHawks play in the National Association of Intercollegiate Athletics. The teams

Photo by John J. Watkins.

The annual Gary Air Show attracts
about 400,000 visitors to the lakefront.

take their name from the red-tailed hawk that can sometimes be seen soaring above the Indiana Dunes.

Lake Street Gallery
613 Lake St.
219/938-4566
If you're looking for artwork native to Northwest Indiana, a stop at this gallery in Gary's Miller neighborhood is in order. While the gallery carries an impressive selection of items from around the country, it specializes in local pieces and hosts several shows a year devoted to the works of new area artists. Items on display range from contemporary works to pottery to jewelry.
Open Mon.–Wed., Fri. 10 a.m.–6 p.m., Thu. 10 a.m.–7 p.m., Sat. 10 a.m.–5 p.m.

EVENTS

Gary Air Show
Gary/Chicago Airport (6001 W. Industrial Hwy.)
Marquette Park (Just east of Lake St. and Grand Blvd.)
219/949-9722
219/881-1314
Held annually over stretches of Gary's lakefront, the air show attracts about 400,000 people over two days to watch the Lima Lima Demonstration Team, the Northern Lights Jet Team, and B-1 Bombers perform. The striking display of military jets over Marquette Park is among the best air shows held on the lake each summer.

And the nice part is it's all free—from the shows to the parking. Just bring a blanket or lawn chair to Marquette Park, stake out a place to relax, and enjoy the spectacle. Vendors are on hand to take care of food and souvenir needs.

The July weekend begins with a fireworks display on Friday night at the airport, and the air show is held Saturday and Sunday afternoon at the Marquette Park beach. Jets take off from the nearby airport, then display their intricate twists and turns.

Those in wheelchairs or who have disabilities that make getting around difficult can still enjoy the show. Several areas with special padding on the ground and accessible restrooms are available.

The Gary/Chicago Airport is also the staging ground for the Chicago Airshow that is always held soon after Gary's. If you want a preview of the jets as they head a few miles west for Chicago's show, stake out a spot near the airport.

Blues Fest
Genesis Center Plaza
Fifth Ave. and Broadway
219/881-1314
This one-day event, sponsored by the city of Gary the Friday before Labor Day, brings a variety of great Chicago-area blues artists onto stages outside the Genesis Convention Center. Recent performers have included The Kinsey Report, Carl Weathersby, and Millie Jackson. The only thing you have to bring is an interest in some terrific music. Plenty of food vendors are on hand to take care of hearty appetites.

DINING

Miller Bakery Café
555 Lake St.
219/938-2229
The name sometimes throws first-time visitors. They come

expecting a place that will serve fresh cookies and cakes, and then are wowed by a sophisticated, white-table-cloth restaurant serving a wide range of excellent entrees, including pasta, fresh shrimp, duck, and rack of lamb.

The Miller Bakery Café is housed in the old Miller Bakery building. For more than a decade this has been one of the area's finest restaurants. The secret is out, and diners from Chicago to South Bend have been coming to this corner of Gary for a menu that consistently surprises even longtime customers.

And just because this isn't really a bakery anymore doesn't mean the pastry chef doesn't know how to make a great dessert. The flourless chocolate cake and Irish crème cheesecake are among the items that shouldn't be missed. But, like the entrée menu, the choices are always evolving.

Open for lunch, Tue.–Fri. 11:30 a.m.–2 p.m.; for dinner, Tue.–Thu. 5 p.m.–9 p.m., Fri.–Sat. 5 p.m.–10 p.m. Directions: From I–80/94 or I–90, exit at U.S. 12 east. Take U.S. 12 to Lake Street and go north (right). Follow Lake Street into the business district of the Miller neighborhood. The restaurant is on your right.

Miller Pizza Station
622 1/2 S. Lake St.
219/938-7071
www.millerpizzacompany.com
Housed in a one-time freight station, this is a nice place to stop for a sandwich and watch a ballgame on the big screen TV. And right outside you can feel the rumble of the trains as they roll by.

The menu is filled with sandwiches, including a juicy Italian beef. But most come here for the pizza. The deep dish is terrific, and the stuffed Chicago style can compete with some of the best you'll find in the windy city. But don't dismiss the thin crust. It's tough to make a good thin crust pizza—too many places serve something akin to tomato sauce on a Saltine. Here, they've got the recipe perfected.

There are actually several Miller Pizzas in the area: another in Gary, in Merrillville and Valparaiso. This is the original, though. And it's a friendly place to stop if you're visiting the Miller neighborhood and looking for a good lunch.
Open Mon.–Sat. 11 a.m.–10 p.m., Sun. 3 p.m.–9 p.m.

Miller Beach Café
903 Shelby St.
219/938-9890
www.beachcafemiller.com
Don't confuse this neighborhood favorite with the Miller Bakery Café, which is located nearby. The Beach Café is well known to local beach visitors. It's a comfortable place, with a fireplace and décor that invokes the feel of an old time yacht club. There's a well-stocked bar, but this is also a place you can bring the kids. A special family buffet is served until 2 p.m. on Sundays. The menu is packed with good eating. Be sure and try the barbecued ribs. The rib eye is also good, as is the perch, walleye, and catfish. There's a great seafood sampler platter for those who just can't make up their mind.
Open Mon.–Thu. 11 a.m.–9 p.m., Fri.–Sat. 11 a.m.–10:30 p.m., Sun. 10 a.m.–9 p.m.

Vanzant's Ribs on the Run
1907 W. 11th Ave.
219/883-1429
Some of the best ribs around can be found at this family-owned institution. Vanzant's has a huge menu, which includes steaks, chicken, and daily specials that are often salmon, lamb, or Cornish hens. But the beef ribs are what keep many customers coming back again and again. Regulars know to ask for the cornbread to go with these choices. Side dishes include mixed vegetables and macaroni and cheese, but better options are the

mixed greens or black-eyed peas with okra. And save room for the signature dessert, peach cobbler. Carry out is available. *Open Mon.–Thu. 11 a.m.–8 p.m., Fri 11 a.m.–sunset., Sun. noon–8 p.m. Closed Sat.*

Café 444
444 S. Lake St.
219/939-0444
Chef and co-owner Carl Lindskog has worked in the kitchen of some of the Chicago area's best restaurants, including Spago, Green Dolphin Street, and Nick & Tony's Chophouse. The restaurant he's opened in the Miller neighborhood has an eclectic menu. Don't visit without trying the fried green tomatoes. The salads are excellent, and the offerings are always changing. If you visit at lunchtime, try the schnitzel sandwich; at dinner, the filet au poivre or salmon.
Open for lunch, Mon., Wed.–Sat. 11 a.m.–2:30 p.m.; for dinner, Mon., Wed.–Thu. 5 p.m.–9 p.m., Fri.–Sat. 5 p.m.–10 p.m., Sun. 5 p.m.–9 p.m.

● ● ● ● ● ● ● ● ● ● ● ● ● ● ●

Courtesy of the Calumet Regional Archives at Indiana University Northwest.

MICHAEL JACKSON

Michael Jackson and his famous brothers and sisters spent the earliest years of their lives growing up in a one-story clapboard house at 2300 Jackson St. in Gary. The two-bedroom home around the corner from Roosevelt High School is still there, but don't knock on the door asking when the next tour is. The former Jackson family home remains a private residence.

"The earliest memories I have of my father are of him coming home from the steel mill with a big bag of glazed doughnuts for all of us," Michael wrote in his 1988 autobiography *Moonwalker.* His father, Joe, was in a local band, the Falcons, that played venues in Northwest Indiana and Chicago.

The Jackson sons began performing locally at their father's urging. Their first big break came when they won a citywide talent competition on the stage at Roosevelt when Michael was eight. The boys scored with their rendition of the Temptations' *My Girl.* Later they performed at Mr. Lucky's, then a popular Gary nightspot.

In 1967 the Jacksons won an amateur competition at New York's famed Apollo Theater. The next year, the Jackson Five's (the word would be replaced with a "5" soon after) first single, *Big Boy,* debuted on Steeltown Records, a Gary label. It wasn't long before Motown Records founder Berry Gordy spotted the talented youngsters. In October 1969, Motown released the single *I Want You Back.* It became a smash hit.

With their success, the Jackson family left Gary and began touring nationally. They were now living in southern California, and their next visit to Gary was for a performance in early 1971. Someone had hung a sign on a tree outside their former home: "Welcome Home Jackson 5; Keepers of the Dream."

Nine children were raised by Joe and Katharine Jackson in the small house on Jackson Street: Maureen Reilette (Rebbie), Sigmund Esco (Jackie), Toriano Adaryll (Tito), Jermaine LaJuane, LaToya, Marlon David, Michael, Steven Randall (Randy), and Janet. Janet was about three years old when her brothers' success began and the family moved west.

A common mistake is assuming Jackson Street is named for the famous family that once lived there. It's not. Many of Gary's streets carry the name of former presidents, and this one was named for Old Hickory.

● ● ● ● ● ● ● ● ● ● ● ● ● ● ● ● ● ● ●

● ● ● ● ● ● ● ● ● ● ● ● ● ● ● ●

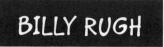

Nearly a century after he died, not many people remember the story of Billy Rugh, the disabled newsboy whose death was mourned across the nation. As many as 20,000 crowded the streets of Gary on October 20, 1912 for Billy's funeral procession.

Even today, the story of Billy Rugh sounds like a tale cooked up by an overly sentimental short-story writer. But it's all true.

He was a newsboy—that's what people called him even though he was 41 years old when he died—in the then-young city of Gary. He read about a woman in town, Ethel Smith, who had suffered severe burns in a motorcycle accident and needed skin grafts. Billy approached doctors with an offer that stunned people when they heard it. He asked the physicians to amputate his bad leg and use the skin to provide Miss Smith the grafts she needed.

The young woman soon recovered after the surgery, but Billy developed pneumonia and died. His story was front-page news for days.

Billy died "just when the printing presses in a hundred cities were grinding out millions of papers that again told the story of his sacrifice and precarious condition," the *Lake County Times* wrote.

Mayor Thomas E. Knotts wrote to the *Gary Tribune* urging that the "name of William Rugh should be remembered in Gary as long as the city shall last. The hearts of all are torn today when we realize that his act of noble heroism, his unselfish willingness to suffer that another might enjoy health and life, has culminated in the supreme sacrifice."

Between 10,000 and 20,000 (press accounts vary) turned out for the funeral, which was covered by many midwestern newspapers.

The Billy
Rugh
Funeral.

*Courtesy of the
Post-Tribune and
the Calumet
Regional
Archives.*

The crowd was so large that plans to hold services inside the church were abandoned. Instead, mourners gathered in the street while a minister climbed on top of the funeral car to perform the service.

Four brass bands played and honorary pallbearers included Mayor Knotts, school superintendent William Wirt, W.P. Gleason, general superintendent of Illinois Steel, and George M. Hunter, general manager of the American Bridge Company.

Afterward, there was great demand for a statue to honor the newsboy, but it was never built. For a time, there was a plaque in the city's Memorial Auditorium, but that building has been gutted by fire and largely destroyed.

It's not known if the memorial to Billy Rugh survived.

• • • • • • • • • • • • • • •

Sledders at Griffith's Oak Ridge Prairie, a popular spot for winter fun.

GRIFFITH

• • • • • • • • • • • • • • • • •

Incorporated: 1904
Population: 17,334
Median age: 35.8
Motto/Nickname: The Town that Came to the Tracks
Size: 8.72 square miles

Although the exact origin of the town name remains unclear, local historians agree it probably came from the surveyor who set the grade for the **Grand Trunk Railroad** in the 1870s. The man's name was Griffith, and train engineers simply attached his name to the area they traveled through.

Jay Dwiggins and Company of Chicago, a real estate developer, laid out the community in the 1890s, and the town experienced a temporary population boom for a few years. The growth was stalled by a depression in 1893 that forced many to leave in search of jobs. The only stable work left was with the railroads that crisscrossed the town.

In the twentieth century, Griffith grew into a residential community with some small industry. But the town has kept its links to its railroading past. At one time it was a busy place with more than 180 trains coming through each day, according to the Griffith Historical Society. That pace has slowed considerably, although strong ties to the railroading past still exist with the **Canadian National** and **Elgin, Joliet & Eastern (EJ&E)** lines running through Griffith each day.

Hoosier Prairie Nature Preserve
Kennedy Ave. and Main St.
317/232-4052
www.state.in.us/dnr/naturepr/npdirectory/preserves/hoosierprairie.html
To imagine what much of Northwest Indiana looked like just a few hundred years ago, visit this tallgrass prairie on the edge of Griffith. The Hoosier Prairie has one of the most diverse collections of plants in a single spot anywhere in the country, a fact even more amazing considering the preserve is only 430 acres. This small piece of land has sand prairie, wet prairie, sedge meadows, and marshes. A hike through the prairie showcases the diversity of plant life and birds such as sparrows and yellowthroat warblers. Wildflowers first appear in June and remain until August or September.

The preserve can also be a sobering reminder of how much the area in general has changed from the natural wonder it once was. There are industrial storage tanks beyond one edge of the property, and a road bisects the land.

The prairie is under the jurisdiction of the Indiana Dunes National Lakeshore and is maintained by the Indiana Department of Natural Resources.
Directions: From I–80/94, take Indianapolis Boulevard south to Main Street in Highland. Go east (left) on Main Street to Kennedy Avenue. Parking is available on Main just past Kennedy.

Oak Ridge Prairie
301 S. Colfax St.
219/769-PARK (7275)
Oak Ridge Prairie, all 687 acres, is a popular spot for picnics and nature walks, and a good place for bird-watching. Birders try at dusk to catch a glimpse of the male woodcock that will soar 300 feet then plummet while zigzagging back and forth. According to the Lake County Park Department, which maintains this park, sighting the woodcock's rituals "are the perfect

way to celebrate the coming of spring, just as surely as seeing the first robin."

During the summer months, guided tallgrass prairie hikes take visitors through areas resembling the plains that greeted the first white settlers in the 1800s. Fish ponds with largemouth bass, carp, rainbow trout, and bluegill are open to anglers who are county residents for $7, non-residents $9. Children and senior discounts are available. No license is required.

In winter, the park fills with cross-country skiers. Ski rentals are available, and the trails provide a good workout. Just as popular is the giant sledding hill, high enough to build up some speed, but not so imposing that younger children are intimidated. Plenty of parking is available.
Directions: From I–80/94 take Cline Avenue south to Main Street. Go left (east) on Main to Colfax Avenue. Turn right (south) for about a half-mile. The prairie entrance is on Colfax.

Griffith Historical Park and Depot Museum
201 S. Broad St.
219/924-6013
www.lakenetnwi.net/org/griffithhistsoc/table.htm
This museum complex maintained by the Griffith Historical Society offers a look at the history of the railroads and the days when climbing aboard a train was the only way to travel long distances. The museum itself is in the Grand Trunk Railroad Depot, the last of Griffith's four depots. It was saved from demolition in 1979, moved to its current site in 1980, and restored and open to the public by 1981. The grounds contain several restored railcars that visitors can walk through. Among the highlights are a Pullman Company sleeping car and Caboose 503, rescued from a service yard in Gary (after new technology made it obsolete) and restored to look like when it was the place railroad workers stayed on long runs.
Open Sun. 2 p.m.–4 p.m., Memorial Day–Labor Day; by appointment

the rest of the year. Directions: From I–80/94, take Cline Avenue south to Main Street. At Main go east (left) to Broad Street. Turn south (right). The museum is located just before the first set of railroad tracks.

EVENTS

Park Full of Art
Central Park
600 N. Broad St.
www.griffithindiana.com/art.htm
Held annually since the mid-1970s, this two-day, juried show every July attracts over 115 artists from throughout the Midwest, who bring a huge selection of paintings, sculptures, jewelry, arts and crafts, and custom-made furniture to display and sell—and art lovers from just as far who come to buy it. The caliber of work is unusually high. Central Park is the year-round home of the **Griffith Veteran's Memorial** and a vintage World War II Army Tank.
Open 10 a.m.–5 p.m. Admission is free.

Griffith Railroad Fair
Griffith Historical Park and Depot Museum
201 S. Broad St.
219/924-2155
www.lakenetnwi.net/org/griffithhistsoc/rrfair.htm
Railroad buffs, collectors of toy trains, or just those in search of fun come to Griffith for this celebration on the grounds of the town's train museum the last weekend in September. Because it draws railroad memorabilia dealers, the fair is a good place for toy and train collectors to pick up hard-to-find items. Even if you're not a railroad aficionado, this is a great place to meet people who spent their lives working on the railroads. A variety of vendors provide lunch and dinner options. Be sure to save some room for the fair's famous Hobo Stew.

DINING

Corner Cafe
101 N. Broad St.
219/922-9596
This is the traditional corner restaurant right in the center of downtown, where everyone keeps coming back for the satisfying food, large portions, and relaxing atmosphere. The menu is filled with soups, sandwiches, and burgers. There's plenty for kids to choose from and special deals for seniors (which may explain why you often see grandparents with their grandkids here).
Open Mon.–Fri. 5 a.m.–8 p.m., Sat.–Sun. 5 a.m.–2 p.m.

Photo by the author.

Part of sculptor Alfonso Iannelli's Art Deco doors
that graced Hammond City Hall from 1931 to
1976. They now have a home at Purdue Cal.

HAMMOND

• • • • • • • • • • • • • • • • •

Incorporated: 1884
Population: 83,048
Median age: 33.9
Size: 22.95 square miles

For years, Hammond had a reputation as a tough place to leave. Not because of the great attractions, but because the numerous rail lines that converged there made crossing the tracks without being stopped by a train seemingly impossible.

The building of a downtown overpass and removal of some lines in recent years has largely eliminated that headache. Now, many come to Hammond to take their chances at the gigantic **Horseshoe Casino** (p. 228), to enjoy the **Hammond Marina** (p. 217), or to spend a day windsurfing at **Wolf Lake** (p. 97).

Ernest and Caroline Hohman settled in what became Hammond in 1851 after fleeing a cholera epidemic in Chicago, according to local history. The area became known as Hohmanville. That changed soon after Detroit butcher George Hammond arrived in 1869 and built a slaughterhouse. Hammond, the inventor of the refrigerated boxcar, took advantage of the livestock industry already established on Chicago's neighboring south side.

A fire destroyed the slaughterhouse in 1901, but city leaders quickly attracted a variety of industry to fill the economic void. For decades downtown Hammond was one of the area's retail centers. That has changed, with the downtown becoming more of a service district. A new federal government building that

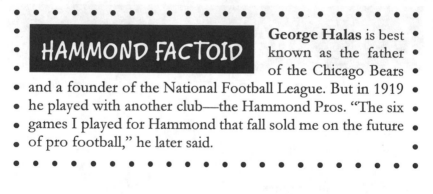

HAMMOND FACTOID George Halas is best known as the father of the Chicago Bears and a founder of the National Football League. But in 1919 he played with another club—the Hammond Pros. "The six games I played for Hammond that fall sold me on the future of pro football," he later said.

features a 64-foot-high vaulted central hall and a sculpture by Dale Chihuly dominates it.

If you're downtown, stop by the **Hammond Rotunda**, a 27-foot-tall sculpture on Hohman Avenue. The fountain has become a favorite lunchtime gathering spot. "Rain" seems to

Photo by the author.

The installation of David Black's Rotunda, a "pavillion sculpture," helped kick off Hammond's downtown arts movement.

pour from the center of the pavilion into a pool. Columbus, Ohio, artist David Black calls his creation "a pavilion sculpture."

The rotunda was just the first step in beginning an arts movement downtown. In 2001 Hammond unveiled a 20-foot-tall mural reproducing a famous painting by Salvador Dali. Many cities have downtown murals on the side of a building. What makes this reproduction of *Persistence of Memory* (it depicts melting timepieces) unique is that it's 80 feet in the air. It was the inaugural painting in the **Midwest Wall of Classics**, an attempt to surround people with works of art. Ultimately, there will be 10 such reproductions downtown, city officials say.

One more note. The northernmost portion of Hammond is known locally as **Robertsdale**. This section is closely linked to the neighboring city of Whiting; most in Robertsdale use Whiting as their mailing address. To make things easier for readers, businesses in the Robertsdale section are all listed in the Whiting chapter (see pp. 151–158).

Wolf Lake Park
121st St. and Calumet Ave.
Located about a mile south of Lake Michigan, Wolf Lake reaches into both Indiana and Illinois and is a favorite summer playground for windsurfers and boaters. Many like to head to the small island in the center of the lake for exploring or a little privacy.

Wolf Lake Park is a year-round, 453-acre attraction. Boat rentals, fishing, and miniature golf bring crowds in the summer, while winter provides cross-country skiing and ice skating. The playground area is popular when kids have had enough of the water. Several small convenience stories are nearby, a godsend for picnickers who forgot the ketchup or run low on ice.
Directions: From I–80/94, exit Calumet Avenue north to 119th Street.

From the Chicago Skyway, exit Indianapolis Boulevard south and follow U.S. 41. There's plenty of parking.

Gibson Woods Nature Preserve
6201 Parrish Ave.
219/844-3188
www.in.gov/dnr/naturepr/npdirectory/preserves/gibson.html
Want to spot a rare Karner blue butterfly or dune goldenrod? This treasure in the middle of the city is the place to go. The Lake County Parks and Recreation Department operates this nature conservancy, a prime spot for birdwatchers. Look for black-throated, blue, and magnolia warblers. Animal inhabitants include gray foxes, weasels, minks, and the endangered Franklin's ground squirrel.

The 130-acre preserve has four trails and contains the longest intact inland dune ridge in the Midwest outside of the National Lakeshore. Some of the trails at Gibson Woods are on a boardwalk and are accessible to wheelchairs. The **Environmental Awareness Center** provides programs, lectures, and information about all trails.
Open daily 11 a.m.–5 p.m.; the nature center is open 11 a.m.–4 p.m. Directions: I–80/94, to Cline Avenue. Go north to 165th Street, then east to Parrish Avenue. Go north on Parrish, which dead ends at the preserve.

The Little Red Schoolhouse and Museum
Hessville Park
Kennedy Ave. and 173rd St.
219/844-5666
www.ci.hammond.in.us/community/littlered.htm
Opened in 1869 as the Joseph Hess School, this one-room schoolhouse has been painstakingly restored to resemble a classroom from over a century ago. The building had a short life as a schoolhouse, only about three decades, but it was used for nearly a century, first as a meeting hall and later a residence. In the early 1970s the **Hessville Historical Society** purchased

the building and moved it down the street to its present location in Hessville Park. Now, the schoolhouse hosts tours, an annual festival in late June and early July, and a holiday visit from Santa. For Hammond's Hessville neighborhood, the Little Red Schoolhouse has become a gathering point, a place that many of the local festivals include in their celebrations. *Call for hours. Directions: From I–80/94, take Kennedy Avenue north to 173rd Street.*

Purdue University Calumet
2333 171st St.
219/989-2400
www.calumet.purdue.edu
Residents call it Purdue Cal to distinguish it from the main campus about 100 miles south in West Lafayette. The Calumet campus is the largest of Purdue's regional campuses with more than 9,000 students. It offers master's, bachelor's, and associate degrees in more than 85 areas of study. Purdue Cal's Lakers and Lady Lakers compete in the Chicagoland Collegiate Athletic Conference. For information about sports, theater, and art exhibits at the school, check out the calendar on the Web site.

If you're on campus, stop in the library to see a stunning piece of Hammond history. Beautiful Art Deco doors designed by sculptor Alfonso Iannelli graced the entrance to Hammond City Hall from 1931 to 1976. The huge doors were so heavy they were found to be a safety hazard and had to be removed. Rather than put them in storage, they were given a home at Purdue Cal in 1978. Iannelli, who once worked with architect Frank Lloyd Wright, designed the doors with graphics that pay tribute to the laborers who built Hammond. One side shows a man at work on large machinery, while the other depicts a worker pulling the rope of a bell, a nod to the workers' spiritual needs.
Directions: From I–80/94, exit Indianapolis Boulevard north to 173rd

Street. Take 173rd east. A large parking lot is on the south end of the campus.

Substation No. 9
435 Fayette St.
219/933-0200
The building is small and has no large sign out front, but you can't miss it. It's the one with huge cover-the-whole-side-of-the-building murals depicting the diversity of the people of Northwest Indiana on three of its sides.

Substation No. 9 is one of the Northern Indiana Arts Association's satellites. It was once an electrical utility substation, and a large transformer is still fenced in back. But inside there's a different kind of power at work. In addition to a variety of exhibits, the substation offers classes and community outreach programs. Special programs are offered for seniors and children. In addition to traditional art classes, there are sessions in Web design and using a computer to produce works of art. The building is outfitted with wireless Internet service.
Open Tue.–Sat 10 a.m.–5 p.m. Directions: From I–80/94, exit at Calumet Avenue north. At 165th Street turn left (west) to Hohman Avenue and turn right (north). At Fayette Street, turn right (east). Free parking is available next to the building.

Firefighter Memorial
6110 Calumet Ave. (at Conkey St.)
Many communities have firefighter memorials, but few have sculptures that incorporate the materials that Hammond's does. The moving sculpture of a firefighter rising above twisted steel beams was made from scrap recovered from a warehouse fire that took the life of a local firefighter.

Fred P. Biedron died in the blaze on Dec. 16, 1991. What made his death even more shocking was that he was the son of a Hammond firefighter—Fred W. Biedron—who died in the line

Photo by the author.

Ramojus "Ray" Mozoliauskas's Firefighter Memorial in
Hammond stands next to the city's central firehouse.

of duty on March 18, 1968. In all, eight Hammond firefighters
have lost their lives doing their jobs.

Sculptor Ramojus "Ray" Mozoliauskas created the touching
sculpture, which was dedicated in 1994. It depicts the ghostly
visage of a firefighter; beneath him is the wreckage left by a
blaze. It stands next to the city's central firehouse.
Directions: From I–80/94, exit Calumet Avenue north.

LeRoy Neiman Mural
Mercantile National Bank
5243 Hohman Ave.
219/932-8220
Artist LeRoy Neiman is famous for his paintings of entertain-
ers, of Muhammad Ali throwing a fierce hook, horse racing,
and Olympic competitions. His works have graced magazine
covers, hang in galleries around the world, and bring top dollar
from art collectors.

Before he was known internationally for his bold use of color and expressive design, Neiman worked on a series of murals. One of them hangs behind the tellers in downtown Hammond's **Mercantile National Bank.**

The mural, a huge 8 feet by 56 feet, is called *Afternoon at the Indiana Dunes.* On the left, the Chicago skyline is visible in the distance. Steel mills can be seen on the right. In between are beach goers enjoying an afternoon in the sun. The bank commissioned the work by the then unknown artist in 1966, a controversial choice. Note that it includes the John Hancock center, not open until 1970.

The bank lobby is open Mon.–Fri. 9 a.m.–5 p.m. Directions: From I–80/94, exit Calumet Avenue north. At 173rd Street turn west to Hohman Avenue. North on Hohman.

Hammond Public Library
564 State St.
219/931-5100
www.hammond.lib.in.us
If you ever shopped in downtown Hammond during the mid- to late-twentieth century, you probably remember the ornate clock that hung inside Goldblatt's department store. It was big and fancy, and generations of shoppers made plans to meet by the clock before heading out to lunch.

Goldblatt's is gone, but in 2001 the clock returned. It now hangs in the recently-renovated main library building: a four-sided timepiece, about 30 inches across and 34 inches high. Bronze ornaments decorate its exterior. Its age remains a mystery. It hung in what was originally the Kaufman and Wolf building when that business opened in 1927. When the building was later sold to Goldblatt's, the clock remained. Some experts have said its design appears to resemble clocks made in the late nineteenth century, but there is no record of when it first came to Hammond.

If you enjoy local history and stop to see the clock, also make plans to visit the library's **Calumet Room**. History buffs will find a variety of local histories, old high school yearbooks, newspaper articles, and other documents that tell the story of Hammond and many surrounding communities.

Open Mon.–Thu. 9 a.m.–9 p.m., Fri.–Sat. 9 a.m.–5 p.m., Sun., Sept.–May 1 p.m.–5 p.m.; the Calumet Room is open Mon.–Thu. noon–5 p.m., Wed. noon–9 p.m. Directions: From I–80/94, exit Calumet Avenue north. At 173rd Street turn west to Hohman Avenue. North on Hohman to State Street. East on State to the library.

EVENTS

International Culture Festival
219/844-8219
This September festival offers a terrific look at just how culturally diverse Northwest Indiana is. The ethnic heritages are evident in the performers, who showcase traditional works from Mexico, Ireland, Germany, and Israel, to name just a few. You can also sample the cultural differences by stopping at some of the different food booths. Try a little Greek food, followed by Hungarian. And save room for Chinese. Some of the booths are run by local churches with strong ethnic ties. Each year the festival hosts a naturalization ceremony, swearing in immigrants as U.S. citizens.

The festival has been held annually since 1973, when it was conceived as a way to foster understanding between different cultures. It has grown to more than 20,000 visitors over the two days. The event is wheelchair accessible.

The festival committee is currently choosing a new location for this event. Call for more information.

DINING

Phil Smidt's
1205 N. Calumet Ave.
800/FROG-LEG (376-4534)
www.froglegs.com
It has been decades since the Smidt family owned Phil Smidt's, but owners over the years have known not to mess with a good thing. Since it opened in 1910, the restaurant has been considered among the best in greater Chicago. The frog legs and lake perch, served swamped in butter, are still the signature meals; the décor is still a soft rose color, and the mural of roses remains. All entrees come with their traditional spread of coleslaw, cottage cheese, beets, kidney beans, rolls, and choice of potatoes. Their acclaimed gooseberry pie still tops a list of appetizing desserts.

Phil Smidt's was the only Northwest Indiana restaurant to make *Gourmet* magazine's list of the nation's best eateries in 2000. *USA Today* also named it one of the nation's finest. The restaurant is near the Hammond Marina, and from inside you can see Lake Michigan. Because of its popularity, reservations are recommended.
Open Tue.–Thu. 11:15 a.m.–9 p.m., Fri.–Sat. 11:15 a.m.–9:30 p.m., Sun. 1 p.m.–7 p.m. Directions: From the Chicago Skyway, exit at Indianapolis Boulevard and turn north at Calumet Avenue; from I–80/94, exit Calumet Avenue north. Phil Smidt's is on Calumet Avenue, just south of the Amtrak station.

McGee's Restaurant and Speakeasy
142 Rimbach St.
219/852-8500
There's a lot of truth in this restaurant's name. Local legend says that back during prohibition, this building was a speakeasy serving bootleg liquor. Eighty-plus years later, it's a good steak

and sandwich spot. For lunch, try the Reuben, a patty melt of the special, a Big Mike. They aren't kidding—there's three-quarters of a pound of meat between two buns. At dinnertime, the porterhouse is recommended. There's also a good selection of seafood on the menu, including shrimp, perch, catfish, and orange roughy.

Open Mon. 11 a.m.–7 p.m., Tue.–Sat. 11 a.m.–2 a.m. Dinner served Tue.–Thu. until 9 p.m., Fri.–Sat. until 10 p.m.

El Taco Real
935 Hoffman St.
219/932-8333
The best Mexican restaurant in the area, El Taco Real draws long lines on weekends from diners who can't wait to try this authentic Mexican food. Many of the recipes have been handed down generation to generation in the owner's family. First-time visitors might want to order one of the sample plates to try several of the excellent dishes.

Call for hours. Directions: From I–80/94, exit Calumet Avenue north to Hoffman Street. Turn right. From the Chicago Skyway, exit at Indianapolis Boulevard. Go south at Calumet Avenue to Hoffman Street and go east.

Ludwig's Club Café
7206 Calumet Ave
219/933-4477
You're not going to find a restaurant that does a better job of representing the various ethnicities that make up Northwest Indiana. Looking for a place that makes authentic Spanish-style dinners. You've got it here. How about Croatian? They can do that. Hungarian and Mexican, too. They can also prepare a great steak or a terrific platter of fresh perch.

There's a lot to recommend here, There specialties were learned in the kitchens of Europe, and the authenticity shows. First time visitors should be sure and try the Weiner Schnitzel. The goulash is also great, and for a real treat try the coq au vin—chicken smothered in bacon and onions and drenched in wine.

Ludwig's is great for an evening out, but not too fancy. They serve beer and wine, and the menu can accommodate children. *Open 7 a.m. daily; Mon.–Thu. until 9 p.m., Fri.–Sat. until 10 p.m., Sun. until 8 p.m.*

• • • • • • • • • • • • • • • •

Courtesy of the Calumet Regional Archives.

It was always hard to tell how Jean Shepherd really felt about his hometown. In his books and on his New York radio show in the 1960s, Shepherd told stories about a place called Hohman, Indiana. But anyone who knew him knew he was really writing about growing up in Hammond. He simply substituted the name of Hohman, a major north–south roadway on Hammond's west side.

"Hohman, Indiana, is located in the extreme northwestern corner of the state where the state line ends abruptly in the icy, detergent-filled waters of that queen of the Great Lakes, Lake Michigan," he wrote in *In God We Trust, All Others Pay Cash.* "It clings precariously to the underbody of Chicago like a barnacle clings to the rotting hulk of a tramp steamer."

He would go on to deride his hometown as a "place people never really come to, but mostly want to leave."

But he could also be nostalgic about the place. He drew on his memories of growing up in Hammond when he worked on the holiday film classic *A Christmas Story*. It was adopted from his short stories, and Shepherd is the unseen narrator in the movie. When he died in 1999, he was remembered as a great storyteller. "He was in the tradition of the old-time storytellers like Mark Twain, except he told stories of the twentieth century," writer Studs Terkel told the *Chicago Sun-Times*. "His stories came out of an industrial town—smelly and oily and dirty, and he could invoke childhood. He was an American original."

Shepherd went to Hammond High and worked at Inland Steel. But his great fame came when he went east and hit it big in radio. He was on WOR, an AM station that could be heard up and down the Eastern seaboard. Most didn't believe his stories about that mythical place called Hohman.

"One time our scoutmaster took us out on a hike through Hohman," Shepherd wrote in one of his books, "and hand-painted moss on the north side of all the fireplugs, so we could blaze a trail to the vacant lot behind the Sherwin-Williams sign."

In 1970 Shepherd came home. He was filming a new public television series on America, and he wanted to do a story on Inland Steel. Talking to a *Chicago Daily News* reporter, he began telling another story. Like many of Shepherd's stories, it's not clear how much was true.

He recalled working at Inland as a young man and seeing one of the huge, legendary mill rats. "Chester Gotch said his cat could beat anything in the house," Shepherd told the reporter. "So he brings in that tough S.O.B. cat that night. The next day we found the cat dead.

"It's a true story, and all of a sudden just then I realized I was in a tough business."

• • • • • • • • • • • • • • • •

HIGHLAND

● ● ● ● ● ● ● ● ● ● ● ● ● ●

Incorporated: April 4, 1910
Population: 23,546
Median age: 39.8
Land area: 6.8 square miles

Settled in the mid-1800s by an Ohio couple, Michael and Judith Johnston, Highland's name comes from its physical location. Thousands of years ago, when Lake Michigan reached further inland, this was high land. Homes built on a steep, sandy incline along Ridge Road sit on what was once the high piece of ground near the lakeshore. Today the beach is about seven miles away, but the ridge remains.

For most of the first part of the 20th century, Highland was known for its large Dutch community. It has evolved into a town celebrated for its extensive 19-park system. The biggest, and a focal point for the community, is **Main Square Park** (3001 Ridge Rd., just east of downtown), noted for its impressive white gazebo and immense playground.

Highway of Flags
U.S. 41 has been designated the Servicemen's Highway. If you're from one of the seven states that U.S. 41 rolls through—Wisconsin, Illinois, Indiana, Kentucky, Tennessee, Georgia, and Florida—you might want to stop for a moment at the **Highway of Flags Servicemen's Memorial** (U.S. 41 and Ridge Rd.). It opened May 26, 1975, to honor members of the armed services. The memorial consists of a plaque for each branch of the military and a flag from each state on the Servicemen's Highway. Parking is available around the rear of the monument.

Wicker Memorial Park
Indianapolis Blvd. (U.S. 41) and Ridge Rd. (Hwy. 6)
Dedicated by President Calvin Coolidge in 1927, 350-plus-acre
Wicker Park is one of Lake County's biggest playgrounds.
Picnic grounds, volleyball courts, walking trails, and a pavilion
that's always booked for a reception or anniversary party attract
thousands of people annually. Its most popular asset is the golf
course.

Wicker Park is dedicated as a living war memorial with an
eternal flame that burns for those who died in service. The
flame was installed in the 1990s to replace a wooden cross that
was removed after complaints that represented government-
sponsored endorsement of religion. The cross was relocated a
few miles east on the grounds of **St. James the Less Catholic
Church** (9460 Kennedy Ave.).

The Town Theatre
8616 Kennedy Ave.
219/838-1222
www.towntheatre.net
Grownups like going to the Town not to see adult movies, but
to watch movies without the distraction of children running
down the aisle or loudly demanding more popcorn during an
crucial moment in the film. Children under 12 are not admitted
with or without parents.

Many of the movies are art, independent, and foreign films
although the Town does show some second-run mainstream
films. It has one other attractive feature, an intermission.
Halfway through the movie, the film is stopped, the house
lights come on, and everyone is invited to the lobby for a free
slice of sheet cake and a cup of punch.
*Directions: From I–80/94, exit Kennedy Avenue south. Free parking is
available in a lot across from the theater.*

Lincoln Center

2450 Lincoln Ave.

219/838-0114

This former school building attracts crowds each year for events ranging from home improvement shows, to computer expos, to card and comic book shows. Events vary from week to week, but something is scheduled most weekends. Call for details.

Directions: From I–80/94, exit Indianapolis Boulevard south to Lincoln Avenue. Turn East on Lincoln.

Highland Historical Society

2450 Lincoln Ave.

219/838-2962

http://users.rootsweb.com/~inlake/highland.htm

In its offices at Lincoln Center, the historical society works to preserve the community's history. Exhibits range from glacier rocks, left behind thousands of years ago by the icy behemoths that carved out the community, to a sign from the first train depot that called the town Highlands. Native American artifacts, pictures, and one of the stools that spectators sat on during Coolidge's visit to Wicker Park are also on display.

Open Sat. 9:30 a.m.–11:30 a.m. and by appointment

EVENTS

Fall Fest

Main Square Park

3001 Ridge Rd. (Hwy. 6)

219/923-3666

One of the largest and most popular of its kind in Northwest Indiana, Highland's annual September festival is a chance to kick off the fall with a bang. There are carnival rides, games, an arts and crafts area, and plenty of food.

DINING

Miner–Dunn Restaurant
8940 Indianapolis Blvd.
219/923-3311
One of the area's oldest restaurants, Miner Dunn opened in 1932. The menu has expanded, but the basics are still the same: good hamburgers, chili, and meat loaf. Most people order fries, but regulars know to ask for the excellent onion rings. Meals always come with a small cup of sherbet, which makes the kids happy and ensures you don't walk out with onion-ring breath. Carryout is available and reservations are not needed.
Open daily 10:30 a.m.–11 p.m.

Blue Top Drive-In
8801 Indianapolis Blvd.
219/838-1233
Stop by the Blue Top on a summer evening and you'll see something out of an old episode of *Happy Days*, with carhops running out to take your order for a burger and a shake.

Be there on a weekend night in the spring and summer, and it looks like a used car lot. A very nice used car lot. The Blue Top is a magnet for classic car buffs. If you want to see souped up Chevys and classic Thunderbirds, this is the place. Many of the car owners will park, pop the hood, and take out a rag to begin polishing their car and swapping classic car restoration stories.

And here's the best part—the food's pretty good, too. The Blue Top restaurant opened in 1936, so they have to be doing something right. The specialty is the Big Ben Burger: two huge patties with cheese; the Blue Top is Big Ben with no cheese.

The Town Club Restaurant & Lounge
2904 45th St.

219/924-5227

The Town Club was founded just after World War II and has a reputation for serving big steaks and tasty fish. The fried shrimp is well-known in the area as being among the best. The Town Club also serves, without a doubt, the area's best martini. Reservations are usually needed, especially on the weekends. *Open Mon.–Sat. 11 a.m.–2:30 p.m. and 4:30 p.m.–10 p.m.*

Photo by John J. Watkins.

The Deep River Grinders playing 19th-century-style
base ball in Hobart's Deep River Park.

HOBART

Incorporated: 1889 (town), 1921 (city)
Population: 25,363
Median age: 37.7
Nickname/motto: The Friendly City
Size: 15.45 square miles

If you like shopping, this is the place to be. Not that it's all shopping malls and parking lots. Hobart also has a attractive downtown with some quaint shops.

Englishman George Earle bought the land for this community from the Potawatomi. He founded Hobart in 1849, naming it for his brother, Frederick Hobart Earle, of Falmouth, England. Earle opened a grist mill and built a dam on **Deep River**, creating **Lake George**. The lake remains one of the biggest attractions today.

The main industry in early Hobart was timber, much of which was shipped to Chicago builders. In the last part of the nineteenth century Hobart became one of the great brick-making cities in the Midwest. Clay from Hobart lacked impurities, which made the bricks highly sought after by builders.

The brick industry is gone, but Hobart has developed into a bedroom community known for a variety of recreational and shopping options. It has grown considerably through the annexation of **Westfield Shoppingtown Southlake** and many other nearby shopping centers. See the Shopping chapter (pp. 275-277) for what some of those retail centers have to offer.

Deep River Park
9410 Old Lincoln Hwy.
219/947-1958

This 1,400-acre park holds a piece of area history—**Wood's Mill**, a nineteenth-century, three-story grist mill on the National Register of Historic Places. Inside is a working 4,000-pound grindstone, just like the one that was used a century ago to grind corn, rye, and wheat into flour and meal.

John Wood, a Massachusetts farmer, built the first mill here in the 1830s. In 1876, his son Nathan built the present one. According to local history, Wood's Mill was the first ongoing industry in Lake and Porter Counties.

The Lake County Parks Department which runs the mill replaced the old grindstone several years ago. When the mill was home to a thriving business, all three stories were used for the mechanics of the stone and the storage of corn and finished flour.

Much of the space now is used for other purposes. The mill has a weaving area and displays that give a glimpse of life in the latter half of the nineteenth century. The exhibits include photos, furniture, and period quilts.

Next door, in a white, wood-frame building is the **Gift Shoppe and Visitors' Center**, previously a church once used by the Wood family and, until the early 1970s, the Deep River Church of Christ. For sale are old-fashioned toys, fresh syrups, preserves, and Indiana souvenirs.

The park has a canoe put-in just downstream of the Old Lincoln Way bridge. The trip ends about six miles, and usually two to three hours, later at the Arizona Avenue Bridge. The Deep River can get muddy, but the trip does go past some pretty countryside and through some dense forest. The Indiana

Department of Recreation recommends spring canoeing; in summer, water levels are often too low.

Other park amenities include an apple orchard, bridle paths, picnic facilities, fishing, hayrides in the fall, cross-country skiing in the winter, and a beautiful gazebo that has become a popular spot for weddings.

The park is open daily, year-round 7 a.m.–dusk; the mill and visitors center is open daily, May 1–Oct. 31, 10 a.m.–5 p.m. Directions: U.S. 30 to Route 51. Go north to Old Lincoln Highway (the first stop sign). Go east 2.5 miles.

Deep River Grinders Base Ball Club
Deep River Park
Grinder Field
9410 Old Lincoln Hwy.
219/947-1958
www.vbba.org/teams/grinders.html
Want to see how they played baseball in the old days? The Deep River Grinders play ball the way they did in the mid nineteenth century. The emphasis is on showmanship and gentlemanly behavior, so players don't slide and no one is going to get into a shouting match with the umpire. The pitcher is called a "hurler"; the batter, a "striker"; and the fans, "cranks." Players are in period costumes, and no gloves are used. The rules are slightly (OK, more than slightly) different from today. After a "striker" scores, he has to stop by the scorer's table and ring a little bell. Otherwise the run, called an "ace," doesn't count.

It's not simply a re-enactment, these guys play for real as charter members of the Vintage Base Ball Association. Among their opponents: the Berrien County (Michigan) Cranberry Boggers; the Elkhart County (Indiana) Bonneyville Millers; and the Rock Springs Ground Squirrels from Decatur, Illinois.

The team is sponsored by the Lake County Parks Department. *The season runs from June through September. Call for a game schedule.*

Hobart Historical Society Museum
706 E. Fourth St.

219/942-0970

Known as the "town's attic," the museum has historic documents, Ice Age fossils, Native American artifacts, items from the old brickyard, a model blacksmith shop, and a brochure for a walking tour that gives the background of mid-nineteenth through early twentieth-century buildings. One of the places mentioned is the English Renaissance-style museum building itself. Built in 1914 with a grant from Andrew Carnegie, it was once Hobart's library.

Open Sat. 10 a.m.–3 p.m., but call ahead because hours sometimes vary; other times by appointment.

Brickie Bowl
Hobart High School

36 E. 8th St.

If you're in the Hobart area on a fall Friday night, stop by the Brickie Bowl to see the kind of high school football hysteria that's indigenous to small towns. Elementary schoolboys talk about how they want to play for the Brickies someday. A giant schedule of games is even posted on the front of city hall.

The Brickies get their name from the brick-making industry that was a mainstay in Hobart from the 1880s until the 1960s. Under coach Don Howell the team won state titles in 1987, '89, '91, and '93. The field is now named for the late Howell, who retired in the late 1990s and died a short time later.

Directions: From I–80/94, exit at Indiana 51 south (Ripley Street). Follow 51 south as it winds through Hobart to Eighth Street. At Eighth, go west.

Skystone N' Silver

1350 Lake Park Ave.
219/942-9022
www.skystonensilver.com

The only store in Northwest Indiana that specializes in Native American art and jewelry, Skystone boasts that it carries nothing but authentic pieces. Items available here include Pueblo pottery, Navajo rugs, sculpture, toys, knives, and shields. Appraisals are also available.

Open Mon.–Tue., Sat. 10 a.m.–7 p.m., Wed.–Thu. 10 a.m.–5 p.m.

Festival Park

111 E. Ridge Rd.
219/942-2987

Home of the annual Lakefront Festival, Festival Park sits on **Lake George** in the center of downtown Hobart. It is a popular spot for lunching next to the water and feeding the ducks before heading back to work.

A pathway next to the water includes a covered footbridge and a wheelchair-accessible canoe launch. The park is also home to the **Revelli Band Shell**, site of several summer concerts. In 1925, William D. Revelli established the Hobart High School Band, which won three national championships. Revelli left for the University of Michigan in 1935, but his impact in Hobart was never forgotten.

The **Lakefront Festival**, held every August, draws people from all over the area who come for the rubber duck race (don't laugh, this is a lot of fun), the pig roast, and music. In recent years it has included several nights of bingo, a laser light show, and a beer garden.

EVENTS

Serb Fest
4101 W. 49th Ave.
219/942-2233
Roasted lamb and pig don't get any fresher than this—sliced right off the spit. Get a plate of *sarma* (stuffed cabbage) and end the meal with some of the fresh-made *palachinke* (crepes). Then the *tamburitza* music will set the mood for the evening.

Several local churches sponsor ethnic festivals, but Hobart's Serb Fest is one of the best. Held in late July, it's sponsored by **St. Sava Serbian Orthodox Church**, and its reputation has grown since it began in the early 1980s.

DINING

Bright Spot Diner
332 Main St.
219/947-1196
This is the downtown spot all the locals stop in to eat—for breakfast, lunch, and dinner. If you're looking for breakfast, there are plenty of egg and pancake choices on the menu. The Denver and broccoli omelets are among the best you'll find anywhere.

If it's later in the day, try the chicken and noodles, the sort of meal that puts the "comfort" in comfort food. Another favorite is the Hungarian goulash. It's not on the menu every day, but if it's one of the specials when you visit, don't pass this up.
Open Mon.–Sat. 5:30 a.m.–8:30 p.m., Sun. 6 a.m.–2 p.m.

Red Rooster Restaurant

1151 W. 37th Ave.

219/942-4615

It's not hard to spot the Red Rooster Restaurant—the only one in town with a giant rooster out front. It's been around for more than three decades and has earned a reputation as a fine place for dinner. Order the lake perch or fried chicken (with a name like Red Rooster, you just know chicken has to be one of the specials, right?).

Open Sun.–Thu. 6 a.m.–10 p.m., Fri.–Sat. 6 a.m.–midnight.

Lowell's 25-foot-high Civil War Memorial, erected in 1905,
is one of the state's oldest war memorials.

LOWELL

● ● ● ● ● ● ● ● ● ● ● ● ● ● ● ● ●

Incorporated: June 10, 1868
Population: 7,505
Median age: 34.2
Size: 3.85 square miles

Melvin A. Halsted settled Lowell in the 1840s, building a sawmill in 1848 and adding a flourmill a few years later. The town was named after Lowell, Massachusetts.

For most of its existence, Lowell has been a quiet town in southern Lake County. Some excitement came in 1933, according to town historian Richard Schmal, when members of the Dillinger gang robbed the local bank.

Today it is known for its collection of antique stores and small downtown setting. The community's other big attraction is a historic farm.

Buckley Homestead
3606 Belshaw Rd.
219/696-8969
The Buckley family emigrated from Ireland in the mid-nineteenth century. Their farm is now operated by the Lake County Parks Department, which has divided the homestead into three distinct areas: the 1850 pioneer farm, complete with log cabin; a restored, turn-of-the century schoolhouse; and a large 1910 farm with the Buckley's farmhouse, barn, milk house, orchard, and farm animals. Actors, trained in the ways of pioneer farm life from sheep shearing to detailed farming methods, perform for visitors. A picnic area and gift shop are

also on the site.

Pageantry at the homestead differs according to the time of year. Christmastime means singing carols and making plum pudding. Horse-drawn bobsled rides are offered in January and February. The popular **fall festival** includes wood carvers, bagpipes, craftspeople such as wreath makers and spinners, entertainment with a turn-of-the-century feel, and storytelling. There is the annual retelling of the *Legend of Sleepy Hollow*, as a tour guide takes visitors on a search for Ichabod Crane and the Headless Horseman (misplaced from New England!). Also in the fall, Buckley Homestead demonstrates how to cook with apples, including apple cobbler and apple pie. In October there's **Butchering Day on the Farm**—a chance to see how the farm prepared for winter. If you've ever wondered what else a pig is good for besides pork chops, stop by. And, while several area parks offer tractor-driven hayrides every fall, Buckley Homestead has horse-drawn hayrides.

Park is open daily 7 a.m.–dusk; buildings are open Sat.–Sun. 10 a.m.–5 p.m. May–Oct., for special programs, and by arrangement.

Three Creeks Monument
Commercial Ave.

Many communities in Northwest Indiana have war memorials, but few have one this old. Lowell's went up in 1905. The 25-foot-high monument was erected in honor of those who served in the Civil, Mexican, and Spanish-American Wars, and the War of 1812 according to an inscription at the 9-foot granite base. The memorial has the name of one woman, Mrs. Abbie Cutler, a Civil War nurse.

The memorial sits in **Old Town Square**, just east of the downtown business district, in a park filled with picnic benches and a gazebo.

EVENTS

Labor Day Parade

Lots of communities in Northwest Indiana have Labor Day parades, but few are as long-running as Lowell's, the state's oldest dating from 1919. That was the year Prohibition was enacted, the Chicago White Sox threw the World Series, and veterans returned home from World War I.

The Lowell parade is a family event that turns out crowds from the area. No celebrated guests, but plenty of floats made by local groups, high school marching bands, and the usual assortment of clowns. In recent years it has featured floats with Mexican themes, an appearance by the Northwest Indiana Pipes and Drums (a group of bagpipers from Valparaiso), and dancing horses.

DINING

Hawkeye's Restaurant
420–B E. Commercial
219/696-5864
The folks who run Hawkeye's are fans of old films, especially *Gone With the Wind*. Posters and pictures cover the wall, and it's hard to look in any direction without seeing Clark Gable or Vivian Leigh staring back at you.

The menu items are also named after Hollywood stars or have references to their films, such as the Adams Bar-B-Que Baby Back Ribs (inspired by the Spencer Tracy–Katharine Hepburn film *Adams Rib*) or the Veronica Lake Perch. Dinners run $5.95–$13.95.
Open Sun.–Fri. 11:30 a.m.–8 p.m., Sat. noon–8 p.m.

Zuni's Restaurant and Lounge
149 W. Commercial
219/696-8986
219/696-3565

Formerly Dante's, this restaurant has it all—a family dining area, a bar and restaurant, and a banquet room. Zuni's is both the sort of place where a family can take the kids or adults can go alone to get away from their kids for the evening. While their specialty is Italian, the menu carries a variety of items. Favorites include the broasted chicken or pork chops. On the weekends, the bar area has live entertainment and dancing.

Open Mon.–Sat. 11 a.m.–10 p.m., Sun. 9 a.m.–9 p.m. (until 2 p.m. for brunch).

MERRILLVILLE

Incorporated: December 30, 1971
Population: 30,560
Median age: 37
Size: 38.5 square miles

Although Merrillville wasn't incorporated until 1971, its history reaches back more than a century. In the 1830s it was part of a region controlled by the Potawatomi Indians. In the decades that followed it was known as McGwinn Village, then Wiggins Point, and later Centreville. In the 1850s, two brothers, William and Dudley Merrill, successful businessmen, settled in the area, and it soon became known as Merrillville.

An abundance of shopping, entertainment, and dining options make Merrillville a must-visit place in the area. It has more restaurants per capita than any other community in Indiana, the state's largest indoor shopping mall, and a noted live entertainment theater.

Star Plaza Theatre
U.S. 30 and Interstate 65
219/769-6600
773/734-7266
www.starplazatheatre.com
The Star Plaza is a concert destination for people from all over the Chicago area. It features a huge stage, great seating, convenient location, plenty of parking, and a stellar lineup of performers. Recent years have brought the likes of B.B. King, Ted Nugent, Anita Baker, Kenny Rogers, and the Oak Ridge Boys.

The Star Plaza is also one of the homes of the **Northwest Indiana Symphony** (219/836-0525, www.nwisymphony.org), a 70-plus-piece orchestra whose popularity has taken off in recent years. Kirk Muspratt, an Alberta, Canada, native who worked with orchestras in St. Louis, Pittsburgh, and Utah, was named music director and conductor in 2000. The orchestra's chamber music series takes place at the small, more intimate **Center for Visual and Performing Arts** in nearby Munster (see p. 134), but the symphonic and pops performances are on the Star Plaza stage. Guest artists in the past couple years have included pianist Andre Watts, violinist Judith Ingolfsson, and performer Frank Sinatra Jr.

Radisson Hotel at Star Plaza
I–65 and U.S. 30
219/769-6311
800/333-3333
www.radisson.com/merrillvillein
The Radisson is the area's largest hotel. Its huge indoor pool, great food, and beautiful atrium make it popular with out-of-town visitors who come to shows at the adjoining Star Plaza Theatre and stay to avoid the drive home right after a concert.

If you come for the weekend, make a reservation to enjoy the Sunday brunch at J. Ginger's American Grille. In addition to ham, prime rib, waffles, and eggs cooked to order, breakfast will feature live entertainment. Brunch is $16.95 and is served from 10 a.m. to 2 p.m.

For a fun evening, visit **Wisecrackers Comedy Club** (219/769-6311, x. 73, www.wisecrackerscomedy.com), Northwest Indiana's only standup venue for comedians. Known throughout the Midwest, Wisecrackers is located inside the Radisson Hotel and has shows Fridays and Saturdays at 8:30 p.m. and 10:00 p.m.

Merrillville–Ross Township Historical Museum

13 W. 73rd Ave.

219/756-2042

http://users.rootsweb.com/~inlake/ross.htm

This museum, which is maintained by the Merrillville–Ross Township Historical Society, is located in the former town hall offices. Built in 1896, the two-story brick building was originally a school for what was then the very rural Ross Township community. Items on display include military uniforms, nineteenth-century farm equipment, an old-fashioned school room, and a map from the 1800s that recorded the arrival in the area of different pioneer families. Tours are available.

Open Sun. 1 p.m.–4 p.m., May–Oct.

Deep River Waterpark

9001 East U.S. 30

219/947-7850

www.deepriverwaterpark.com

Sixty foot slides where swimmers can zoom along at 30-plus miles per hour have made Deep River Waterpark an area favorite. The park features the 800-foot "Bayou River Ride" for tubers, the Dragon speed slide, the Whitewater Run tube slide, Pipeline Express and Slide-winder, and the Rip Tide wave pool, as well as a children's play area.

At a concession area with chips, tacos, and other snacks save room for Dip and Dots, dubbed the "ice cream of the future." Visitors can bring in food, but no glass bottles or alcohol. Kids a year old or younger get in free. Little ones still in diapers must wear waterproof swim diapers.

Deep River has a gift shop and tube and locker rentals. On hot days plan to get there early to be sure to get a tube. Tuesday is Tubin' Tuesday, with later hours, discounts, and a disk jockey. The park is part of the Lake County Park Department system.

Open daily 10 a.m.–6 p.m., late May–Aug. Admission is $14 for adults

10 a.m.– 2 p.m., $12 after 2 p.m. Admission for those under 46" tall is $7 all day. Spectators pay $7, which is refunded upon departure. Indiana residents can get a $2 discount by showing identification. Group discounts and season passes are available. Directions: From I–65, take U.S. 30 east about 4.5 miles.

SS. Constantine and Helen Greek Orthodox Cathedral
800 Madison St.
219/769-2481
The stained glass and Byzantine mosaic work make a visit to this Greek Orthodox church worthwhile. The rotunda is more than 100 feet across and 50 feet high, with over two dozen pieces of stained glass artwork ringing the interior. To tour the church, call ahead to ensure a guide.

Each July the gold-domed church hosts one of the area's largest Greek fests. Opaa! You don't have to be Greek to enjoy the authentic food, beer garden, kiddy rides, and bands.
Directions: U.S. 30 to Madison Street, then north on Madison

EVENTS

Northwest Indiana Festival of Lights
Hidden Lake Park
6355 Broadway
219/769-8180
The new Christmas tradition of driving through Hidden Lake Park to view beautiful lighted displays add a unique dimension to the magic of the holiday season.
Open weekends (evening hours) starting in late November, weekday hours start in mid-December. Admission is $3 per car. Directions: From I–80/94, exit Broadway south to entrance of the park. The entrance is visible soon after 61ˢᵗ Street.

DINING

Cafe Fondue
281 W. 80th Pl.
219/793-1511
Who knew there were so many kinds of fondue? You might start with a cheese fondue, then move on to dipping veggies. Or, choose a main course from among several cuts of meat, poultry, or seafood, and flavor the morsels yourself with a battery of sauces. Dessert is pastry and fruit dunked in chocolate. A huge wine selection is available to compliment every course.

Cafe Fondue is a little pricey (meals range from $16.95 for the vegetarian fondue to $27.95 for the seafood lover's delight), but it is a memorable experience.

Youngsters will love cooking their own dinner and dipping into the various sauces, but those with small children should remember that the sauces are often hot and the fondue bowls can be tipped over.
Open Mon.–Thu. 5 p.m.–9 p.m., Fri.–Sat. 5 p.m.–10 p.m. Directions: From U.S. 30, take Broadway north to 80th Place. Turn west (left) at 80th Place. Reservations are recommended. Cafe Fondue is very busy on weekends.

Café Venezia
405 W. 81st
219/736-2203
The Zagat Survey of Chicago-area restaurants has called this the best Italian restaurant in Northwest Indiana. In addition to its renown for world-class pasta, Café Venezia has a reputation for seafood, veal, and unusual specials, not to mention the homemade sorbet and generous cappuccinos for capping off the meal right. It has no children's menu, but small plates of pastas

are available for the kids.

Café Venezia is easy to miss if you're not looking for it. It's tucked away inside the Ross Plaza strip mall on U.S. 30. Don't be fooled by the location, this is upscale dining with the atmosphere and prices to match. Reservations are strongly suggested.
Open for lunch Mon.–Sat. 11:30 a.m.–2:30 p.m.; for dinner Mon.–Thurs. 5 p.m.–9 p.m., Fri.–Sat. 5 p.m.–10:30 p.m.

MUNSTER

Incorporated: July, 1907
Population: 21,511
Median age: 42.9
Motto/Nickname: Town on the Ridge
Land area: 7.44 square miles

Settled by the Dutch in the early 1800s, Munster was first known as a stopping-off point for travelers on their way to Chicago who grabbed dinner and a pint of beer at the Brass Tavern, opened in 1845 by Allan and Julie Brass. Its name comes from Eldert Munster, who ran the local post office.

Munster's fastest growth came in the years after World War II as a bedroom community for industrial workers in Hammond, Gary, and East Chicago. Today it has one of the highest per capita incomes in the state, as many professionals call this town home.

Many assume Munster's nickname comes from Ridge Road, a busy thoroughfare that cuts through residential areas and the business district. The "Ridge" in Town on the Ridge (and the source of the road's name) comes from the natural ridge of land that separated the Little Calumet River from what was once called Cady Marsh. This was literally where the ridge of the glaciers that formed Lake Michigan once reached.

Recreation lovers feel right at home in Munster. The town has an extensive park system and a 20-plus mile bike path.

The Center for Visual and Performing Arts
1040 Ridge Rd.
219/836-1930
219/836-3255 (box office)
www.cvpa.org

With two art galleries, a rehearsal hall, banquet room, and a 500-seat theater that attracts a variety of dramas, musicals, and concerts, this 70,000-square-foot center is a cultural jewel for the entire area. It is home to the **Northwest Indiana Symphony's chamber group**, the **Northern Indiana Arts Association (NIAA)**, and the **Ridgewood Arts Foundation**.

Stop in the building's Atrium Gallery and the 5300-square-foot William J. Bachman Gallery, named for the architect who designed the center, who also was a founding member of the NIAA. Both galleries are maintained by the **Northern Indiana Arts Association** (219/836-1839) spotlight works of a variety of artists: Sometimes the exhibit will showcase the works of students from a local university or high school, another time it might be watercolors, photographs, or the work of a silversmith.

Advance tickets to shows are available at the center's box office, also a Ticketmaster outlet. The center also has a gift shop where artists' works, books, posters, and other items can be purchased.

If you plan to be in the area on a Sunday, call the **banquet hall** (219/836-1950) and make reservations for the brunch, which includes great food and live entertainment (Adults, $17.50; children, $8.75).

Galleries open Mon.–Fri. 10 a.m.–5 p.m., Sat. noon–5 p.m., Sun. 11 a.m.–4 p.m. Brunch Sun. 11 a.m.–2 p.m. Directions: From I–80/94 or I–90, take Calumet Avenue south to Ridge Road. Go east on Ridge Road; the center will be on your right. Ample parking is available.

Carmelite Monastery Shrines
1628 Ridge Rd.
219/838-7111
Founded by Polish Carmelite Friars in the early 1950s, these shrines have attracted visitors ever since with their beauty and the message preached by the fathers and brothers who live and work here. The Carmelites served as chaplains for the Polish Free Army in World War II. They fled the country after it became a Soviet satellite.

The monastery, hidden from busy Ridge Road by evergreen trees, draws the faithful from throughout Northwest Indiana and Chicago each Sunday. Masses are in English, Polish, and Latin.

The grounds have an arboretum and an abundance of places to rest and reflect. There are nearly two dozen shrines on the six acres, including stunning chapels and grottos. They are built with sponge rock and stone, and adorned with crystals and other stones. When the sun hits them at certain angles, the rocks seem to move. Special lighting is used to enhance the magical appearance.
Directions: From I–80/94 or I–90, take Calumet Avenue south to Ridge Road. Go east on Ridge Road. The monastery entrance is on your right. Parking and admission is free.

Bieker Woods
Ridge Rd. at Columbia Ave.
219/836-6920
http://members.aol.com/ ht a/oldmunster/mhstree
Hikers and history fans will appreciate Bieker Woods. The beloved small forest is home to the nineteenth-century Kaske House, one of the few structures left from Munster's earliest days. The **Munster Historical Society** (219/838-3296) maintains the house and has a museum here.

The structure, which is listed on the National Register of Historic Places, takes its name from Hugo and Wilhelmina Kaske who lived there in the early twentieth century. Wilhelmina was the daughter of Johann and Wilhelmina Stallbohn, who ran the Stallbohn Inn at this site in the latter half of the nineteenth century. According to the historical society, a telegraph that ran to the inn was the way local residents learned of President Lincoln's assassination in 1865.

The best time of year to visit Bieker Woods is late October for the annual **Haunted Woods** attraction. Walk down the woody paths and you'll run into a motley collection of ghosts, goblins, and vampires, a collection of older school kids recruited for the effort. These monsters jump out as groups pass, ensuring shrieks of terror (mixed in with some giggles) from younger visitors and their parents.

Three Floyds Brewery
9750 Indiana Pkwy.
888/266-0294
www.threefloyds.com
Three Floyds is a popular brewery whose selection includes Robert the Bruce Scottish Ale, Black Sun Stout, and Calumet Queen, German-style ale. Hour-long tours are offered for $5 and include a tasting of some of the brewery's work.
Open Fri. noon–7 p.m., Sat. noon–5 p.m. Directions: I–80/94 to Calumet Avenue south. Go west on Superior Avenue, then south on Indiana Avenue.

Community Veterans Memorial
Calumet, Columbia, and Superior Aves.
www.communityveteransmemorial.org
The Community Veterans Memorial features life-size sculptures of the nation's service men and women, in battle scenes from World Wars I and II, Korea, Vietnam, and the Gulf War. The Community Hospital donated the land and, working with the

Photo by the author.

Holley Ores's "Worker's Sculpture" in Munster's Rotary Park.

town, spearheaded the effort to raise $3 million for the memorial. The principal sculptors are Julie Rotblatt–Amrany and her husband Omri Amrany, two artists from Highland Park, Illinois, the same pair who did the soaring Michael Jordan statue at Chicago's United Center and the Harry Caray statute that greets visitors to Wrigley Field.

Directions: From I–80/94, take Calumet Avenue south.

Worker's Sculpture
Rotary Park
Ridge Rd. at Columbia Ave.
In a tiny park, across Ridge Road from Bieker Woods, is one of the area's most distinctive sculptures. Holly Ores's work depicts the region's heritage with metal stick figures of three men—a Native American, a farmer, and a steel worker. The piece was dedicated on July 4, 1976.

Photo by John J. Watkins.

A scene from Munster's annual jazz and blues festival.

EVENTS

Blues, Jazz and Arts on the Ridge
Munster Town Hall Lawn
1005 Ridge Rd.
219/836-5549
The annual (and free!) July fest, second in the area only to Chicago's jazz festival, brings some of the best local blues and jazz artists together and attracts between 8,000 and 10,000 to the town hall grounds for great music and food. Performers in recent years have included Coco Montoya, the Steepwater Band, Dixie Dogs, and Kenny Neal. Food vendors' wares are not limited to burgers and hot dogs; you can dine on such delicacies as alligator and barbecue. Alcohol is not served.

Ice Carving Competition
Community Park
Calumet Ave. and Ridge Rd.
219/836-4582

The Community Hospital sponsors this event, which attracts dozens of championship ice carvers to Munster each January as part of the larger **Winter Magic Festival**. Their masterpieces, stunning works that resemble cut glass, are on display in a **Magic Garden of Ice Sculptures**. The weekend of family fun includes a pancake breakfast, indoor craft fair, horse-drawn carriage rides, snow wall painting, mini ice-golf, and more.

Courtesy of The Community Hospital.

An artist at Munster's annual ice sculpting event.

DINING

Café Elise
435 Ridge Rd.
219/836-2233

Appearances can be deceiving. From the outside, Café Elise, named for the daughter of owners Scott and Sue Dixon, looks like a tiny restaurant in a small shopping center. But inside is one of the best restaurants in the area—readers of *The Times* recently voted it "Best Gourmet Restaurant" in the region. The menu is innovative and always changing, but always includes salads, homemade soup, fresh fish, and pasta. The specialty is rack of veal with honey-wine glaze.

Café Elise's reputation has spread throughout Northwest Indiana and Chicago, and getting a table on a weekend without a reservation has become an impossible dream. Stop by during the week though to have an easier chance at a table. The entire restaurant is non-smoking. An appetizer, entree, and dessert will run the average diner $20–$35.

Open for lunch, Tue.–Fri. 11:30 a.m.–2:30 p.m.; for dinner, Tue.–Sat. 5 p.m.–10 p.m., Sun. 4 p.m.–8 p.m. Directions: From I–80/94 or I–90 take Calumet Avenue south to Ridge Road. Go west on Ridge Road. Café Elise is in the Harrison Ridge shopping center. Ample parking is available in the rear.

Giovanni's
603 Ridge Rd.
219/836-6220
Giovanni's has been called one of the best Italian restaurants in greater Chicago by the *Chicago Tribune*. Pro LoDuca, a native of Sicily who wanted to bring authentic dishes of his home to the area, opened the café in 1965. The menu's main attractions include veal scallopine Toscana, chicken vesuvio, and sautéed scampi. Giovanni's also offers pizza, with toppings like sun-dried tomatoes, prosciutto ham, and plum tomatoes.

On Friday and Saturday night a piano player provides entertainment in the bar. Giovanni's atmosphere is casual—jackets and ties, dresses, or jeans are equally acceptable. Children are welcome, but there is no children's menu and selections for them are limited. Dinner reservations are recommended.

Open for lunch, Mon.–Fri. 11 a.m.–3 p.m.; for dinner, Mon.–Thu. 3:30 p.m.–10:30 p.m., Fri. 3:30 p.m.–11:30 p.m., Sat. 5 p.m.–11:30 p.m. Directions: From I–80/94 or I–90, exit Calumet Avenue south. At Ridge Road, go west. Giovanni's is on your right.

Old Town Hall
805 Ridge Rd.
219/836-0600
Just as the name promises, this restaurant is located inside the building that was once home to town government. The walls are decorated with historic photos from the early twentieth century.

Food offerings vary, with an array of sandwiches, stir frys, steaks, chops, and more. A small bar tucked in the corner of the dining room helps ensure this is a popular spot for dinner. Prices are reasonable. The Old Town Hall is also a preferred breakfast spot, with some of the best omelets around.
Open daily 6:30 a.m.–11 p.m. Directions: From I–80/94 or I–90, take Calumet Avenue south to Ridge Road. Free parking is available on the side and around back.

Schoop's
215 Ridge Rd.
219/836-6233
When you walk into Schoop's Hamburgers, don't think this is one of those trendy diners made up to recall a place from the 1950s and early 1960s. Schoop's has the feel of an old-fashioned diner because that's exactly what it is. There has been some expansion over the past few decades, and the songs on the jukebox have changed, but this is still a place where the emphasis is on the basics—hamburgers, hot dogs, chili, and soup. If you're hungry, try a Mickey—a double cheeseburger—then wash it down with a chocolate soda.

In recent years Schoop's has opened in several Midwestern cities and in Florida. But this is one of the originals. The atmosphere is laid back and great for kids. If you're in a hurry, call ahead for takeout.
Open Mon.–Sat. 11 a.m.–10 p.m., Sun. 11 a.m.–10 p.m. Directions: From I–80/94 or I–90, exit Calumet Avenue south. At Ridge Road, go west. Look for the storefront on your right, just before Hohman Avenue. Parking is in the back.

SCHERERVILLE

Incorporated: 1911
Population: 24,851
Median age: 37.2
Motto/Nickname: Crossroads of the Nation
Size: 12.97 square miles

For most of its existence, Schererville has been a quiet bedroom community, although its nickname "Crossroads of the Nation" comes from its place at the intersection of U.S. 41 and U.S. 30, two heavily traveled routes. It lacks a bustling downtown area, but retail growth has burgeoned over the past decade.

The town is named for Nicholas Scherer, a German settler who came here in 1866. With land purchased from Aaron Hart, who founded neighboring Dyer, Scherer laid out the town that now bears his name.

Illiana Motor Speedway

7211 U.S. 30
219/322-5311
www.illianaspeedway.com

Auto race fans head for one of the most popular speedways in the Chicago area on Saturday nights all year long to see a variety of events, including championship series. Every October the track hosts the **Tony Bettenhausen Memorial,** named for the Tinley Park, Illinois, native and championship driver who was killed test-driving a car at the Indianapolis Motor Speedway in 1961.

The Illiana Speedway, a half-mile, oval track, has hosted races

since 1945. It was first paved in 1961. It features races of late models, mid-Americans, super stocks, and street stocks.
Directions: From I–90 or I–80/94, exit U.S. 41 (Indianapolis Boulevard) south. At U.S. 30, go east. The track will be on your right. Plenty of parking is available.

EVENTS

Corn Roast
Redar Park
Austin and Gregory St.
219/322-5412 (Chamber of Commerce)
Schererville has hosted a well-attended, crowd-pleasing corn roast the last Friday in July since 1963. When it was a tiny town amidst corn-growing farms, the roast was a natural. Today, most of the farms have been paved over and Schererville is fast-growing with new subdivisions. The corn is still grown locally—**Elzinga Farm Market** has a special crop slated just for the fair. Besides thousands of ears of corn, visitors consume mounds of sauerkraut and barrels of beer. Entertainment and craft shows round out the event.

DINING

House of Kobe
1961 Wicker Blvd.
219/322-1919
Sushi, chicken and steak teriyaki, and hibachi shrimp are House of Kobe's specialties. Chefs prepare the food right at your table, using their sharp knives and forks like magic wands. A second restaurant has opened in Merrillville (8101 Broadway, 219/791-9500) that also has lunchtime hours. Reservations are advised,

especially on weekends.
Open Mon.–Thu. 4:30 p.m.–9:30 p.m., Fri.–Sat. 4:30 p.m.–10:30 p.m., Sun. 11:30 a.m.–9 p.m.

Jalapeños
200 U.S. 41
219/864-8862
Jalapeños bills itself as "the hottest Mexican restaurant." Your server will warn you when a dish is prepared with super-hot peppers: If it sounds like too much, you can ask for milder substitutes. Among the recommended dishes are the mole, burritos, and carne con chile. A huge lunch buffet is a good way to sample the many specialties.

The menu is reasonably priced and the atmosphere is terrific. A mariachi band provides entertainment on weekends.
Open Sun.–Thu. 11 a.m.–10 p.m., Sat.–Sun. 11 a.m.–11 p.m. The bar is open Sun.–Tue., Thur. until midnight ; Wed., Sat.–Sun. until 3 a.m. Directions: From I–80/94, exit U.S. 41 south.

Schererville Lounge
48 E. Joliet St.
219/322-5660
The locals know this is as the place for great-tasting perch or frog legs. Steaks, ribs, and a host of sandwiches fill out their menu. Even the children's menu offers kiddie-sized portions of perch and frog legs alongside the burgers. Reservations are often not needed, but it's a good idea to call ahead just in case.
Open Mon.–Sat. 11 a.m.–10 p.m. Directions: From U.S. 30, exit Joliet Street north.

Teibel's
U.S. 30 and U.S. 41
219/865-2000
Teibel's has been family-run since 1929. Although located at a highly-traveled intersection, it hasn't thrived for 70 years just

because it's convenient. Diners return again and again to the upscale dining rooms to feast on steaks, perch, fried chicken, and good down-home food. Lunches run about $6–$10, dinners about $11–$23. Live entertainment performs in the lounge. *Open Mon.–Sat. 11 a.m.–10 p.m., Sun. 11 a.m.–8 p.m. Directions: From I–80/94, exit U.S. 41 (Indianapolis Boulevard) south.*

Tandoor
1535 U.S. 41
219/865-9511
Zagat's restaurant survey calls Tandoor "the only Indian in Indiana." A slight exaggeration, but the food is absolutely authentic. The breads are prepared each day in a clay oven and many of the main courses are stewed in a clay pot over an open flame. Ask about the chef's specials. The daily lunch buffet, as well as the Monday night buffet, includes more than a dozen items.

Open daily 11 a.m.–2:30 p.m. and 5 p.m.–10 p.m. Directions: From I–80/94, exit U.S. 41 south. Tandoor is located about a block north of U.S. 30.

SCHNEIDER

Incorporated: 1915
Population: 317
Median age: 33.1
Size: 0.9 square miles

Schneider, settled in 1835, has remained a tiny farming community, and just outside its limits is of one of the state's most diverse nature preserves.

LaSalle Fish & Wildlife Area
U.S. 41 at Indiana 10
219/992-3019
http://www.in.gov/dnr/fishwild/publications/lasalle.htm
Named after the French explorer Robert Cavelier, sieur de LaSalle, the state-maintained 3,648-acre preserve stretches from Lake County south to Newton County. LaSalle and his fellow explorers came down the Kankakee River in the late 1600s searching for a waterway route to the Pacific Ocean. He explored the Grand Marsh of the Kankakee, now mostly gone. The preserve is all that remains, with ducks, geese, herons, egrets, snakes, and frogs among the birds and small animals that visitors will spot.

The **Kankakee River** flows through the site, and just west of the Illinois line is a boat launch. Four miles further, just before the river runs under U.S. 41, is a picnic area and primitive campground, and on the preserve's southern half, near **Beaver Lake Ditch**, is a rifle range.

You can hike on service roads running through the property

Photo by John J. Watkins.

LaSalle Fish & Wildlife Area.

with the best one being the longest. It begins in parking area 3A at the southern end of the Kankakee River and cuts through swamps, giving an up-close look at the wildlife.

The marsh is a popular spot with waterfowl hunters. Access to portions of the preserve is restricted during the October through January hunting season. Call ahead for details.
Directions: From I–65 exit at Indiana 10 and go west about 12 miles.

ST. JOHN

Incorporated: 1911
Population: 8,382
Median age: 38.6
Land Area: 6.09 square miles

The first settler in St. John was John Hack, a German immigrant who began farming in 1837. In its earliest days, the community was known as St. Johns. The "s" was dropped by the time St. John was incorporated as a town in 1911. Since then it has grown from a small farming community into a thriving mini-metropolis. The growth has meant an increase in retail shops, with strip malls replacing many of the corn and soybean fields.

St. John Evangelist Church
9300 Wicker Ave.
219/365-5678
When driving U.S. 41 you can't miss St. John Evangelist Catholic Church, one of the tallest buildings in town. You might not notice the tiny log cabin in the church cemetery. Now the church's **Eucharistic Adoration Chapel,** many locals call it the pioneer church. Built in 1839 by John Hack, it may be the first church built in Lake County. Many of the town's earliest settlers are buried in the cemetery here.

Statue in a Field
This large statue of Blessed Mother Mary rising out of a farm field on U.S. 41 just south of town causes many drivers to slow down, look, and often stop to reflect and rest. There is no church next door, no religious school; the statue just sits there.

Photo by John J. Watkins.

The historic St. John church, built in 1839 by John Hack,
is now St. John's Eucharistic Adoration Chapel.

The statue was erected in 1956. An inscription at the base reads:
*In loving memory of Rev. C.P. Brogan, past diocesan spiritual leader of the
Legion of Mary.* It is not maintained by any local church, and the
Gary Diocese plays no role in its upkeep. In fact, the diocese
has tried to find the family who takes care of the statue's
upkeep and has been told only that they want to maintain their
privacy.

WHITING

• • • • • • • • • • • • • • •

Founded: 1895 (as a town), 1903 (as a city)
Population: 5,137
Median Age: 35.9
Nickname: Little City on the Lake
Size: 1.76 square miles

Tiny Whiting on the shores of Lake Michigan was originally known as Whiting's Crossing. Herbert L. "Pop" Whiting was a train engineer who had a reputation for taking risks. In 1869, at a spot about 100 yards south of the current Whiting Park, Whiting intentionally derailed his train to make way for an oncoming passenger train.

To avoid a reoccurrence, the railroad put in a sidetrack and called it Whiting's Siding. When **Standard Oil** came to the area in 1889, the name was shortened to Whiting. A marker now stands in Whiting Park to honor the city's namesake. The city's name "preserves the memory of one of the humblest men that ever pulled a throttle or ditched a train," it says.

With the population growing rapidly with the arrival of Standard Oil, Whiting became a town in 1895 to avoid being annexed by Hammond to the south. It became a city eight years later. Today, with less than two square miles, it is Indiana's smallest city but is home to the nation's largest inland refinery. The refinery's name has changed over the years, from Standard Oil to Amoco, then to BP–Amoco and, in 1999, to just BP.

Whiting and Standard Oil played a small but crucial role in the **Manhattan Project**, the code name for the development of the atomic bomb in the 1940s. Workers spent time at an obsolete boiler plant on the Standard Oil of Indiana grounds, where they experimented with ways to separate boron isotopes.

Another important scientific discovery has a local tie. Whiting native Ferid Murad won the Nobel Prize in 1998 for his discovery that nitric acid is a signal carrier for the cardiovascular system. That work was instrumental in the development of Viagra.

Whiting Lakefront Park
Located just east of Hammond's Whihala Beach on the Michigan lakefront, locals call it simply Whiting Park. It's not a good choice for swimming because large rocks line much of the shoreline, but it's a great place to bring lunch, chill out, and view the majesty of the lake and admire the Chicago skyline. The park also treats visitors with a garden, volleyball and tennis courts, a children's playground, and walking paths.

Free concerts by the **Whiting Park Festival Orchestra** are held on Saturday nights during the summer. A **Fourth of July celebration** is always one of the area's best because it comes at the conclusion of a weeklong carnival. And in the fall, the **Haunted Pavilion** is a Halloween favorite for kids. For information on park festivals, contact the **Whiting/Robertsdale Chamber of Commerce** (219/659-0292).

Parking is free for residents, $5 for those from Robertsdale (the name given the northern most section of Hammond), $7 for all those from other places in Indiana, and $10 for out-of-staters. The parking lot closes at 10 p.m. No dogs allowed. Access is off Park Road, but you have to cross several sets of train tracks so delays are possible.

City Hall
1443 119th St.
219/659-7700
If you think there is something somber, or even spiritual, about

the look of the Whiting City Hall, there's a good reason. The halls of local government were once home to a church that later became a National Guard Armory. Above the main doorway, *Indiana National Guard Armory* is etched into the brick front, which was added to the original structure. The oldest part of the building was built in 1894 by the Plymouth Congregational Church, later altered in 1927 when the National Guard bought it, and changed again in 1936 by the Works Progress Administration.

In the late 1990s one of the original pieces of stained glass was taken out of storage from the attic and put on display in the building's side entrance. In 1999, a small garden was opened next door. Named **Binhammer Commons**, it honors Carl Binhammer, former president of State Bank of Whiting. The garden has benches on which to sit and admire a swan sculpture by Christopher Diersen called *Grace*.

If you stop to take a look at City Hall, take time to grab a snack at the **Calumet Bakery** (1446 119th St., 219/473-9560) across the street. It's one of the area's best.

Hoosier Theatre
1335 119th St.
219/659-0567
From the outside, this theater looks like any other old movie house. But once inside you'll see that it's the area's last remaining movie palace. The Hoosier Theatre opened in 1924 and remains a classic, ornate shrine to the days when going to the movies was an experience. A historic pipe organ thunders before shows. Instead of the shoebox screening rooms found at multiplexes, the Hoosier has a sky-blue ceiling dome, crystal chandeliers, and a huge, thirty-two-foot screen. This was the way movies were meant to be seen. Even a bad film seems better in these surroundings.

The Hoosier opened as a vaudeville and silent movie house. After decades of neglect, the interior was renovated by owner John Katris and turned into a community treasure. Plans are underway to restore the theater's stage to feature live productions.

Prices are low, and when *The End* flashes on the screen, you are right downtown within walking distance of several good restaurants.

Lake Michigan Winery
Calumet Ave. at 119th St.
219/659-WINE
888/TNT-WINE
www.lakemichiganwinery.com
Looks can be deceiving. Drive too fast past this building and you might mistake it for a gas station. At one time it was. Don't let that stop you from checking out the only winery in Lake County. It's received rave reviews from around the Chicago area.

The Lake Michigan Winery specializes in wines from Indiana and Michigan. It is in the heart of a busy urban area, but after tasting what flows out of this tiny winery, you will think you're in the middle of wine country. Free tours are available, and be sure to save some time afterwards to relax before the wood stove in the tasting room. For a local treat, ask for a glass of the Whiting White. The winery has become a popular stopping place for those who want to enjoy a glass of wine and some conversation without the noise and distractions of a bar.

The winery is actually in a section of north Hammond known as Robertsdale, but it has a Whiting mailing address.
Open daily 1 p.m.–7 p.m. Directions: From I–80/94, exit Calumet Avenue north. From I–90, exit at Indianapolis Boulevard , and then south at Calumet Avenue.

Cornerstone Art Center
Centier Bank
1500 119th St.
219/473-9881
The gallery in the local bank features the work of area artists. The displays usually last several weeks.
Open Mon.–Fri. 9 a.m.–5 p.m., Sat. 9 a.m.–noon.

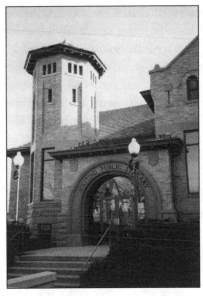

Photo by the author.

Whiting Public Library
1735 Oliver St.
219/473-4700
www.whiting.lib.in.us
A now faded cornerstone remembers the man who built it with the inscription, *The gift of Andrew Carnegie A.D. 1905.* Bloomington, Illinois, architect Paul Moratz's design included a large rotunda for the circulation desk. The exterior has a stately look, with stone and brick topped off by a barrel tile roof. The building sits on land donated by Standard Oil.

An addition was built in 1982 with care taken to preserve the look of the historic structure. The library still has the fireplaces and reading alcoves that were part of the original design.
Open Mon.–Thu. 9 a.m.–8 p.m., Fri.–Sat. 9 a.m.–5 p.m.

Whiting Community Center
1938 Clark
219/659-0860
www.whitingindiana.com/comm_center.html
Originally known as the Memorial Community House, this

two-story, red-brick building on the National Register of Historic Places was dedicated in 1923 as a memorial to Standard Oil employees who served in World War I. Standard Oil provided the land and $300,000 toward construction, while John D. Rockefeller contributed $100,000 and John D., Jr. added another $50,000, according to *The Calumet Region*, a local history published in 1959.

Built with an eye to southern Italian architecture, Standard Oil's founder hoped the building would help foster a sense of culture in the community. It included an auditorium, gymnasiums and pool, and billiard and reading rooms.

The center continues to serve the community with its meeting rooms, gymnasium, and bowling alley. Each December it is home to an annual community Christmas celebration. *Open Mon.–Fri. 8 a.m.–8 p.m., Sat. 8 a.m.–3 p.m. (closed Sat. June–Sept.). Daily fee is $3 for residents, $5 for non-residents ($1.50/$2.50 for seniors), and $1 for a children's swim pass.*

EVENTS

Pierogi Festival
Downtown Whiting
219/659-0292 (Whiting–Robertsdale Chamber of Commerce)
www.whitingindiana.com/pierogi.html
In many of Indiana's small towns, young girls grow up hoping to be queen of the county fair. Only in Whiting can a young boy dream of being named Mr. Pierogi, who, dressed like a giant Polish dumpling, makes his appearance every July during Pierogi Festival. Walking with him in the **Pierogi Parade** are the dancing Pieroguettes.

The festival is a good-natured celebration of the area's ethnic

Photo by John J. Watkins.

Pieroguettes at Whiting's annual Pierogi Festival.

heritage. It's also one of the most popular local festivals, attracting crowds who can't wait for a plate filled with fresh pierogi and sauerkraut. After stuffing oneself with ethnic delights, you can visit a huge beer garden, dance to polka bands, and play bingo and Eastern Bloc Jeopardy.

DINING

Dimitri's Cake and Steak
1342 119th St.
219/659-1390
Where the elite (city officials and business owners) meet to eat steak and cake, as well as burgers, ribs, a variety of salads, and shish kabobs.
Open daily 6 a.m.–8 p.m.

Keith's
1872 Indianapolis Blvd.
219/659-4444
The building used to be a neighborhood tavern; now it's one of the area's better restaurants, with a cozy setting and an elegant menu. Appetizers include smoked trout and Portobello mushrooms. Ask about the chef's daily special. Other choices include shrimp anisette, rack of lamb, and smoked shrimp pasta. Save room for some key lime pie. Try the Burger From Hell; it's huge and it's good. Keith's is not a large restaurant, so call ahead for reservations.
Hours vary by the season. Open for lunch and dinner. Call for details.

PORTER COUNTY

Porter County 161

Beverly Shores 163
Chesterton 167
Hebron 173
Kouts 177
Ogden Dunes 179
Portage 181
Porter 185
Town of Pines 189
Valparaiso 191

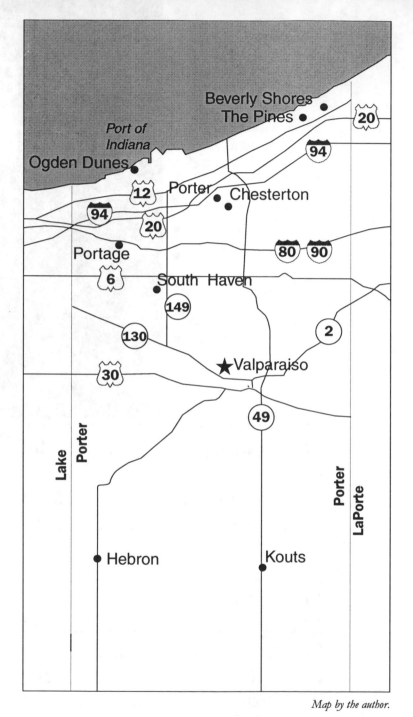

Map by the author.

Porter County, Indiana

PORTER COUNTY

Created: February 7, 1835
Named after: U.S. Navy Commander David Porter
County Seat: Valparaiso
Population: 146,798
Median age: 36.3
Land area: 418 square miles

Porter County is home to some of the Midwest's most beautiful natural sites with both the **Indiana Dunes National Lakeshore** (p. 250) and **Indiana Dunes State Park** (p. 260). And in the middle of the traditional country towns and acres of farmland is **Valparaiso University** (p. 192), consistently ranked among the Midwest's best small universities.

Porter County was home to Potawatomi Indians until Joseph Bailly, the first white settler, arrived in 1822. By the 1850s, rail lines ran through the area providing links to Chicago and the East. State lawmakers created and named Porter County for Commander David Porter, a naval hero in the War of 1812.

Convention, Recreation & Visitor Commission
800 Indian Boundary Rd.
Chesterton
219/926-2255, 800/283-8687
www.casualcoast.com
If you're planning a visit, this is the best place to start for information about festivals and other events. They'll also suggest places to stay and provide details of special travel packages. *Directions: From I–90, exit Indiana 49 south to Indian Boundary Road. Go east.*

Courtesy of the Porter County Convention, Recreation & Visitor Commission.
A day at the Porter County Fair.

Porter County Fair
Porter County Fairgrounds and Expo Center
Indiana 49, at Division Rd., one mile south of Valparaiso
www.portercofair.org
The first Porter County Fair was held in 1851. In the 150-plus years since it has grown into a 10-day event that is part carnival, part concert, part agricultural exhibition. The first fair cost $528.97 to put on and made $26.48 profit, according to local history. Today, it's a multi-million-dollar extravaganza that draws region-wide attendance every July. Attractions include a midway, rodeo, livestock shows, petting zoo, demolition derby, and the crowning of the queen. The Grandstand has hosted such performers as the Doobie Brothers, Travis Tritt, and REO Speedwagon.

BEVERLY SHORES

• • • • • • • • • • • • • • • • • • •

Incorporated: 1947
Population: 708
Median age: 50.8
Land area: 3.58 square miles

The Bartlett Realty Company, founded by two brothers who were Chicago developers, planned Beverly Shores in the late 1920s as a fancy resort community in the dunes for Chicago's upper class. Beautiful homes were constructed on the dunes overlooking Lake Michigan, and it was named after Fredrick Bartlett's daughter.

Beverly Shores never grew into a vacation destination. Instead, it became a year round community known for the homes tucked into the majesty of the surrounding dunes. Deer wander through the forested area, and many of the homes are close enough to the lake to hear waves lapping onto the shore. It's remained a small community and has no business district. Still, there are some good reasons to visit.

Lakefront Road runs, as the name implies, along the lakefront, with a public parking area, an adjoining deck with picnic areas, public bathrooms, and steps down to a small stretch of beach that's part of **Indiana Dunes National Lakeshore** (p. 250). A wheelchair lift makes this beach accessible. Further east on Lakefront is parking for residents and small telescopes for looking out at the water and at the Chicago skyline.

Consider spending a morning on the beach, then trekking over to these other sites worth seeing.

World's Fair Homes

The 1933–34 World's Fair was one of the biggest events in Chicago's history and brought millions to the city. Many toured the Home and Industrial Arts Exhibit where they saw the latest in home-building technology.

When the Fair closed, most of the structures were dismantled. Robert Bartlett, one of the developers of Beverly Shores, bought six of the homes and transported them to his development. Five still stand, all between State Park Road and Broadway on Lake Front Drive. Now listed on the National Register of Historic Places, they comprise the **Century of Progress Architectural District**.

Driving east, the first house is the **Wiebolt–Rostone House**, named for the materials used for its exterior. Next is the **Armco–Ferro House**, a porcelain steel frame structure. Then comes the striking **House of Tomorrow**, a 12-sided home that resembles a giant wedding cake. Across the street is the Florida **Tropical House**, with an Art Deco design. Finally, east of the Tomorrow home, is the **Cypress Log Cabin**, built of timber and resembling a mountain lodge.

Bartlett also purchased 10 buildings from the fair's Colonial Village exhibit and brought them to Beverly Shores. One remains: The **Old North Church**, a replica of Boston's church of Paul Revere fame. The buildings are not generally open to the public, but walking tours detailing their history are available.

Contact the **Porter County Convention, Recreation and Visitor Commission** (219/926-2255, 800/283-8687) for more information.

Beverly Shores Depot Museum and Gallery
525 Broadway
219/871-0832
You won't find a more beautiful train station in which to wait for your morning commute to work. It is on the National Register of Historic Places and is located next to the Indiana Dunes National Lakeshore. This Mediterranean Revival-style depot is the South Shore Line's stop in Beverly Shores and also houses a museum and art gallery. The Bartlett brothers teamed up with financier Samuel Insull, the owner of the South Shore Line, to develop and promote the depot. Architect Arthur Gerber designed the building, which has a striking pink stucco exterior and a barrel tile roof.

The museum features maps and documents relating to the development of Beverly Shores; the art gallery focuses on the work of area artists, many of whom are influenced by the dunes. At the gift shop, you can purchase postcards, books, and posters on the South Shore Line and Dunes region, many

Photo by the author.

The historic Beverly Shores train station.

produced in a 1920s style.

The museum, gallery, and gift shop are open Sat.–Sun. 1 p.m.–4 p.m. Admission to the museum and gallery is free, but donations are encouraged. Directions: Take I-94 or I-80/90, to State Road 49 and go north to U.S. 12. Take U.S. 12 east 4.5 miles to Broadway and go north.

CHESTERTON

● ● ● ● ● ● ● ● ● ● ● ● ● ● ● ●

Incorporated: October 5, 1869
Population: 10,488
Median age: 36.7
Motto/Nickname: Gateway to the Dunes
Land area: 7.09 square miles

Chesterton's history dates to the 1830s when the area was known as Coffee Creek, and later Calumet. The region began to grow in the 1850s with the arrival of the Michigan Southern Railroad. The name Chesterton was adopted in 1869 when the community incorporated.

Today Chesterton is known for its access to the dunes and its collection of antique and specialty shops. If you're here on a Friday night June through August, come to **Thomas Centennial Park** (Calumet Rd. and Broadway Ave.) at dusk for the free Movie in the Park Night. Details are available from the **Westchester Public Library** (219/926-7696).

Wizard of Oz Fantasy Parade and Festival
Calumet Rd. and Broadway Ave.
219/926-7048
219/926-5513
http://www.chestertonchamber.org/Community.html
How did a city in Indiana become so identified with the *Wizard of Oz*? The book wasn't written here, wasn't set here, and neither author L. Frank Baum nor those involved in the famous MGM film ever called Chesterton home.

But one of the people who fell in love with the story did. Jean

Photo by John J. Watkins.

Wizard of Oz characters at Chesterton's Oz Fantasy Festival.

Nelson opened The Yellow Brick Road Shop in 1978. Four years later, the annual Oz Fantasy Festival began. Now, each September, the festival attracts 50,000-plus Oz fanatics to Chesterton.

They come to meet some of the original movie Munchkins, many of whom return every year for the celebration. You might also want to take a chance in the monkey drop. In tribute to the flying monkeys in the *Wizard of Oz*, participants buy chances on stuffed monkeys that are dropped from a hot air balloon onto a yellow brick road where Dorothy's ruby slippers sit. The winner is the person whose monkey lands closest to the magical shoes. The event raises money for local charities. There are Dorothy, Scarecrow, Lion, Tin Man, Toto, Glinda and Wicked Witch look-a-like contests, a Wicked Witch cackling contest, and theater performances of Oz-inspired works. The fest is also a hot spot for Oz memorabilia dealers and collectors.

Even if it's not Oz Fest time, it's worth stopping by **The**

Yellow Brick Road Shop (109 E. Yellow Brick Road, at Indiana 49, 219/926-7048), home to the Oz Museum, which includes costumes worn by Munchkins, autographs, and more. Hours vary with the season, so call ahead.

Lustron Home
400 block of Bowser Ave.
As distinctive in its own way as the **World's Fair Homes** (p. 164) in nearby Beverly Shores, Lustron was supposed to be the home of the future. The house is all steel, with steel panels attached to a steel frame. Pictures were hung with magnets, since pounding nails into steel walls is slightly impractical.

The Lustron Corp. built the homes in the late 1940s and early '50s to provide housing for World War II veterans. The porcelain-enameled buildings couldn't rot, termites couldn't destroy them, and fire couldn't burn them down. They were high tech, with built-in dishwashers that doubled as clothes washers, and low maintenance. Taking care of the exterior meant hosing the building down.

About 2,500 Lustron homes were built, with about 150 shipped to Indiana. Several are still in use. Chesterton's is unique because it is one of the few *three*-bedroom homes. It's easy to spot—it's the only one on the block with an exterior and roof that's made out of the same stuff used to make a kitchen stove.

Indian Oak Resort
558 Indian Boundary Rd.
219/926-2200
800/552-4232
www.indianoak.com
Indian Oak Resort is on **Lake Chubb,** a private lake that attracts a variety of waterfowl. The resort has a fitness room, lap pool, and sauna. Massages and body wraps are available in the spa. Some rooms have fireplaces and whirlpools. In a wooded

area, it offers plenty to do outdoors, including bike trails. *Call for rates.*

Station House Pottery
321 Broadway Ave.
219/926-7781
Station House Pottery boasts nine rooms of pottery by over 60 American artists. There are decorative items here, along with pottery for cooking and serving food. Not merely beautiful bowls, plates, and pitchers, these are truly works of art. *Hours vary with the time of year. Call for details.*

EVENTS

Chesterton Art Fair
Hawthorne Park
500 Ackerman Dr.
Porter
219/926-4711
The Chesterton Art Fair has been attracting the work of artists from all over the U.S. two days each August for more than 40 years. The juried fair includes oils, watercolors, and sculptures, and has been ranked by *Sunshine Artist* magazine among the top 100 in the nation for three consecutive years. A major supporter of the fair is the **Chesterton Art Center** (115 S. Fourth St., www.chestertonart.com), a gallery that showcases the work of hundreds of artists.

Northwest Indiana Storytelling Festival
Indiana Dunes State Park Nature Center
1600 N. 25 E.
219/926-1390
Storytelling is indeed an art that is very much alive in this annual October talkfest and contest in the **Indiana Dunes State Park**

(p. 260). In addition to children's stories, there is always a good mix of local legends and ghost stories. *Call for details on the next festival.*

DINING

Lucrezia Cafe
428 S. Calumet Rd.
219/926-LUCY (5829)
www.lucreziacafe.com
Named for the infamous Lucrezia Borgia, Lucrezia Cafe is a wonderful Italian restaurant in a brightly painted Italianate house built in 1876. The specialty is Northern Italian cooking, and chicken vesuvio, rigatoni with smoked chicken, and fettuccine salmon are among the recommended items. The intimate and homey interior includes a main dining room for non-smokers and families with children, and a bar area where smoking is allowed. During the warmer months, diners also sit outside in a garden setting. Lucrezia does not take reservations. Dinner entrees run $8–$18, with appetizers and salads at $2–$6. *Open Sun.–Thu. 11 a.m.–10 p.m., Fri.–Sat. 11 a.m.–11 p.m.*

Wingfield's Restaurant and Irish Pub
Indian Oaks Mall
558 Indian Boundary Rd.
219/926-2200, x. 5
This is one of those places where you can stop in anytime, get a good meal, and run into people you know in the community. It's got a reputation as a place with hearty breakfasts, satisfying dinners, comfortable surroundings, and an adjoining Irish Pub. If you come in the morning, ask for one of the omelets. At lunchtime there are huge salads and juicy burgers. In the evening try one of the steaks, pasta, or the fresh fish special. There are items the kids will like on the menu, and be sure to

save room for dessert. Reservations are recommended, especially on the weekend. A brunch buffet is served on Sundays, with carved meats, blintzes, customized omelets, and other breakfast and luncheon dishes.

Temporarily under renovation; call for hours. Directions: From I–94, exit Indiana 40 south to Indian Boundary Line Road. Go west, and the mall is immediately on your left.

HEBRON

Incorporated: 1886
Population: 3,596
Median age: 32.9
Land area: 1.38 square miles

Hebron's past is linked to efforts to travel long distances as fast as possible, first by stagecoach and then by train.

In the early nineteenth century, Native Americans mainly populated the area that would be known as Northwest Indiana. The first white settlers came to the Hebron area in the 1840s. Within a few years, they built a hotel ere for travelers to stop as they traveled from Detroit to Chicago.

Stagecoach Inn Museum
Panhandle Depot
127 N. Main St. (Rte. 2)
219/996-5678
The Stagecoach Inn, built in 1849, was a stop on the stagecoach line that operated through Northwest Indiana. The wood-frame structure has been restored and is used as a museum that recalls the days when travel by stage was the way to go.

Next door is the **Panhandle Depot**, a place to learn about the early days of railroading when the depot was the first place to get news as people gathered around its wood-burning stove. Built in 1867 for Pittsburgh, Chicago, and St. Louis Railroad, this building was used as a train depot for decades. When trains no longer came through town, it was sold and turned into a restaurant building. In the 1990s, it was acquired by the Hebron

Historical Society, which already operated the Stagecoach Inn, and moved next to the inn. Tours of the inn and depot are by appointment.

Directions: From I–65, exit U.S. 231 east to Main Street. South on Main.

Grand Kankakee Marsh County Park

21690 Range Line Rd.

219/552-0033

This 1,901-acre park was the first county fish and wildlife park in the state, according to Alan McPherson's *Nature Walks in Northern Indiana.* It stretches about three miles along the northern bank of the Kankakee, making it the place to be if you want to hike near the river. The park also has channels and ponds and access to the Kankakee if you're interested in some challenging fishing.

Grand Kankakee is very rural and lacks some of the family-friendly programs held at other Porter County parks. Late in the year, it closes to the general public for hunting season. Call ahead for details. Archery season begins in October. In addition to hunting with conventional weapons, the county also allows the use of muzzleloaders in season.

Open daily 7 a.m.–dusk, Jan.–Sept. Directions: From I–65, take Route 2 to Range Line Road, then south for five miles.

Hebron Public Library

201 W. Sigler St.

219/996-3684

http://www.pcpls.lib.in.us/Branches/brhebron.htm

Hebron's library building was built in 1917 with an Andrew Carnegie grant. There have been additions, but care has been taken to retain the early architectural feel. The original entrance remains, as well as the magazine racks built into the wall and much of the original woodwork and windows. Original reference tables and the circulation desk, cut down to be a reference table, are still in use.

Open. Mon. 1 p.m.–9 p.m.; Tue.–Fri. 10 a.m.–6 p.m., Sat. 9 a.m.–5 p.m. Directions: From I–65, exit Indiana 2 east to U.S. 231 north. Go west at Sigler Street (Indiana 8).

Is Dunn's Bridge, in Kouts, a piece of carnival history?

KOUTS

Incorporated: 1921
Population: 1,698
Median age: 35.6
Land area: 1.08 square miles

Settlers drawn to the hunting and fishing along the Kankakee River founded Kouts in the 1860s. When the railroad came through the fledgling community, it was called Kouts Station, after the Barnhardt Kouts family, then shortened to Kouts.

In October 1948, President Truman's whistle-stop campaign tour pulled into Kouts after a political rally in Hammond. Most of the town turned out to greet the president's train. Truman, his wife, Bess, and daughter Margaret, stood on the rear platform and waved to the crowd. When someone asked Truman to make a speech, the president declined. "I've said too much already," he replied, according to a history compiled for the 100th anniversary of the town's founding. A photo of Truman leaning down from the train's rear platform was snapped by a *Life* magazine photographer and appeared just weeks before the election.

Dunn's Bridge
At first glance this bridge over the **Kankakee River** looks only like a dilapidated old steel bridge. But is it much more, perhaps a piece of carnival history?

Local legend has it that this bridge is a link to Chicago's famed White City—the community built for the Columbian Exposition at the 1893 World's Fair. Some believe the bridge was built with steel salvaged from the giant wheel built by George W. G. Ferris—inventor of the Ferris wheel. There is evidence to indicate the bridge was made with remnants of structures built for the fair, and the steel is rounded like that on a Ferris wheel, but experts disagree on whether this is all that's left of the famous wheel-ride that garnered international attention.

The Porter County Parks Department has said it cannot confirm where material for the bridge came from. Officials only know it has been there for about a century.

So is this a piece of history? The answer appears lost to antiquity. Judge for yourself. But be careful! Signs warn that the bridge is not safe, and roadblocks are in place to keep people from driving over it. The road now swings by the old bridge, and cars travel over a more modern structure. But Dunn's Bridge is still there. It's located south of Kouts, across the Kankakee River at County Road 500 East. It's about seven miles south of Indiana 8.

EVENTS

Pork Fest
Downtown Kouts
219/766-2867
Pork Fest, a one-day, late-summer Kouts tradition, is not simply an opportunity to pig out on the "other" white meat; it includes a four-mile run, almost 100 arts & crafts and food vendors, tractor pulls, a parade, square dancing, and more entertainment.

Christmas Open Houses
800/283-8687
Many Kouts residents open their homes for holiday treats and craft sales during Christmas week.

OGDEN DUNES

Incorporated: 1925
Population: 1,313
Median age: 48.7
Land area: 0.73 square miles

Named for Francis A. Ogden, the owner of the lakefront property that became a town after his death. He hoped the region would one day become a great tourist attraction, but that dream died with him. Instead, it became a small community of summer homes and year-round residences.

Ogden's estate was purchased and platted by developers in 1923. The tiny town incorporated because residents wanted to ensure there would be a crossing built over the New York Central Railroad giving them access to Dunes Highway (U.S. 12). At the time, they worried about being boxed in by the railroad.

The **Indiana Dunes National Lakeshore** (p. 250) surrounds Ogden Dunes on three sides. Although it has no commercial development, from 1928 to 1932 it was home to one of the nation's longest ski jumps. The steel-and-wood structure was built by the **Ogden Dunes Ski Club** to promote winter sports on the dunes.

For a time the club was successful. Every winter for five years the jump attracted international competitors and crowds of 10,000 or more. The nearly 600-foot slide was built on a 295-foot sand dune. When they flew off the slide, skiers would either glide or fall nearly 300 feet. One account compared it to jumping off of a 30-story building.

After the 1932 competition, the slide was dismantled. In 1997 the Indiana Historical Society placed a marker on **Ski Road Hill** to commemorate the ski jump.

PORTAGE

• • • • • • • • • • • • • • • •

Founded: 1959 (as a town), 1968 (as a city)
Population: 33,496
Median age: 35.4
Size: 20.83 square miles

Until 1959, most thought of Portage as a little place in the country just east of Gary. That year the National Steel Company chose the area for its new plant and the town incorporated for the first time. One unusual feature of the incorporation was the zoning of the entire lakefront section of the new town for industry. In 1961, the state began developing its new Great Lakes port here.

Port of Indiana–Burns Harbor
U.S. 12 and Indiana 249
219/787-8636
www.portsofindiana.com
This port is among the busiest on the Great Lakes, welcoming ships from around the world that have made their way through the St. Lawrence Seaway. The port was dedicated in 1970, and today more than 6 million tons of cargo move in and out of it annually. Come and watch commercial vessels from Poland, Finland, Canada (Quebec), and other countries. A good view of the ships is available from the fishing dock. Parking is free, restrooms are available, and the pier is wheelchair accessible.

Indiana's other ports, Southwind Maritime Center and Clark Maritime Center, are on the Ohio River. The facility at Burns Harbor is the oldest public port in the state. It's named after Randall W. Burns, a developer who pushed for development of

Photo by the author.

The International Port of Indiana in Portage.

a ditch that would drain some of the swampy land east of Gary and make it suitable for development. Burns began his efforts in 1908. Legislative and legal wrangling held up development of the ditch until 1923.

Directions: From I–94, take Indiana 249 north. Follow the signs into the port and to the public parking area along the lake.

Imagination Glen Park
2775 McCool Rd.
219/762-1675
The Hoosier Chapter of the Sierra Club has called this an exceptional urban park. It's densely wooded with hiking trails that become a challenging cross-country skiing course in winter. The park also offers an eight-mile course for off-road bicycling, that has been used for the **Outback Trail Mountain Bike Challenge**.

Imagination Glen also has ball fields and an access point for canoeing on the **Salt Creek**. This creek is popular with anglers

who fish for chinook, salmon, coho, and northern pike.
*Directions: From U.S. 20 go south on Indiana 149 to Lenburg Road. Go
west to McCool Road. Go north on McCool Road to the park entrance.*

Countryside Museum
Countryside Park
5250 E. U.S. 6
219/762-8349
Home of the **Portage Community Historical Society,** the
museum is in the turn-of-the-century house built by Charles
Trager, one of the area's earliest settlers. Tours are available
with advance notice. Although the museum has limited hours,
Countryside Park is open daily and has a playground, picnic
facilities, fishing pond, and a tubing hill.
Open Sat. 11 a.m.–3 p.m.

DINING

Hot or Not
2782 Willowdale
219/762-1984
www.hotornotcajun.com
The area's best Cajun and Creole cuisine and one the best blues
and jazz clubs in Indiana. The menu features specialties like
Louisiana yard-dog posterior (blackened alligator tail), crawfish
etouffée, and excellent pork baby-back ribs. First-time visitors
should try the Cajun Creole sampler platter.

As good as the food is, the music is even better. Performers
who have taken the stage here include Melva LeBlanc, Barrel-
house Chuck and Buzz Kilman.

Diners typically order from the "Open Menu," with entrees
priced between $8 and $16. When there's entertainment, everyone eats from the "Premiere Menu" that allows guests to

sample several entrees and enjoy the music for a flat fee of $20. Reservations are recommended, especially on the weekend. *Open Thu. 5 p.m.–9:30 p.m., Fri.–Sat. 5 p.m.–10:30 p.m. Directions: Take I–80/94 east to the Ripley Street south exit. Take Ripley to Central Avenue. Go east on Central about two miles to Willowdale Road, then south on Willowdale.*

PORTER

Incorporated: 1908
Population: 4,972
Median age: 32.7
Land area: 6.32 square miles

Porter owes its beginnings and name to the Michigan Central Railroad. It was a stop on the train's route and was named after a railroad executive.

Over the years Porter attracted other small industries such as a brickmaker. But when the area expanded, the largest growth came further south in neighboring Chesterton. Reminders of Porter's long history are in the oldest section of town, which still has many buildings built in the late nineteenth and early twentieth centuries.

The town was among those that lost land and millions in property tax revenue when the **Indiana Dunes National Lakeshore** (p. 250) was established. Porter gave up about 1,000 acres, or about a third of the town, to the new federal park.

If you're planning a day at the dunes, there are several attractions that make Porter a destination.

Dune Ridge Winery
U.S. 20 at Beam St.
219/926-5532
www.duneridgewinery.com
This family winery opened in 1998 and specializes in small batches of painstakingly prepared wines. Specialties include a

Chardonnay and a local favorite, Lakeshore Red. Dune Ridge has had several medal winners, including its Chardonnay Reserve 1997, the Chardonnay Semi-dry 1998, and the Vidal Blanc Semi-dry 1997.

Make an afternoon of your visit to best enjoy the picnic area, gift shop, and free wine tasting. Don't worry about Indiana's ban on Sunday alcohol sales. It doesn't apply to wineries.
Open Wed., Fri.–Sat. 11 a.m.–5 p.m., Sun. noon–5 p.m.; weekends only Jan.–Apr. Directions: I–80/90 to State Road 49. Go north to U.S. 20, and head west to Beam Street.

Splash Down Dunes

150 E. U.S. Hwy. 20
219/929-1181
www.splashdowndunes.com
Some of the tallest water slides in Indiana and the Midwest's largest wave pool—30,000 ft.^{2}—make this water park a favorite summer stop. **The Tower** is a 68-foot monster that the park promises is like sliding down the side of a six-story building. **The Twister** is a series of slides that wrap around each other on their way down. And the **Lazy River** is 1,200 rambling feet long.

Photo by John J. Watkins.

For youngsters, there's **Sandcastle Bay** for those four feet and under, an indoor play area, and an arcade filled with video games. Try the beach volleyball courts when you've had enough of the water.

The Splash Down complex provides showers and lockers, a picnic area for vacationers with bag lunches, and the Carousel Cafe, which serves hamburgers, hot dogs, Polish sausages, and other fast food items.
Open daily 10 a.m.–8 p.m. Memorial Day–Labor Day; hours may be shorter near the end of the season. Admission is $17 for those four feet and taller and $10 for those shorter than four feet; children three years and younger get in free. Directions: From I–94 east, take U.S. 20 east (exit 22B). From I–80/90 or I–94 west, exit at 49 north and follow it as it merges into U.S. 20.

Midnight Parade
Downtown Porter
If you're in Porter on July 4, come by for what promises to be the first Independence Day parade in the area: The **Porter Veterans of Foreign Wars** holds its parade at midnight. Organizers hit upon the idea more than a decade ago as a way to beat the heat, and the event now attracts thousands who want to get an early start on the holiday.

DINING

Wagner's Ribs
361 Wagner Rd.
219/926-7614
Wagner's slabs are huge and not too spicy. Add a pile of onion rings and a big bowl of coleslaw, wash it all down with a beer from a huge selection, and you've got a meal fit for a discerning glutton. If you're not in the mood for ribs, dine on burgers or

steaks. Wagner's doesn't take reservations, and it can get pretty crowded on weekends.

Open Mon.–Sat. 11 a.m.–10 p.m., Sun noon–10 p.m.

TOWN OF PINES

Incorporated: 1955
Population: 798
Median Age: 40.1
Size: 2.28 square miles

Yes, "Town" is officially part of this tiny community's name, though most simply shorten it to "Pines" or "The Pines." The name comes from the sprawling pine forest that once covered this section of northern Porter County. For a time there was a thriving timber industry here, but that ended when the supply of trees dwindled. Town of Pines is mostly residential and is home to the giant dune, **Mount Baldy** (p. 259).

DINING

Pumps on 12
3085 W. Dunes Hwy. (U.S. 12)
219/874-6201
Stopping at this old-time roadhouse for a burger and beer has become a tradition for those on their way to or headed home from the beach. It owes its unusual name to it's being a renovated 1920s-era filling station on U.S. 12; vintage gas pumps are still on the premises. Besides the burgers, the soup, pasta, and "hub cap" thin-crust pizzas are recommended. It also offers steaks, ribs, fried fish, and a large selection of local microbrew beers. Lunch and dinner are served.
Open Mon.–Thu. 11 a.m.–10:00 p.m., Fri.–Sat. 11 a.m.–10:30 p.m., Sun. noon–9 p.m. (dinner all day).

The Chapel of the Resurrection on the
campus of Valparaiso University.

VALPARAISO

Incorporated: February 13, 1851
Population: 27,428
Median Age: 32.7
Motto/Nickname: Vale of Paradise
Land area: 10.15 square miles

Valparaiso dates to the earliest settlement days of Northwest Indiana when it was on the trail that ran from northern Illinois to present-day Detroit. In the early 1800s the Potawatomi lived here, along with a few fur traders.

As the county seat of Porter County, it was originally known as Portersville. In 1837 it was renamed Valparaiso—or Vale of Paradise. The link to Commander David Dixon Porter, a hero in the War of 1812 and the man for whom Porter County was named, was not lost when the city's name was changed. One of Porter's most famous battles was near the port of Valaparaiso, Chile.

The town sits on a glacial moraine—a mound of earth and rock pushed into place by a glacier. This one is called, not surprisingly, the **Valparaiso Moraine**.

Today, Valparaiso is a community with a growing population. Many are attracted by its vibrant downtown with a good mix of retail stores and first-class restaurants.

The city's national profile has also been raised by the success of **Valparaiso University**, which has attracted attention for academic and athletic successes, most notably on the basketball court. Tickets to basketball games are hard to come by , but you can try giving the athletic ticket office a call (219/464-5233). While not a university town in the sense that everything revolves around the school, VU is a great source of pride for those in the Valparaiso area.

Valparaiso University
U.S. 30
219/464-5000
www.valpo.edu
Valparaiso, a private, Lutheran college, has a beautiful 310-acre campus. Its 3,600 students, drawn from around the world, attend a university that *US News & World Report* has consistently ranked among the best comprehensive universities in the Midwest.

Valpo (as it is affectionately called) has a graduate division, the area's only school of law, and five colleges: Arts & Sciences, Business Administration, Engineering, Nursing, and Christ College—the Honors College.

It began as Valparaiso Male and Female College in 1859, one of the first coeducational institutions in the United States. It closed in 1871, but was reopened two years later as Northern Indiana Normal School. By the end of the first term, the phrase "and Business Institute" was added to the name.

In the late nineteenth century, the school had earned a reputation as "The Poor Man's Harvard." In 1900, the name was changed to Valparaiso College, and six years later it was rechartered as Valparaiso University. In the years during and after World War I, VU went through some tough times: changes in leadership, financial problems, dwindling faculty, and dropping enrollment.

After an unsuccessful offer to sell the school to the state, a buyer stepped in and tried to get control of the privately-held school. Unfortunately for VU the buyer was the Ku Klux Klan, ready to buy the school for $350,000, according to Powell A. Moore's history, *The Calumet Region*. The deal fell through when the Klan's national leaders decided owning a school would not be such a great idea.

The institution's owner made one more unsuccessful offer to the state in 1925 to take the school off his hands. That same year a buyer stepped forward. The Lutheran Church of the Synod of Missouri wanted the school. The Lutheran University Association was formed and purchased the school for $176,500.

Today, the campus sits along U.S. 30 in the heart of Porter County. Its most stunning building is the **Chapel of the Resurrection**, dedicated in 1959, with a great organ, 94-foot-high Mundeloh stained glass windows, and the Brandt Campanile, a bell tower 140 feet tall.

The **Center for the Arts** is home to the **Duesenberg Recital Hall** and the **Brauer Museum of Art** with more than 2,500 works in its collection. The nineteenth-century gallery features the works of Hudson River School painters, including Junius Sloan. Among the twentieth-century gallery artists are Georgia O'Keefe, Ansel Adams, and Frank V. Dudley.

In 2000, VU opened its newest building, the Kade-Duesenberg German House and Cultural Center, a residence for German-speaking students and a venue devoted to programs about German history and culture.

Memorial Opera House
104 Indiana Ave.
219/548-9137
www.memorialoperahouse.com
When the Porter County chapter of the Grand Army of the

Republic wanted to build a memorial to the men who fought in the Civil War, their choice was a magnificent opera house, something the entire community could enjoy.

The theater and concert hall built in 1893 by architect Charles Lembke is still in use by local groups, including Valparaiso's **Community Theatre Guild** (p. 280). In the mid-1990s the red brick building with red, white, and blue stained glass windows underwent repair and renovation to restore some of the luster lost over the decades. The building is on the National Register of Historic Places.

In 1896, famed orator and presidential candidate William Jennings Bryan spoke here. Two years later, John Philip Sousa led a concert at the Opera House, and in 1919 the Marx brothers took the stage. A variety of shows and performances are mounted at the opera house, and tours are available. Call for a current lineup.

One more note: Beulah Bondi, the veteran Hollywood actress whose performances included playing Jimmy Stewart's mother in *It's a Wonderful Life*, grew up in Valparaiso and got her start in shows at the Memorial Opera House.

Old County Jail Museum
153 Franklin St.
219/465-3595
http://home.attbi.com/~hspc/
From 1872 to more than a century later, this building on Franklin Street is where convicted criminals in Porter County were jailed. Together with the adjoining brick house that once was the sheriff's residence, they are on the National Register of Historic Places.

Since 1975, the buildings have served as a museum, maintained by the **Historical Society of Porter County**, that shows how crooks were treated generations ago. The collection includes local Native American artifacts, the skeleton and tusk of a mastodon found on local farmland, tree stumps embedded with Civil War cannonballs and shot, and an invitation and dress worn to Lincoln's inaugural ball. There are also items connected to Commander David Porter, the county's namesake.

Some of the exhibits are on display in the old jail cells. You won't believe how small they are. Architecture buffs will find the building itself interesting. The jailhouse portion of the building resembles a castle with high brick walls. The sheriff's home is an Italianate brick design.
Open Wed., Fri.–Sat. 1 p.m.–4 p.m. Tours are available.

Anderson's Orchard & Vineyards
430 E. U.S. Hwy. 6
219/464-4936
www.andersonsvineyard.com
This 45-acre orchard, packed with more than 5,000 fruit trees (and a sculpture garden), is not the local secret it once was. More and more visitors have wanted to enjoy the hospitality of this family-owned farm. The winery's Million Bubbles Millennium, a sparkling wine, has won several gold medals. Other specialties include Dune Country Golden Harvest, a sweet apple wine; the Vidal Blanc; and Orchard Blue, the state's first blueberry wine. In addition to free tastes of several premium wines, fresh fruit, homemade jellies and jams, fresh bread, and other items are available. Tours of the winery and orchard can be scheduled, and cellar master David Lundstrom offers a wine appreciation series.

Anderson's also sponsors an event in June that you won't find with most orchards: a medieval festival with combat demonstrations, a masked ball, and huge feast. In the fall visit the pumpkin patch, and a few months later try cross-country skiing.
Open Jan. 1–Mar. 21 Tue.–Sat. 10 a.m.–5 p.m., Sun. 11 a.m.–4 p.m.;

Mar. 21–Dec. 31 Mon.–Sat. 10 a.m.–6 p.m., Sun. 11 a.m.–5 p.m.
Directions: I–80/90 to Route 49. Go south five miles to U.S. 6. Go east
on U.S. 6 about three miles.

Indiana Aviation Museum
Porter County Airport
U.S. 30 and State Rd. 49
219/548-3123
www.indianaaviationmuseum.org
Founder James Reed used his own aircraft collection to help this museum get off the ground. The exhibits include a 1945 P-51D Mustang, a 1941 PT-17 Stearman, and a 1945 F4U-5N Corsair. Many of the items in the collection are available for airshows.

Unlike at many museums, you can do more than look at these beauties. For a $150 donation, the museum will take you up for a 20-minute ride in one of its vintage fighter planes. They call it "the warbird experience." The museum's motto is, "Where history flies." During a visit here, you can, too.
Call for hours and to schedule a flight. $5 for adults; $4 for seniors and veterans; kids under 12 are free.

Art Barn
695 N. County Rd. 400 East.
219/462-9009
Located in an 1870 barn on a 69-acre farm, this is one of the most noteworthy gallery and art schools in the state. The Art Barn had three large galleries: one devoted to oils, another to watercolors, and a third, in the entryway, to its latest exhibits. Classes are offered for both adults and children on such subjects as oils, pastels, water colors, acrylics, jewelry, and ceramics It also hosts workshops, daylong programs that include lunch and an in-depth discussion on a topic or artist's work.

The Art Barn has a gift gallery and can be rented for gatherings

such as wedding receptions. It also sponsors the annual **Sunflower Festival** in October, a chance to see and purchase pieces by various artists.
Open Mon.–Sat. 10 a.m.–4 p.m.

Hoosier Bat Co.
4511 Evans Ave.
219/531-1006
800/228-3787
www.hoosierbat.com
The bats produced here are used by some Chicago Cubs, including Sammy Sosa, and a lineup of other big league players. The 52,000 bats made each year include a special slugger made of three different woods: ash in the handle, hickory in the hitting area, and maple on the bat end. The company calls it the most durable bat available. Unfortunately, if you go to a Major League game, the only place you'll see that bat is during batting practice. Three months after the bat was introduced, Major League Baseball rewrote the rules and outlawed it. Now, it's used in the minor leagues. The players in the big league clubs who use a Hoosier Bat during a game are carrying the traditional bat made of ash.
Tours available Mon.–Fri. 9 a.m.–11 a.m., and must be scheduled four days in advance. Participants must be eight years old or older.

WINTER FUN

When it snows, Valparaiso has much to offer, especially skiing.

Pines Peak Family Ski Area
674 N. Meridian
219/477-5993
The only ski resort in Northwest Indiana, the Pines has eight ski runs that use snowmaking equipment to assist Mother Nature

when necessary. Built on the Valparaiso Moraine the glaciers left behind, it's large enough for advanced skiers—the longest run is 1,200 feet—a great "bunny" hill for first-timers and youngsters, and snowboard and tube runs. Slopes are lighted at night. The Pines also has a huge lodge to warm up before the fire with a cup of hot chocolate.

Pines Peak offers lessons and a variety of seasonal, daily, and family rates; a full array of equipment is available for rental.
Open in season, usually late Nov.–early Mar., Mon.–Fri. 5p.m.–9 p.m., Sat. 10 a.m.–9 p.m., and Sun. 10 a.m.–6 p.m. Directions: From I–80/90 or I–94, exit Route 49 south to Route 6. Take Route 6 west to Meridian. Go south (left) on Meridian about one mile.

Sledding and Tubing
Rogers–Lakewood Park
North Campbell St. (Meridian Rd.) and Lakeview Rd.
219/462-5144 (Valparaiso Park District)
Valparaiso has **Derby Downs** in Rogers–Lakewood Park, one of the area's most popular sledding spots. That means it's sometimes one of the most crowded, so be extra-watchful with small children.
Directions: From U.S. 30 go north on Washington Street to Lincolnway. West on Lincolnway to Campbell Street. North on Campbell.

Forest Park
1158 Harrison Blvd. (at Campbell St.)
219/462-5144 (Valparaiso Park District)
Another popular spot for sledding, tubing, and cross-country skiing.

Sunset Hill Farm County Park
Meridian Rd. and U.S. 6
219/465-3586
This 200-plus acre park on the site of a former dairy farm includes a picnic area, shelters, restrooms, and hiking trails. It's

a popular spot for cross-country skiers because parts of the trail are pretty difficult.

Directions: From I–94, take Indiana 49 south to U.S. 6. Go west to Meridian Road.

ENTERTAINMENT

49er Drive-In Theatre
675 Calumet Ave.
219/462-6122
www.49erdrivein.com

In a lot of areas drive-in theaters are a thing of the past, replaced by sprawling multiplexes with two dozen screens and paper-thin walls. Valpo still has a drive-in theater, and it can be a pretty popular place.

And here's a deal you won't get at a theater: kids under eleven get in free. Nothing beats packing the kids into the care on a summer night, getting a huge tub of popcorn (Orville Redenbacher of course!), and pulling into your space before that giant screen.

The 49er shows double features every night. If you arrive early, there's plenty of open areas around the drive-in lot to throw around a Frisbee or baseball. Once the show starts you don't have to worry about the speaker not working. The sound is broadcast in stereo and can be heard at 88.5 FM on your radio.

If the film isn't very good, the concession stand has plenty of items available to keep the kids occupied. Specialties include nachos, hamburgers, barbecue sandwiches, and pretzels.

Gates open at 7 p.m.; movies start at nightfall, usually around 8:30 p.m. Open Fri.–Sun. Apr.–May, Sept.–Oct.; Open nightly June–Aug.

Front Porch Music
505 E. Lincolnway
219/464-4700
www.frontporchmusic.com
Not only is this the best place in the Northwest Indiana to buy a guitar, it has a huge selection of string instruments that include banjos, dulcimers, autoharps, and mandolins. Many come here for instruction or to have an instrument repaired. Even those who don't know the first thing about playing a guitar keep returning here for the music. The lower level of the store is a great coffee house that hosts live music a few nights each week. Some concerts are free, but most run $5–$10. Open stages invite all ages, all instruments, and all musical styles; performers pay $2, listeners $3.
Store is open Mon.–Fri. 10 a.m.–8 p.m., Sat. 9 a.m.–4 p.m. Concerts usually start at 8 p.m.

EVENTS

Popcorn Festival
204 E. Lincolnway
219/464-8332, 800/283-8687
www.popcornfest.org/popcorn.html
The traditional Valparaiso Popcorn Festival was inspired by the longtime presence of Orville Redenbacher's popcorn farm and plant. The factory is gone but the festival lives on! The area's connection to popcorn actually pre-dates Redenbacher. According to local historians, French traders found Native Americans in Northwest Indiana in the early 1600s growing popping corn that was sometimes used in popcorn soup.

Held every September on the Saturday after Labor Day, the festival kicks off with the Popcorn Panic 5M Run and Popcorn 5K Walk. Don't miss the opening day parade. Each float has to incorporate popcorn in at least 20 percent of its decoration.

The parade is followed by a weekend of entertainment and food—lots and lots of food! The crowning of the Popcorn Queen, bands, a production by the Community Theatre Guild, a talent show, and the Kiwanis Club's hot air balloon show are all part of the fun.

Duneland Woodcarvers Woodcarving Show
Porter County Expo Center (just south of Valparaiso)
215 E. Division Rd. (at Indiana 49)
800/283-8687
An annual April show that's been happening for almost three decades: Visitors can buy the offerings of more than 80 carvers and carving tools; learn about the art of woodcarving; win door prizes; and even commission their own wooden sculptures.
Admission is $3 for adults. Children twelve and younger get in free.

Colonel Murray Memorial Kite Festival
Sunset Hill Farm County Park
U.S. Hwy. 6 and Meridian Rd.
219/465-3586
Held every May, the festival includes kite-making workshops, special programs for kids, and lots of kite flying. One of the highlights is the mass ascension, when everyone lets their kites soar at the same time. The fest has an arts and crafts show, flea market, pony rides, plenty of food concessions, and hours worth of live country music.
Admission is $3 for adults. Children 6 and younger get in free.

Porter County Home & Garden Show
Porter County Expo Center (just south of Valparaiso)
215 E. Division Rd. (at Indiana 49)
219/464-2944
www.pcbaonline.com
Hundreds of professional craft workers assemble for four days

each March to display new items for the inside and outside of the home. There are plenty of opportunities to swap home-remodeling stories or seek gardening advice from experts. *Admission is $4.*

DINING

Bistro 157
157 W. Lincolnway
219/462-0992
www.valparaiso.com/dining/pages/bistro157/
Formerly known as Sole, Bistro157 is in beautiful downtown Valparaiso. The decor is elegant without being flashy. Butcher paper covers the tablecloths for children to draw with crayons, and original artwork festoons the walls. The menu is varied and always changing, with French, Asian, and traditional American influences. Known in part for game and fresh seafood, try specials like pan-seared duck breast or Atlantic salmon. Bistro 157 lacks a children's menu, but the kitchen can improvise.
Open for lunch, Tue.–Fri. 11 a.m.–2 p.m.; for dinner Tue.–Thu. 5 p.m.–9 p.m., Fri.–Sat. 5 p.m.–10 p.m., Sun. 4 p.m.–8 p.m.

Restaurante Don Quijote
119 E. Lincolnway
219/462-7976
The best place to find tapas (Spanish appetizers) in Northwest Indiana, specialties include *pinchos morunos*—Moorish-style skewered veal and pork served with yellow saffron rice. Or try the *paella marinara*, prepared with jumbo shrimp, flounder, clams, and crab legs. The wine menu is extensive, and the desserts are outstanding. Tables are candlelit, and a guitarist plays on Saturday. A children's menu is available.
Open for lunch, Mon.–Fri. 11 a.m.–2 p.m.; for dinner, Mon.–Thu. 5 p.m.–9 p.m., Fri.–Sat. 5 p.m.–10:30 p.m.

Strongbow Inn
2405 E. U.S. 30 East
219/531-0162
800/462-5121
www.strongbowinn.com

No matter the time of year, it always smells like Thanksgiving at the Strongbow Inn, known to regular travelers of U.S. 30 since 1940 as the place for one of the best turkey dinners around. If you're not in the mood for turkey, there's a full menu with steak and seafood dishes. Before dinner, you may want to stop in their on-site bakery for fresh baked goods, or their aeronautically-themed **Blue Yonder Lounge** for a cocktail or glass or wine. Tuesdays hold specials for senior citizens, Wednesdays is the evening Turkey Buffet (5 p.m.–8 p.m.)

Open for lunch, Mon.–Sat. 11 a.m.–4 p.m.; for dinner, daily after 4 p.m.; for brunch, Sun. 10:30 a.m.–2 p.m.

Aberdeen Brewing Co.
210 Aberdeen Dr.
219/548-3300
www.aberdeenbrewingco.com

One of the area's few microbrew restaurants. Every day there are four flagship beers available (selections include County Porter and Aberdeen Scottish Ale) and one to four specialty brews (such are Barley Wine and English Pale Ale). Accompany your beer sampling with pub classics like fish and chips, cottage pie, and Scotch eggs (a hardboiled egg encased in seasoned sausage, rolled in bread crumbs, and deep fried!), or more upscale alternatives like rack of lamb or blackened tuna. Sandwiches run $7–$10, entrees $11–$24. Daily specials and a children's menu are available.

Open Tue.–Thu. 11:30 a.m.–10 p.m., Fri.–Sat. 11:30 a.m.–midnight, Sun. 11:30 a.m.–9 p.m.

Valpo Velvet Shoppe
57 Monroe St.
219/464-4141
An old-fashioned ice cream parlor, complete with soda fountain and ice cream made right on the premises. The recipe for Valpo Velvet has been in the family of owners Mike and Mark Brown since their grandfather opened a dairy three generations ago in 1947. From the moment it touches your tongue you know you're tasting something special.

If you're one of those who never get enough ice cream, try the Valpo Velvet Viking—scoops of five different ice creams, toppings, bananas, whipped cream, nuts, and cherries. Gooey and great! Valpo Velvet Shoppe also has sandwiches and salads. For lunch, order the Popeye—a vegetable submarine sandwich made with spinach leaf, cucumbers, red onion, and more. The spinach cream cheese makes it special.

Open Mon.–Sat. 11 a.m.–10 p.m. Inquire about group tours of the plant.

RECREATION

Antiques.................................... 207
Boating..................................... 217
Christmas Trees 223
Gaming.....................................225
Golf Courses 235
Lakeshore.................................247
Shopping 275
Theater 279

Pair a weekend of antiquing in Northwest Indiana
with small town activities or seasonal festivals.

ANTIQUES

Antique hunters will discover a fine array of antique shops in Lake, Porter, and LaPorte Counties. Some communities have developed antique districts in historic sections of town, where you can readily find such treasures as Hoosier cabinets, Shaker furniture, beautiful glassware, and precious old books.

The following list is by no means complete, but it provides a good sample of what's available. County tourism offices can provide the names of additional dealers. Be aware that stores close, move, and change their hours, so call ahead to make sure the shop will be open when you arrive. Happy hunting!

BEVERLY SHORES

Dune Antiques & Interiors
4944 W. Dunes Hwy. (U.S. 12)
219/879-2368
Rustic furniture, antique hickory furniture, folk art, and pottery. *Open Sat. 10 a.m.–5 p.m.; Sun. 11 a.m.–5 p.m. Call ahead.*

CHESTERTON

Antiques 102
402 Broadway Ave.
219/395-8899
More than 24 dealers. Books, sterling silver, furniture, and

artwork are among the huge selection.
Open Mon.–Sat. 10 a.m.–5 p.m., Sun. noon–5 p.m.

Carol's Antiques
214 S. Calumet Rd.
219/926-4757
Carol's variety includes Victorian pieces.
Open Tue.–Sun. 10:30 a.m.–6 p.m. Call ahead.

Estate Liquidators
123 N. 4th St.
219/926-3697
Neon signs, estate furniture, toy trains, dishes, and collectibles.
Open daily 10:30 a.m.–6:30 p.m., but call ahead.

Kathy's Antiques
1599 S. Calumet Rd.
219/926-1400
Jewelry, lamps, and an assortment of furniture, including china cabinets and library tables. Kathy is a licensed appraiser.
Open Tue.–Sat. 10 a.m.–4 p.m.

Russ & Barb's Antiques
222 Lincoln Ave.
219/926-4937
Pottery, china, glassware, and more.
Open daily 10 a.m.–5 p.m.

Schoolhouse Shop & Antiques
278 E. Porter County Rd. 1500 North
219/926-1551
www.schoolhouseshop.com
One of several shops located in the former Furnessville school-house built in 1886, the large selection of antiques includes toys and glassware. Other shops in the schoolhouse sell gourmet food store and gifts.
Open Mon., Wed.–Sat. 10 a.m.–5 p.m., Sun. 11 a.m.–5 p.m.

Yesterday's Treasures
700 W. Broadway
219/926-2268
An antique mall with more than 120 dealers spread over two floors.
Open Mon.–Sat. 10 a.m.–5 p.m., Sun. noon–5 p.m.

CROWN POINT

Antique Shoppe
Courthouse Square
219/663-1031
Located on the lower level of the old courthouse, this store's inventory includes a large selection of furniture, books, and lamps.
Open Mon.–Sat. 10 a.m.–5 p.m.

Heritage Galleries
5511 W. 109th Ave.
219/663-9616
A dealer in fine antique furniture.
Open by appointment only.

Old Town Square Antique Mall
103 W. Joliet St.
219/662-1219
More than 80 dealers occupy the three floors in this building on Crown Point's historic downtown square. Furniture, books, pottery, and glassware are among the items available.
Open Mon.–Sat. 10 a.m.–5 p.m., Sun. noon–5 p.m.

GRIFFITH

Sampler Square Antiques
121 E. Main St.
219/922-8443
This store is so crowded with items that the proprietor boasts it would be hard to fall down in the aisle here even if you tried. Toys, furniture, lamps, blue glass, and more. And there's always a cup of coffee waiting for visitors.
Open Tue.–Sat. 10 a.m.–5 p.m.

HEBRON

Carol's Antique Mall & Howard's Militaria
108 N. Main St.
219/996-4655
Toys, glassware, antique fishing tackle, and military items, including uniforms, collectible firearms, patches, and medals.
Open Tue.–Sat. 9 a.m.–6 p.m. Call ahead.

Old Farmhouse Antiques
409 S. Main St.
219/996-5329
A lovingly-restored 1893 farmhouse with a nice collection that includes clocks, glassware, and furniture. And be sure to ask the owners how to make an old farmhouse look like new again— they've got plenty of experience.
Open Mon., Thu.–Sat. 10 a.m.–3:30 p.m., Tue. 1 p.m.–3:30 p.m., Sun. noon–3:30 p.m. Closed Wed.

HOBART

Treasure House Antiques
402 N. Hobart Rd.
219/942-1947
A one-person shop with a variety of items, including lamps, books, and knick-knacks.
Open Fri.–Sat. 10 a.m.–5 p.m., Sun. noon–5 p.m. Call ahead.

KOUTS

Kouts Antique Market
107 S. Main St.
219/766-2777
While a variety of antiques are sold here, Kouts Antique Market specializes in Hoosier Cabinets, the kitchen cabinets made at the turn of the century. Also available is furniture from estate sales, including items that had been built into homes, such as buffets and cabinets.
Open Mon., Wed.–Sat. 10 a.m.–5 p.m., Sun. noon–5 p.m. Closed Tue.

LAPORTE

Antique Junction Mall
711 Lincolnway
219/324-0363
A range of antiques and artwork sold from a 125-year-old former general store in the heart of the downtown antique district.
Open Mon.–Sat. 10 a.m.–5 p.m., Sun. noon–5 p.m.

Coachman Antique Mall
500 Lincolnway
219/326-5933
Housed in a century-old store, Coachman has a large selection, including furniture and glassware.
Open Mon.–Sat. 10 a.m.–5 p.m., Sun. noon–5 p.m.

Corner Cupboard
108 Lincolnway
219/326-9882
This brick home, more than a century old, is filled with assorted antiques, including glassware, jewelry, and lamps.
Open Mon.–Sat. 10 a.m.–5 p.m., sometimes open Sun. Call ahead.

The Goods
431 Pine Lake Ave.
219/324-5853
Located in the former Interlaken School for Boys building, the antiques and collectibles here includes masks and costumes.
Open daily 10 a.m.–4 p.m.

It's a Wonderful Life Antique Mall
708 Lincolnway
219/326-7432
About 30 dealers are located in this downtown building, which features a multi-story skylight. The selection is large, with glassware, pottery, and collectibles.
Open Mon.–Sat. 10 a.m.–5 p.m. Sun. noon–5 p.m.

Wolfe Musical Instruments and Antiques
510 Lincolnway
219/326-7137
Mannequins from Europe, African tribal masks, antique furniture and paintings, and a large selection of musical instruments, including saxophones, trombones, and violins.
Open Thu.–Sat. noon–5 p.m.

LOWELL

Felicia's
324 E. Commercial Ave.
219/696-1221
Oak furniture, lamps, and collectibles in the heart of Lowell's downtown antique district. A small line of gourmet food is also offered, and some store space is rented to other dealers.
Open Tue.–Sat. 10 a.m.–5 p.m.

The Treasurer Hunt Mall
410 E. Commercial Ave.
219/696-1880
Twenty-five dealers in this century-old building sell furniture, lamps, records, magazines, and knick-knacks.
Open Mon.–Sat. 10 a.m.–5 p.m.

The Vault
316 E. Commercial Ave.
219/696-7375
Dining room sets, drop-leaf tables, other furniture, glassware, hats, and other collectibles are for sale this converted 1903 bank building.
Open Tue.–Sat. 10 a.m.–5 p.m.

MERRILLVILLE

Carriage House
420 W. 73rd
219/769-2169
Carriage House's real appeal is for model train buffs—a huge assortment of Lionel trains and a track cover most of the store.
Open Mon.–Fri. 9 a.m.–5 p.m., Sat. 10 a.m.–4 p.m.

MICHIGAN CITY

The Antique Market
3707 N. Frontage Rd.
219/879-4084
More than 100 dealers in one of the region's largest antique malls.
Open Mon.–Sat. 10 a.m–5 p.m., Sun. noon–5 p.m.

Stocking Bale Antiques
227 W. 7th St.
219/873-9270
Across from the **Lighthouse Place outlet mall** (p. 275), Stocking Bale covers two floors of a late-nineteenth-century Victorian building. Specialties include furniture, art, and lighting.
Open Sun., Tue.–Sat. 11 a.m.–5 p.m. Closed Mon.

PORTER

Rainboutique
300 Lincoln St.
219/926-5001
Two floors of curio cabinets, lamps, clothes, books, and collectible ornaments. Every August, Rainboutique sponsors a huge antique flea market that coincides with the **Chesterton Art Fair** (p. 170) held a few blocks away.
Open Wed.–Sat. 10 a.m.–5 p.m., Sun. 1 p.m.–5 p.m.

ST. JOHN

Rosebud Antique Gallery
8126 Wicker Ave.
219/365-0801
Architectural salvage is their specialty, so if you're looking for a deal on a century-old mantel or built-in cabinet, call them up.
Open daily 10 a.m.–5 p.m.

TOWN OF PINES

Roadhouse Antiques and Collectibles
3900 W. Dunes Hwy. (U.S. 12)
219/878-1866
A little bit of everything: furniture, pottery, books, and glass.
Open Sun.–Mon., Wed.–Sat. 11 a.m.–5 p.m. Closed Tue.

VALPARAISO

Tom's Old Country Barn
147 E. County Rd. 50 South
219/477-6629
Fresh Amish baked goods are delivered here every week. Tom's also features furniture, tools, and crafts.
Open Mon.–Sat. 10 a.m.–4 p.m.

Valparaiso Antique Mall
212 E. Lincolnway
219/465-1869
A 12,000-sq.ft. mall housing 40 dealers.
Open Mon.–Sat. 10 a.m.–5 p.m., Sun. noon–5 p.m.

WHITING

Just Little Things
1600 119th St.
219/659-3438
The shelves and tables are filled with tins, glassware, clocks, watches, lamps, and toys—the "little things," but they do carry some furniture.
Open. Tue.–Sun. 11 a.m.–5 p.m. Call ahead.

BOATING

Some visitors to Northwest Indiana have found the easiest way to get there is to use the one route that is never crowded: Lake Michigan. Boaters have a choice of public marinas at which to dock with a number of conveniences—parking, fuel stations, and showers. Each also has its own distinctive characteristics.

MARINAS

Hammond Marina
701 Empress Dr.
Hammond
219/659-7678
www.ci.hammond.in.us/marina/
The Hammond Marina, only 12 miles from downtown Chicago, has 1,113 slips and winter storage for 200 boats. Amenities include ceramic-tiled showers, fuel stations, and the Ship Store and Deli for last-minute needs before heading out for a day on the lake.

Even if you don't have a boat, you may still want to visit the marina for its beautiful view of the lake, the **Horseshoe Casino** riverboat (p. 228), and the **Harbor Steak House**. Just south of the marina is **Phil Smidt's** (p. 104), a local seafood restaurant established in 1910, which has won national acclaim for its specialties of fried perch and frog legs. A bird sanctuary fills **Lakefront Park** (p. 264) next to the marina.

Fishing is available from platforms on the marina promenade, and anglers can clean their catch at stations located near the launch ramps. You can't swim here because of the danger from the boat traffic. Lakefront Park also prohibits swimming.

The marina's sailing school's instructors are certified by the U.S. Sailing Association. Classes are taught on 20-foot sailboats. Instruction is also available for the physically disabled.
Directions: Take I–80/94 to U.S. 41 north (Calumet Avenue). When U.S. 41 veers west and becomes Indianapolis Boulevard, continue following Calumet Avenue north into the marina.

Pastrick Marina
3301 Aldis Ave.
East Chicago
219/391-8482
The marina, named for Robert Pastrick, East Chicago's longtime mayor, has 294 wet slips, each with hookups for electricity, phone, cable television, and running water. Indoor and outdoor winter storage sites can accommodate more than 400 boats.

As with Hammond, the Pastrick Marina has proven popular with Illinois sailors looking for a convenient spot to keep their boat over the summer. The marina has showers, washers and dryers, launching facilities, fuel stations, a fishing pier that is wheelchair accessible, and fish-cleaning stations.

Although **Inland Steel** is next door to East Chicago, water pollution in the harbor has not been a problem.

Harrah's Casino (p. 227) is moored at the marina, making this one of the most popular gaming spots on Lake Michigan. Besides the dining at Harrah's, the marina is home to several restaurants: the popular **Sails, The Deli**, and the **Boardwalk Cafe**.

The marina is located next to **Jerose Park** (p. 266), which hosts several lakefront parties each year, including the **Waterfront Festival** and **Puerto Rican, African-American Heritage**, and

Mexican Independence Day celebrations (pp. 67–68).
Directions: From I–80/94 or I–90, take Cline Avenue north to the marina exit.

Portage Public Marina

1200 Marina Way
Portage
219/763-6833

The Portage Marina is not on Lake Michigan, but on the **Little Calumet River**, about two miles south of the lakeshore. Boats leave the marina, which is on Crisman Road just off U.S. 12 on Portage's north side, travel up the river, and enter the lake east of Ogden Dunes. The marina, home to the **Marquette Yacht Club**, has 135 slips. Several charter services operate near the marina along the Little Cal. No winter storage is available, although private companies nearby do offer such services.
Directions: From I–90 take Indiana 249 north to Crisman Road. Follow the road to the marina.

Photo by the author.

The Portage Harbor.

Photo by John J. Watkins.

Michigan City's Washington Park Marina.

Washington Park Marina
Washington Park
200 Heisman Harbor Rd.
Michigan City
219/872-1712
The marina, with 597 slips, is part of Washington Park, the sprawling park that dominates the lakeshore in Michigan City. The most picturesque of the area's marinas, the marina is close to the state's only lighthouse on Lake Michigan. Also visible from the water are the **Old Lighthouse Museum** (p. 29) and **Lookout Tower at Washington Park Zoo** (p. 28).

Boaters can fuel up, and anglers can clean fish at the marina. It has no winter storage, although some is available at nearby Trail Creek Marina. The **Blue Chip Casino** (p. 225) uses the **Trail Creek Marina** (700 E. Michigan Blvd., 219/879-4300) on the eastern edge of Michigan City.
Directions: from I–94, take U.S. 421 north into Michigan City. Turn right at Ninth Street to Pine Street. Take Pine north, over the Franklin Street Bridge and into Washington Park. Parking is available.

CHARTER SERVICES

Charter boats offer many fishing and sightseeing opportunities. Each county's convention and visitor's office can provide a list of reputable charter companies. If you've never been on a chartered boat trip before, there are a few things you'll want to ask:

- Does the U.S. Coast Guard license the captain?
- Is the captain experienced? Does he or she know the best fishing spots?
- Is the boat equipped or do you have to bring your own rods and reels?

EMERGENCY NUMBERS

U.S. Coast Guard

⇒ **Calumet Harbor:** 773/768-4093
⇒ **Michigan City:** 219/879-8371

Police

⇒ **Lake County Police:** 219/755-3333
⇒ **Lake County Police Marine Patrol:** 219/398-9033
⇒ **LaPorte County Police:** 219/326-7700
⇒ **Porter County Police:** 219/465-1515

CHRISTMAS TREES

Northwest Indiana has several tree farms where you can choose and harvest your own tree. The Indiana Christmas Tree Growers Association provided the following list of choices:

Egolf Christmas Trees
14594 S. and 700 W.
Wanatah
219/733-2143
A good selection of Scotch and white pines, wreaths, garlands, centerpieces, and grave pieces.
Open year round. Directions: About three miles past U.S. 421 on U.S. 30. At County Road 700 West go south about 2.5 miles. Signs are posted.

Guse Christmas Trees
14685 S. and 600 W.
Wanatah
219/733-9346
White and Scotch pines; Douglas, Fraser, and Canaan firs; wreaths; and garlands.
Directions: Go about four miles east of Wanatah on U.S. 30, then south on Thomaston Road (Country Road 600 west). The farm is about 2.5 miles.

Luers Christmas Tree Farm
5605 W. 91ˢᵗ
Crown Point
Scotch, Austrian, and white pines; Douglas, Canaan, and Fraser firs; spruce; and wreaths.
Directions: From U.S. 30, head south on Burr. The farm is a half-mile

west of the Burr Street and 91ˢᵗ Avenue intersection, just outside of Schererville.

Southard's Christmas Tree Farm
14505 Reeder Rd.
Crown Point
219/663-4675
Scotch and white pines, wreaths, pine cones, garlands, and centerpieces.
Directions: From I–65 go west on Indiana 2 to Indiana 55. North on Indiana 55 to 133ʳᵈ Avenue. Go west on 133ʳᵈ Avenue to Reeder Road. South on Reeder Road.

White's Tree Farm
2788 S. LaPorte County Rd. 425 W.
LaPorte
Douglas fir, spruce, wreaths, centerpieces, and grave pieces.
Directions: From I–80/90 take U.S. 39 south to Joliet Road. West on Joliet Road to County Road 425 West. Go South on CR 425 about a quarter mile.

GAMING

Thousands of people come to Northwest Indiana every day to test their luck at a blackjack table, pull the arm on a slot machine, or try a few hands of poker. Veterans of the Vegas strip or Atlantic City Boardwalk who have never given riverboat gaming a chance might turn up their noses at the notion. After all, they argue, how much can you fit on a boat? Plenty. More games than anyone can play in a single visit, in fact. These boats are like floating buildings.

Each casino boat has its own elements that make it special, and each is constantly changing the games to keep things interesting. There is never a charge to board a boat or for parking. And instructions on how to play the various games are available. Boats are permanently moored, so you can board anytime during operating hours.

Finally beware—you must be 21 years old to gamble in an Indiana casino.

Blue Chip
2 Easy St.
Michigan City
888/879-7711
www.bluechip-casino.com
Michigan City's casino boat boasts more than 1,300 slot machines and 55 gaming tables, spread over three levels. Blackjack, craps, roulette, and all the games you'd expect are here, along with popular new challenges like Caribbean Stud Poker, a new take on the old card game.

Photo by the author.

A Blue Chip Casino boat in Michigan City's Trail Creek Marina.

If you're on the third floor, stop by the **Sapphire Room**, a lounge added to give this area more of a club feel. The Blue Chip isn't as big as some of the region's other boats, so efforts have been made to make up for that with a huge sense of fun.

Regular players will want to join the Blue Chip Rewards plan, which lets you earn credit toward cash and prizes every time you play. Membership also gets you discounts, including deals on some meals.

While deciding where to wager your money, you'll also have to make up your mind about where to stop and eat. Most of the restaurants are in the pavilion. The **Grille on Easy Street** has prime rib and New York strip steaks. Just looking for a sandwich and drink or an ice cream cone? Stop by the **Snack Shack**. The **Ventura Lounge** is the place to relax before or after a session on the boat. The lounge has a large bar and plenty of seating. If you've had a great night and want to celebrate, fresh cigars are available. If you get hungry while aboard the boat, the **Jackpot Deli**, located on the lower level.

Next to the pavilion entrance to the boat is the **Blue Chip Hotel**, a 188-room hotel that includes an indoor pool, Jacuzzis, and an exercise room. If you want to make a weekend of it, this is a great place to stay.

The Blue Chip is the easternmost boat in Northwest Indiana, and the easiest to get to from Michigan or the South Bend area. It's also the only local boat not on Lake Michigan; it's east of downtown Michigan City in the Trail Creek Marina.
Open Sun.–Thu., 8 a.m.–3 a.m., Fri.–Sat. 8 a.m.–5 a.m. Directions: From I–94: take exit 40B (U.S. 35 north) to U.S. 12. From I–80/90: Coming from the east take Exit 49 to U.S. 35 North to U.S. 12; From the West: Take Highway 421 North (Exit 39) to U.S. 12, turn right.

Harrah's
777 Harrah's Blvd.
East Chicago
800/HAR-RAHS (427-7247)
www.harrahs.com
You'll never feel crowded on this boat; Harrah's East Chicago Casino is one of the largest gaming ships in the area, with four levels spread over 53,000 square feet.

More than 1,900 slot and electronic poker machines are available, and games on them range from a nickel to $100 bets. There are also 90-plus gaming tables. While all local boats have lots of video poker choices, Harrah's is the only one with live poker rooms. The 15 tables on the fourth level are popular, so call ahead for reservations (219/378-3000).

Harrah's also prides itself on its themed slot rooms. The newest slots are all in one place, the biggest payout machines in another. It makes finding the games you like easier.

If you plan on coming back, stop and sign up for a Total Gold Card. You can earn points on your card at any Harrah's casino in the nation and ensure the casino notifies you about upcoming promotions. Frequent players should ask if they qualify for the Total Gold Star Card, which brings benefits that include valet parking, priority boarding, and access to the Admiral's Quarters lounge.

When it's dinnertime, try the **French Quarter Room**, a stylish restaurant that specializes in steaks and seafood. Reservations are often needed, and diners need to be dressed appropriately. If you want to watch a baseball or football game on a huge TV screen while eating, stop by the **Winning Streaks Stadium Cafe** for a burger or sandwich. Also popular are the **Fresh Market Square Buffet**, and **Club Cappuccino** for coffee, lattes or fresh baked snacks.

The pavilion includes the 5,000-square-foot Rio Ballroom, meeting rooms, and convention space. There is also a 15-story hotel with 293 rooms. Harrah's pavilion stage has live music on Friday, Saturday, and Sunday evenings, like the recently-featured David Cassidy, Neil Sedaka, and the Together Tour featuring the Platters, Coasters, and Marvellettes.
Open daily 8 a.m.–5 a.m. Directions: From I–80/94: take Cline Avenue north to the Pastrick Marina exit (5C). From the Chicago Skyway/Indiana Tollway: Take Cline Avenue East to Exit 5B (the Pastrick Marina). Parking is available in an adjoining 1,800-space garage.

Horseshoe Casino
777 Casino Center Dr.
Hammond
219/473-7000
866/711-SHOE (7463)
www.horseshoe.com
The entrance to the Horseshoe Casino sits within a few hun-

dred feet of where Chicago's Skyway ends, making it one of the most popular casinos for Illinoisans.

It has four decks and 43,000 square feet of gaming space with 60 gaming tables and 1,600 slot and video poker machines. If you're a regular visitor, you'll want to join the Winners Circle Players Club. The club offers patrons special deals, chances to win prizes, and discounts on valet parking, meals, and items at the gift shop.

The Horseshoe also boasts the highest betting limits in the area. You want to make a $10,000 wager? They can handle that action. High-end gamblers can get in the Inner-Circle Club, which offers access to the VIP room and other amenities. Either club card ensures the Horseshoe will send you information about upcoming promotions.

This was the Empress Casino until mid-2001, and many still call it by that name. The name changed soon after casino owner Jack Binion purchased it. The Horseshoe is docked at the eastern edge of the Hammond Marina. Next door to the boat is a 125,000-square-foot pavilion. Inside is a lounge with a sports bar and meeting rooms that can handle groups ranging from twenty to 300.

The pavilion is where you'd head for a meal before a night of gaming, or to stop for a celebratory dinner afterward. The **Lake Michigan Deli Co.** has sandwiches, and the **Village Square Buffet** has a large salad bar and a variety of items, including pasta and barbecue. But if you're really looking for a big meal, try **Jack Binion's Steakhouse**. Reservations are needed on weekends (219/473-6028). The pavilion also has several gift stores and a smoke shop.

Assuming you're not trying to do it at the peak of rush hour, you can get here in less than 20 minutes from downtown

Chicago via the Skyway

Open daily 8 a.m.–5 a.m. Directions: From I–90, exit at Indianapolis Boulevard and follow the clearly marked signs to the casino's large parking lot. From I–80/94, exit Calumet Avenue or Indianapolis Boulevard north and continue to the lakefront. You can't miss the signs directing you to the casino. The Horseshoe has a large, free multi-story parking facility. An overflow parking lot is also available for peak times.

Majestic Star
One Buffington Harbor Dr.
Gary
888/2B-LUCKY (225-8259)
www.majesticstar.com
One of two boats docked at Gary's Buffington Harbor, the Majestic Star has 1,500 slot and video machines and a huge array of table games, including blackjack, roulette, and mini-

Photo by the author.

The entrance to the Majestic Star and Trump Casino
boats docked in Gary's Buffington Harbor.

baccarat. It also offers some of the newest games, including Pai Gow poker and Caribbean stud poker.

The boat has four levels. It's the only casino boat in Northwest Indiana with a VIP lounge. If you don't qualify for VIP privileges and big action, there are usually plenty of $5 and $10 tables available.

Regular visitors should sign up for a Club Majestic card. Frequent use builds up points for special promotions, including cash-back deals. The card will also get you a 10-percent discount at the gift shop, free valet service, and invitations to special events.

High rollers should ask about the Club Majestic Premier card. Not everyone qualifies, but those whose wagers put them in this class can get a card that will give them preferred boarding privileges, a 20-percent discount at the gift shop, special deals when ordering meals, and access to several VIP lounges—the Signature Room, Royal Court, and Chairman's Suite.

The pavilion and free parking at Buffington Harbor also serve the Trump Casino. Amenities here include **Miller Pizza Co.**, the **South Shore Grill**, and **Harbor Treats**.

Other food emporiums are the **Jackpot Java** coffee shop, and the **Wings N Things**.
Open daily 8 a.m.–5 a.m. Directions: From I–90, exit at Cline Avenue East. Follow Cline Avenue to Columbus Drive/Chicago Avenue (exit 6A). Make a right at the light and follow the signs into Buffington Harbor. From I–80/94, exit at Cline Avenue North. Follow Cline Avenue to Industrial Boulevard/Columbus Drive (Exit 6). Take a left at the light, and make a right at the second light into Buffington Harbor.

Trump Casino
Buffington Harbor
Gary
219/977-7000
888/21-TRUMP (218-7867)
www.trumpindiana.com
Yes, that Trump—The Donald himself—owns it. The Trump Casino features 1,300 slot and video machines. There are also plenty of table games, including roulette, black jack, Pai Gow poker, craps, and Caribbean stud and draw poker. It's the only boat in the area to offer two-cent slots.

Trump has also imported some of the rules and options found in his Atlantic City casino. For example, players can split up to four times (except on aces) in black jack. Trump also promises more $5 tables, so those who aren't in the high roller category don't get left out.

What makes Trump's boat unique is the banquet room on the boat. Other boats have large facilities, but they are located in the pavilion at the dock. The fourth level of Trump's boat is the **Crystal Room**, with red velvet decor, chandeliers, and access to the deck. It's available for wedding receptions, bar mitzvahs, company parties, and other large gatherings. The **Top Deck Deli** aboard the boat specializes in sandwiches of all kinds.

Regular visitors should sign up for a Trump International Card. The free card is good for discounts at the gift shop and other promotions. Players who opt for high stakes more frequently will move up to a Gold Club card and, finally, the Concierge Club card.

Gamblers 55 years and older can take part in the Golden Gamers program. It provides restaurant and gift shop discounts and the opportunity to compete in the weekly slot tourney.

Trump also has free valet parking for visitors and a 300-room hotel with an indoor pool and restaurants, including the turf and surf **Lakeside Café**, and a great view of the lake.
See the Majestic Star entry for directions to Buffington Harbor. Open daily 8 a.m.–5 a.m.

HORSE RACING

Trackside OTB
7610 Broadway
Merrillville
219/755-0000
www.tracksideotb.com/trackside_indiana/merrillville
The closest tracks are all in Illinois, but racing fans can still enjoy their sport and get down a bet at Northwest Indiana's only off-track betting parlor. Trackside lets you watch races from Chicago-area tracks such as Arlington Park, Hawthorne, Balmoral, and Maywood, and also catch the action from some of the nation's most famous venues, including Aqueduct, the Meadowlands, Churchill Downs, and Santa Anita. Until mid-2001, this was known as Churchill Downs Sports Spectrum. The famed Churchill Downs company still owns it.

A daily racing sheet for either thoroughbred or harness racing is $2, and a program is $4. Bets can either be placed at one of several windows or at automated machines. And, just like at the track, you collect your winnings right there.

Trackside is roomy, with over 250 TVs filling nearly every wall. Large non-smoking rooms are available.
Open daily at 11 a.m. Free admission. Call for race times. Directions: From I–65, exit U.S. 30 west to Broadway. Go north on Broadway about a quarter mile. Plenty of free parking.

Photo by the author.

One of Northwest Indiana's oldest golf courses, Wicker Park
Memorial Golf Course opened in Highland in 1927.

GOLF COURSES

Whether you're looking for a championship caliber or a nine-hole course, Northwest Indiana has plenty of options. Here is a list of local public courses:

Beacon Hills Country Club
286 W. Johnson Rd.
LaPorte
219/324-4777
⇒ 18 holes, par 72, 6,040 yards
There are no water hazards on this course, built in 1904, but more than two dozen sand bunkers provide plenty of challenges. It's actually a nine-hole course with 10 greens and 18 tees. Golfers shoot at most of the pins twice, but come at them from different angles, depending on the hole.

Beachwood Golf Course
2222 Woodlawn Dr.
LaPorte
219/362-2651
⇒ 18 holes, par 72, 6,627 yards
Golfers will find a challenge on No. 8, a par 3, 189-yard hole that has a small pond with a green guarded by a bunker on the right side.
Reservations are taken for weekends and holidays.

Brassie Golf Club
1100 Pearson Rd.
Chesterton
219/921-1192
www.thebrassie.com
⇒ 18 holes, par 72, 7,008 (championship tees), 6,445 (regular)

Golf attire required, no metal spikes allowed. The course was designed by Jim Fazio and opened in 1998, playing host to the PGA Indiana Open the next year. The course is laid out over rolling terrain, surrounded by lots of water and deep bunkers. *Reservations can be made up to two weeks in advance.*

Briar Leaf Golf Club

3233 N. State Rd. 39
LaPorte
219/326-1992
877/BRIAR-LEAF (274-2753)
www.briarleaf.com
⇒ 18 holes, par 72, 6,850 yards (championship tees),
    6,300 (regular tees)
Golfers face water challenges on six holes, including the newly renovated No. 3, which features a unique island green. *Reservations can be made up to one week in advance.*

Calumet Golf Course

3920 W. Ridge Rd.
Gary
219/980-9484
www.northwestindiana.com/cities/gary/golf_gary.htm
⇒ 9 holes, par 35, 2,645 yards

Cedar Creek Golf Center

10483 W. 109th St.
Cedar Lake
219/365-2902
www.northwestindiana.com/cities/cedarlake/golf_cedarlake.htm
⇒ 9 holes, par 30, 1,645 yards
A chip-and-putt course, an 18-hole miniature course, and lighted driving range.

Cedar Lake Golf Course
3355 E. 700 North
Howe
219/562-3923
www.cedarlakegc.com
⇒ 18 holes, par 71, 6,230 yards
No. 13 could prove unlucky for some golfers. It's 186 yards, par 3, over water, with an elevated tee and green. Get a good tee shot off or you'll get wet.

The Course at Aberdeen (semi-private)
245 Tower Rd.
Valparaiso
219/462-5050
www.golfataberdeen.com
⇒ 18 holes, par 72, 6,905 yards (championship tees),
   5,670 yards (white).
Golfers must wear collared shirts, no jeans, and soft spikes only. A semi-private club designed by Michael Hurdzan to balance the natural beauty of the area with a challenging round of golf. The natural contours of the land have been incorporated into the design. The elevated tees on Nos. 1 and 10 make it easy to lose sight of your ball as it soars onto the fairway below. Golf carts have global-positioning systems to help judge the distance from ball to pin.
Reservations can be made up to two weeks in advance.

Creekside Golf Course and Training Center
Clifford Rd.
Valparaiso
219/531-PUTT (7888)
www.valparaisogolf.com/creekside
⇒ 18 holes, par 72, 3,250 yards
A great place to learn the game or, for veterans, refine their play. Creekside features several sets of tees, offering significant differences in how difficult each hole is. An indoor training

center offers hands-on instruction and sophisticated video analysis of your swing.

Cressmoor Country Club
601 N. Wisconsin
Hobart
219/942-9300
www.northwestindiana.com/cities/hobart/golf_hobart.htm
⇒ 18 holes, par 71, 6,060 yards (blue tees); 5,681 yards (red)
A fairly wide open course, providing a good challenge for beginners.
Reservations available

Duck Creek Golf Club
636 N. 700 West
Hobart
219/759-5870
⇒ 18 holes, par 70, 5,438 yards
The front nine includes two large ponds.

Forest Park Golf Course
1155 Sheffield
Valparaiso
219/531-7888
219/462-4111
www.valparaisogolf.com/forestpark/forestmain.html
⇒ 18 holes, par 70, 5,642 yards
The course features short holes and wide fairways, but huge bunkers provide a challenge on the front nine with elevated tees and greens on the back nine. Includes the **Creekside Golf Course and Learning Center**, a 50-station driving range and training center.
Reservations can be made up to one week in advance.

Griffith Golf Center

1901 Cline Ave.
Griffith
219/923-3223
www.northwestindiana.com/cities/griffith/golf_griffith.htm
⇒ 18 holes, par 54, 2,700 yards
One of the best 18-hole, par 3 courses in the state; Griffith provides a good challenge for seniors and beginners looking to advance.
Reservations are not required.

Indian Ridge

6363 Grand Blvd. (also called Highway 51)
Hobart
219/942-6850
www.northwestindiana.com/cities/hobart/golf_hobart.htm
⇒ 18 holes, par 72, 6,193 yards (back tees)
A wide-open course with relatively flat terrain, making it ideal for beginners or intermediate golfers.
Reservations are recommended on weekends.

Lake Hills Golfers Club

10001 W. 85th St.
St. John
219/365-8601
www.northwestindiana.com/cities/stjohn/golf_stjohn.htm
⇒ 27 holes, par 70, 6,200 yards (Players Course),
    5,900 yards (Country Course and Club Course)
Lake Hills, one of the area's most storied courses, opened in 1925. The 10th hole is a par 3 over a pond. It's the one you'll remember. On that hole, women tee off from the bridge. The sloped green provides another challenge—stay below the cup or you'll have trouble sinking the putt.
Reservations are required on Sunday.

Lost Marsh
901 129th St.
Hammond
219/932-4654
www.lostmarsh.com
⇒ 9-hole, par 27, youth course
The name comes from where this course was built: on a mound of slag (a waste produce from metal production) in north Hammond. Their **Hammond Youth Golf Academy** has proven popular, and an 18-hole adult course is currently under construction. The multi-use property also has George Lake, wetlands, and a wildlife viewing area.

MacArthur Golf Course
140th St. and Indianapolis Blvd.
East Chicago
219/391-8362
www.golfguideweb.com/indiana/eastchicago/bdeff.html
⇒ 9 holes, par 27, 1,370 yards
Reservations are not required.

Michigan City Municipal Golf Course
4000 E. Michigan Blvd.
Michigan City
219/873-1517 (North Course)
219/873-1516 (South Course)
www.emichigancity.com/cityhall/departments/golf/
⇒ Two 18-hole courses: the North, par 60, 3,351 yards;
    the South, par 72, 6,169 yards
The North Course is the easier of the two. The South provides more of a challenge, requiring good approach shots to hit the small greens.

Mink Lake Golf Course
636 N. Calumet Ave.
Valparaiso
219/462-2585
⇒ 9 holes, par 35, 969 yards
Reservations are not required.

Monastery Golf Course
9800 W. 129th Ave.
Cedar Lake
219/374-7750
www.northwestindiana.com/cities/cedarlake/golf_cedarlake.htm
⇒ 18 holes, par 70, 5,820 yards
One of the more unusual sights you'll see on area courses is the dead tree that sits on the fourteenth green here. The tree was alive when the course was built in the early 1900s and was incorporated into the design.
Reservations are recommended on weekends and holidays.

Oak Knoll Golf Course
11210 Whitcomb St.
Crown Point
219/663-3349
www.oakknollgolf.com
⇒ 18 holes, par 70, 5,803 yards
On No. 18, golfers face an elevated tee shot with trees on the left and right and grass bunkers around the elevated green. The par-3 hole plays 180 yards.
Reservations are available for weekends.

Palmira Golf Course
12111 W. 109th St.
St. John
219/365-4331
www.palmiragolf.com
⇒ 18 holes, par 71, 6,889 yards (blue tees), 6,375 yards(white)

The course is a great value and has made some major revisions, rebuilding 15 holes in the last 10 years. Eleven holes feature lakes or streams, including No. 9 with a lake waiting on the right if you slice your tee shot.

Reservations are can be made up to a week in advance and recommended for weekends and holidays.

Pheasant Valley Country Club
3838 W. 141st St.
Crown Point
219/663-5000
www.crownpoint.net/golfcourses.htm
⇒ 18 holes, par 72, 6,826 yards (championship tees),
     6,456 yards (regular), 6,079 yards (women)
Golfers will enjoy the hilly, wooded course. The No. 7, par-4 hole is a special challenge. It's a long hole, playing 469 yards, and you have to cross a ditch to get to the sloped green. The green slopes from left to right, so you don't want to be on the top side putting down.

Reservations are recommended.

Robbinhurst Golf Club
383 W. 875 N. Robbins Rd.
Valparaiso
219/762-9711
www.golfguideweb.com/indiana/valparaiso/fcdf.html
⇒ 18 holes, par 68, 5,629 yards
A windmill from when this was a family farm in the mid-1800s still stands near the first tee. The course has many mature trees, and watch out for Squirrel Creek

Reservations are required on weekends.

Sandy Pines Golf Course

Highway 231 at County Rd. 1100 North
DeMotte
219/987-3611
www.sandypinesgc.com
⇒ 18 holes, par 72, 6412 yards
The most challenging hole is No. 11, which is a long 545 yards.
Large trees guard the narrow fairway. It opens for the third shot
with a water hazard to the right. The secret here is play for
position, not distance.
Reservations are needed for weekends and holidays. No metal spikes
allowed.

Scherwood Golf Course

600 E. Joliet St.
Schererville
219/865-2554
www.scherwoodgolf.com
⇒ 18-hole and 9-hole courses.:18 hole is par 71, 6,500 yards;
    9 hole is par 30, 1,600 yards.
Management has made some changes to toughen and lengthen
the course. No. 9 is a dog-legged fairway with water all the way
down the right side. The par 4 plays 350 to 410 yards.
Reservations are recommended.

South Gleason Golf Course

3400 Jefferson St.
Gary
219/980-1089
www.northwestindiana.com/cities/gary/golf_gary.htm
⇒ 18 hole, par 71, 6,378 yards
The signature hole is No. 6, par 3, 175 yards, almost all over
water, with just 30 yards between the water and the small
elevated green.
Reservations are required on weekends and can be made up to a week in
advance.

South Shore Golf Course
14400 Lakeshore Dr.
Cedar Lake
219/374-6070
www.southshoreclub.com
⇒ 18 hole, par 70, 5,644 yards
Terrain ranges from flat to hilly. Although the course is relatively short, the 75 bunkers keep things interesting.

Summertree Golf Club
2323 E. 101st St.
Crown Point
219/663-0800
⇒ 18 holes, par 72, 6,596 yards
Watch out on No. 5. There's water on the left, water behind it, and a creek along the right side. With the elevated green, play can get a little testy if you can't decide how the wind's blowing.
Reservations for weekends and holidays can be made up to a week in advance. No metal spikes allowed.

Turkey Creek Golf Course
6400 Harrison St.
Merrillville
219/980-5170
www.turkeycreekgolf.com
⇒ 18 holes, par 72, 6,549 yards
Turkey Creek runs throughout the course and comes into play on 12 of the 18 holes. The hilly, tree-lined fairways provide another challenge.
Reservations are recommended for weekends.

White Hawk Country Club (semiprivate)
1001 Whitehawk Dr.
Crown Point
219/661-2323
www.whitehawkcc.com
⇒ 18 holes, par 72, 7,025 yards (championship tees), 6,470 yards (white tees), 5,255 yards (women)

One of the newest courses in the area, Whitehawk added nine holes in 2001. Nos. 15, 16, and 17 are the area's "Amen corner" with a long par 3 and two difficult par 4s over a marshy area. *Reservations are recommended and can be made up to a week in advance.*

Wicker Park Memorial Golf Course
Ridge Rd. and Indianapolis Blvd.
Highland
219/838-9809
⇒ 18 holes, par 72
Another of the area's oldest courses, Wicker Park opened in 1927.
Reservations are needed for holidays and weekends. No metal spikes allowed.

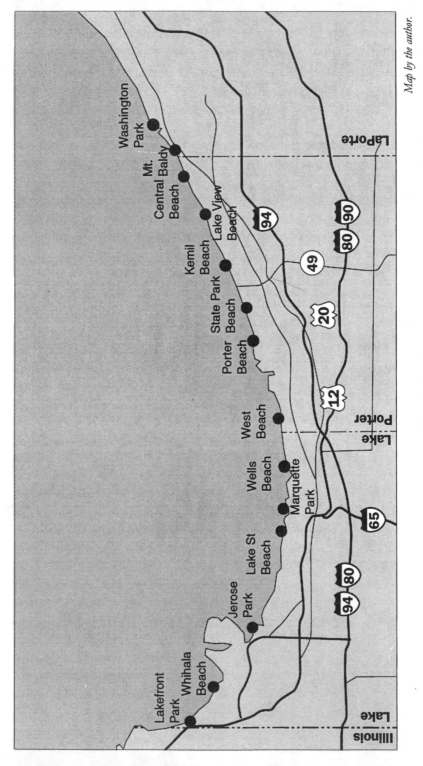

The Lakeshore

Map by the author.

LAKESHORE

• • • • • • • • • • • • • •

The dunes are "symbols of eternity," poet Carl Sandburg wrote
in 1958. "They constitute a signature of time and eternity: once
lost the loss would be irrevocable."

Sandburg lived near Michigan City for years, amid the over-
whelming beauty of the lakeshore. First-time visitors are often
shocked that in an area like Northwest Indiana, a region known
for its industrial might, these graceful, immense mountains of
sand coexist with the steel mills.

The dunes were here thousands of years before the industrialists or the Native American before them. Glaciers, acting like
giant bulldozers as they carved the Great Lakes, pushed the
giant sand piles into place. The glaciers ripped into the ground,
crushed everything in their path, and left behind magnificent
dunes.

Thousands of years later, the dunes provide the greatest uninterrupted stretches of beach in the Chicago area. But the dunes
are more than beaches. There are miles of twisting, turning,
climbing hiking paths that will give you a glimpse of rare plants,
butterfly colonies, and wetlands. And, if you listen closely, you
can hear the "singing sands," a sound unique to the dunes.

The singing comes from the distinctive shape of the sand and
the grinding that takes place when the damp sand is stepped on
near the water's edge. Listen on a quiet evening and you can't
miss it.

Beaches in Indiana begin right at the Illinois line and continue

Above: Photo by the author.
Below: Courtesy of the Porter County Convention, Recreation & Visitor Commission.

The natural beauty and recreational options of the Indiana dunes and lakeshore attract countless visitors to Northwest Indiana.

to Michigan City. At one time much of the land was covered with sand and grasslands, but today the dunes are really first visible on the east side of Gary. By the time you get into Porter County you'll be hiking over land that is known around the world.

Unfortunately, the stretch of dunes is not continuous, nor is the national park that protects them. Steel mills, the **Port of Indiana** (p. 181), a utility, and several communities interrupt what was once a stretch of land comprised of miles of uninterrupted mountains of sand, grass as tall as a grown man, forests, and rare plants. Natural wonders were lost as the area's industry grew throughout much of the twentieth century, but extraordinary efforts, especially by volunteers dedicated to preserving the land, have ensured that areas have been saved—and in some cases reclaimed—for dune lovers.

Industry and development have not been the only enemy of the dunes. Erosion is a problem, and it can be exacerbated by hikers wandering off trails, stomping through areas where dune grass is helping hold the sand in place. Stay on marked trails and you'll help efforts to protect the dunes for future generations.

One more thing to remember: Don't feed the wildlife. Deer, raccoons, possums, and other animals may wander over to see what's in your picnic lunch. These animals may be used to people, but they're still wild animals.

National, state, and local park departments have jurisdiction over the beaches and trails, depending upon where you are. To make things a little easier to navigate, this chapter separates the national and state parks from the local beaches, and gives some detail on each.

Finally, contrary to popular belief, the dunes don't shut down with the close of summer. Some trails are open to cross-country skiing, there's sledding in some areas, and a winter hike offers the chance to see some sites that are obscured by the thick foliage in warmer months. For some, winter is the best time to visit the dunes.

NATIONAL PARK

Indiana Dunes National Lakeshore
219/926-7561
www.nps.gov/indu
It was a senator from neighboring Illinois who was the driving force in Washington pushing lawmakers to give federal protection to a part of the lakeshore. Paul Douglas's efforts earned him the nickname "Indiana's third senator."

Douglas, an Illinois senator from 1948 to 1966, was a liberal Democrat and champion of civil rights. He was also a tireless fighter for the dunes, even if the area was outside his own state. Indiana's own lawmakers were hesitant to protect the dunes, for fear such efforts would impede the growth of industry in the area. In a documentary on his life, Douglas said that early in life, "I wanted to save the world. Then I wanted to save the nation. Now I want to save the dunes." His efforts were successful. The national lakeshore was designated as such on November 5, 1966, and the area under its protection has been expanded several times since.

Visitors should start at the **Dorothy Buell Memorial Visitor Center** (Kemil Rd. and Rte. 12), where park rangers are on duty to answer questions; maps are available; educational programs are offered; and there is even a gift shop in case you want to pick up a volume on bird-watching or nature hikes in the dunes, a souvenir shirt, or postcards. Tip for kids: You can earn a special junior ranger badge by picking up a guide and completing the special activities inside.

The center is named for Buell, who was 65 in 1952 when she founded the **Save the Dunes Council** (219/879-3937), the group instrumental in building public support to protect the lakeshore. A memorial to her in the center's gift shop recalls the

SAVING THE DUNES

There are several groups dedicated to preserving the dunes that can provide more information on the plants and wildlife that can be found there.

Friends of the Indiana Dunes
P.O. Box 166
Beverly Shores, IN 46301
www.duneland.com/friends.htm
A nonprofit organization dedicated to helping people understand and appreciate the dunes.

Save the Dunes Council, Inc.
444 Barker Rd.
Michigan City, IN 46360
219/879-3937
www.savedunes.org
An organization dedicated to conserving the dunes.

Hoosier Chapter of the Sierra Club
212 W. 10th St.
Suite A–335
Indianapolis, IN 46220
www.hoosier.sierraclub.org
The club's publication, *Nature Walks in Northern Indiana*, by Alan McPherson is essential for serious hikers.

Photo by the author.

words she spoke when announcing the council's formation: "We are prepared to spend the rest of our lives if necessary to save the dunes."

The national park is more than 15,000 acres, so there's no way to take in all of the trails, beaches, and historic attractions in a single visit. Even those who have been going for decades to swim, hike, or birdwatch see something new on every trip. Call ahead for information and to plan a trip.

Bailly Homestead and Chellberg Farmhouse
219/926-7561, x. 246
These two attractions are a short walk from each other in the National Lakeshore

The **Bailly Homestead** is what's left of the trading post established in 1822 by French-Canadian trader Honore Gratien Joseph Bailly de Messein, according to a history compiled by the National Park Service. White settlers, Native Americans, missionaries, and others would gather at the Bailly homestead. Bailly eventually built several houses on his property, as he established an area that for a time was known as Baillytown. A trail from the homestead leads to the Bailly Cemetery, a round, raised cemetery where Bailly, his wife, and other family members are buried. Hikers still follow the trails out to the Baillys's resting place, and many stop there to rest and reflect as they make their way through the forest.

Chellberg Farm is less than half a mile from the Bailly Homestead. Anders and Johanna Chellberg established the farm in 1872. Their descendants farmed the property until 1972, when it was sold to the National Park Service. The farmhouse, now open to tourists, was built in 1885. Today, most of the building retains its original appearance, except for the dining room, which reflects the style of the 1930s. A short walk from the farmhouse are a barn, chicken house, and livestock area. Children are able to pet cows and horses and watch them during feeding time. Park employees who work on the farm will take the time to talk with visitors and explain about the care and feeding of farm animals.

In March, the **Maple Sugar Time Festival** brings visitors who want to see how the sap is gathered and made into maple sugar and syrup. Many return in the fall for the **Duneland Harvest Festival**, a program that includes nineteenth-century crafts, music, and plenty of food prepared the old-fashioned way. In December, the farmhouse is decorated for the **Christmas in the Dunes program**.

Paul H. Douglas Center for Environmental Education
Miller Woods, south of Lake St. Beach, north of Gary's Miller neighborhood
219/938-8221
Named for the conservation-minded Illinois senator, the center sponsors programs year-round. In the summer it might be a program on bird watching or spotting rare flowers, while in the winter the focus might shift to a workshop on hiking with

snowshoes. The center also has lots of hands-on exhibits that kids love.
Open Mon.–Fri. 10 a.m.–4 p.m.

Environmental Learning Center and Camp Good Fellow
700 Howe Rd.
Chesterton
219/395-9555
www.nps.gov/indu/learning
A place open to school kids, community groups, business, and industry, the center offers a variety of educational programs and a chance to see the dunes in a way few ever will. The center is a not-for-profit institution run in cooperation with the National Lakeshore. Programs offered include **Frog in the Bog** that brings elementary students to stay at the center and learn about ecology, and **Mighty Acorns**, a program developed with Chicago's Field Museum of Natural History to teach young people about the importance of environmental restoration. The camp has 10 cabins, equipped with heating and air conditioners, which make the center popular year round.
Directions: From I–94, take exit 22B (Highway 20). Go north at Mineral Springs Road, then east at Oak Hill Road. Follow Oak Hill to Howe Road and go north.

Dunewood Campground
219/926-7561, x. 225
Open from April through October, the campground is the only one in the National Lakeshore (although Dunes State Park also has one). Dunewood has 79 sites—54 drive-in sites and 25 walk-in. All cost $15 a night. Reservations are not accepted; sites are available on a first-come, first-served basis. Dunewood has hot showers and a convenience store that can provide wood, ice, and other items. Gathering wood from the floor of the forest is not allowed.

Cowles Bog

Who wants to visit a bog, you're wondering? Well, this may be one of the most impressive sites in the national park. Cowles Bog is named for Dr. Henry Chandler Cowles, the University of Chicago botanist who later said his European counterparts considered the Indiana dunes to be one of the wonders of America. Cowles has been called the nation's first professional ecologist and the dunes the "birthplace of ecology." He studied dune formations around the globe, and called those in Northwest Indiana "the grandest in the entire world."

There is a trail here that makes a five-mile, round-trip hike through the dunes, past ponds and marshes, around rare plants, down to the beach, then back. The contrast between the wetlands and dunes and stretch of beach is incredible.
Directions: In Porter County, take U.S. 12 to Mineral Springs Road. Go north to the Dune Acres park entrance. The trail is clearly marked. Parking is available.

Ly-co-ki-we Trail

Bring comfortable hiking shoes. This 10-mile trail is the longest the National Lakeshore offers. It's also a tough one. The name Ly-co-ki-we comes from the Miami tribe, and it means "sandy ground." Part of the trail is sandy and can make for a tough hike. Take a look at a map; there are several smaller "loops" hikers can make so they don't have to do the whole 10 miles.
Those who venture on this trail will be rewarded. The National Park Service says it's one of the best for viewing fall wildflowers and migrating birds. Rangers lead some of these hikes, pointing out some of the rare plant life that might otherwise be missed.

If you want to make a day of it, the trail does include a shelter, restrooms, and picnic area.
Directions: You can start in one of two places, both of them in Porter County: Kemil Road and Route 12, or U.S. 20 and County Road 275 East. Both places offer parking.

NATIONAL LAKESHORE BEACHES AND TRAILS

These are listed in the order you encounter them as you enter the National Lakeshore from the west heading east. See the entry for the **Indiana Dunes State Park** (p. 262) for what's between Porter and Kemil Beaches.

In April 2001, the Dunes National Lakeshore banned the use of personal watercraft so water and jet skiing aren't allowed along these areas. The ban does not extend to beaches not under the National Lakeshore's control.

West Beach
One of the area's most popular beaches, there are nearly four miles of lakefront beach here, along with more than three miles of dune hiking trails. West Beach is also the most family friendly

Photo by the author.

A stunning National Lakeshore dunescape.

of the National Lakeshore beaches. Lifeguards are on duty in the summer, and there are showers, restrooms, a first aid station, and concessions. Facilities are wheelchair accessible.

West Beach is home to a boardwalk trail that offers a 3.5-mile hike that gives a great view of the dunes. The trail, which slowly climbs to 110 feet, includes a series of benches for stopping and resting on the way. But stay on the trail. If you stray off the boardwalk, you'll harm the rare dune grass and other vegetation below. West Beach trails also offer a hike to **Long Lake**; although if it's swimming you want you'll be better off staying at the beach. Anglers like this lake and have had success going after bass, blue gill, and northern pike.

West Beach is open 9 a.m.–sunset; no fires are allowed. Directions: Take I–94 to Indiana 249 to U.S. 12 and go west. At County Line Road, go north to the park entrance. There is ample parking, although a fee is charged during the summer months, beginning in late May; $4 per carload, 50 cents per person for walk-ins and bicyclists, $25 for bus loads. National Park Passes cannot be used for entry to West Beach.

Porter Beach

Tucked between the community of Dune Acres and the Indiana Dunes State Park, this is a popular beach for swimmers. Lifeguards are on duty and the area is wheelchair accessible.

Directions: From I–94 or I–80/90, take Indiana 49 north. At State Park Road, go west to Waverly Road, then go north. Parking is available.

Kemil Beach

You want secluded? This may be the National Lakeshore beach for you. It's one of the smaller beaches, and the lack of a huge parking lot keeps many would-be visitors away. Kemil is worth visiting though for the hike up the **Dune Ridge Trail**. There's a beautiful view at the top of this small ridge, where an observation platform is waiting.

Directions: In Porter County, take U.S. 20 to Kemil Road. Go north, past the visitors' center, and stay on Kemil to the beach. The parking lot is located about a quarter mile south of the beach, and you'll have to hike down Kemil Road to get to the water.

Lake View Beach

Lake View has a nice spread of open beach, and an elevated picnic area that offers a good view while eating. Restrooms are available. A wheelchair lift makes this beach accessible. A bit further east down Lakefront Road is parking for residents only, their lot has small telescopes for looking out onto the water and at the Chicago skyline on the northwest horizon.

As with Kemil Beach, finding parking here can be tough but worth the effort. There is a lot, but it's not that large. Here's a tip the park department offers to solve parking dilemmas: Dunbar Parking Area is a small lot about a half-mile west of the beach. Also, spots are sometimes available at the South Shore Line train station about a mile south of the beach. You can also park at either of these places and hike back to the beach.
Directions: From U.S. 12 or U.S. 20, go north on Lake Shore Country Road. At Lakefront Road, go west.

Central Avenue Beach

About two miles long and usually not too crowded, Central Avenue Beach can be a great place to bring a group for volleyball or touch football. No lifeguard is on duty and there are only basic restroom facilities. This is also the beach closest to **Mount Baldy** (p. 259), so it's the starting off point for many about to take on that challenge.

Like several of the national parks, Central Beach can sometimes be very rocky along the shoreline when you first step into the water. Don't let that stop you, though. Once your go out a ways you're past the rocky portion and are standing on sandy ground.
Directions: In Porter County, take U.S. 12 to Central Avenue and go north. It's about a quarter mile hike through some underbrush to get to the beach from the parking lot.

Mount Baldy
Here's a fun, challenging hike that even kids can do. Just be ready to take your time and bring a camera. Mount Baldy is a 123-foot high "living" sand dune; the shifting sands make the dune move inland about four feet annually.

The hike up isn't *that* bad. There are wooden steps that make the climb to the summit. Or, hardy souls can try climbing up the dune. At the top you can see the **Michigan City Lighthouse** (p. 29) to the east, the Chicago skyline off in the distance, and the steel mills on the west. After you've taken it all in, the fun starts. Running down the front of the dune, toward the beach, provides a rush that's not available anywhere else on the shore. Because it's not a steep slope, kids can do it, too.

For those who just want to enjoy the water, it's possible to hike to it without climbing to the top of Mount Baldy. Look for the marked trails. This offers more of an opportunity to take in the beauty of the oak, maple, and hickory trees.

Every winter there are a few sledders who hike up Mount Baldy and enjoy the rush of sledding down. They're risking more than a run-in with a tree or sliding out onto thin ice. The National Lakeshore has banned sledding in the national park, and park rangers can cite those who are caught. The ban was not only prompted by concerns that sledders will hurt themselves. Many of them slid over and damage the fragile grass that grows on and next to the dune. That grass helps anchor some of the sand, and when it's lost erosion will follow.

Finally, know why they call it Mount Baldy? Because at the top, this mount has no grass, no trees, no vegetation of any kind. So, it's "bald!"
Directions: In Porter County, take U.S. 12 east until it intersects with Beverly Drive. Take Rice Street north to the parking lot. Picnic facilities are available.

STATE PARK

Indiana Dunes State Park
1600 N. Porter County Rd. 25 East
Chesterton
219/926-1952
www.state.in.us/dnr/parklake/parks/indianadunes.html
The state park, which was created in 1925, is a stretch of land
nearly surrounded by the National Lakeshore. The 2,182 acres
include 16 miles of hiking trails, picnic areas, a beach, and a
nature center. No alcohol is allowed in the state park, and pets
are not allowed on the beach. Pets can go other places in the
state park, but they must be kept on a leash. Tip for kids: The
Park Patch Program lets you earn a special patch by completing a series of fun activities.
*Admission is $4 per carload with Indiana license plates, $5 per car from
out of state; $1 for each person 8 an older entering on foot, bicycle, or
horseback. Annual passes and senior discounts are available.*

State Park Beach
This beautiful, three-mile stretch of beach is also one of Indiana's busiest. There's a huge pavilion with concessions, restrooms, and a beach house for changing, making it one of the
nicest beaches for families. Swimming is allowed only when
lifeguards are on duty, although that rule is sometimes broken.
Be careful, though. The undertow at lakeshore beaches can be
strong, and sudden dropoffs are common, so keep an eye on
children playing in the water. Lifeguards will absolutely not
allow the use of inner tubes and other inflatable devices in the
water.
*The beach and bathhouse open Memorial Day weekend and remain open
no later than Labor Day.*

Begin at the **Nature Center** where you can learn more about
the interesting topography of the dunes, which includes wet-

lands, forest, and sand. Kids can put on puppet shows and will be fascinated by the observation window, where they can record the variety of wildlife that stops by. Hummingbirds, chipmunks, and frogs are among the steady visitors.

 There are seven clearly marked trails, ranging from a moderate, three-quarter-mile walk to a 5.5-mile hike through a "tree graveyard." That's the name given to a grove of trees buried by sand then later uncovered when the sand blows away. Many trails begin right outside the Nature Center.

The trails are numbered, but not one to seven (come on, that would be too easy!). Some trails have been closed over time, so they're no longer listed and their numbers have been "retired." Also, many of these trails intersect and overlap for some stretches, so be sure to pickup one of the park's free trail maps. It's easy to get lost.

Start with **Trail 1**, a tenth-of-a-mile hike that will take you to the lookout tower. If you're in a hurry or have children who aren't up to a more strenuous hike, this is good walk.

Trail 2 is a three-mile walk over mostly flat ground. This one is popular with cross-country skiers.

Trail 3 is a short, three-quarters of a mile. It's also the only trail that's cut off from all the others. According to park personnel, this is the trail to walk in the spring for a look at wildflowers, including prickly pear cactus.

Trail 4 is another three-quarters-of-a-mile hike. This one goes by the base of Mount Tom—at 192 feet, the highest dune on the lakeshore—and passes through dunes covered with black oak forests.

Trail 7 is next. It's 1.1 miles and is the path you'll take if you want

Photo by the author.

The Indiana Dunes State Park beach on a quiet winter day. During the summer, it is one of Indiana's nicest and busiest beaches.

to get from the beach to the Nature Center.

Trail 8 is the most rugged of the walks, but also one of the most rewarding. It's "only" 1.5 miles, but it takes you over three dunes, including Mount Tom.

Trail 9 is a 3.75-mile hike that will take you past the "blowouts." This is also the best trail for a beautiful look over the lake.

Trail 10 is 5.5 miles, but it's one of the most interesting of the hikes. It goes past the bird observation tower, cuts near a grove of white pines, and offers a look at several blowouts.

Calumet Trail
Not one of the numbered trails, Calumet Trail is a 9.2-mile path used by hikers, joggers, bikers, and cross-country skiers. It cuts through a part of the National Lakeshore property, and provides a good link between the state and federal grounds. It runs parallel to Indiana 12, also known as the Dunes Highway. As such, it

doesn't provide magnificent views of the beach. It will take you by some blowouts and through some beautiful areas of plant growth. The trail is on land leased from Northern Indiana Public Service Co., the local gas and electric utility. Access to the trail is off Indiana 49, just south of the park entrance.

Devil's Slide

This hill is steep, and when ice and snow have built up, the ride down is fast. The Devil's Slide is near the beach, just southeast of the concession stand. Unlike the National Lakeshore, there is no ban on sledding in the state park. But that doesn't mean it's encouraged either. You won't find any signs directing you to the best sledding areas. Another challenge is getting to the top of a dune when it's covered with ice and snow. What can be a difficult hike in July becomes a nearly impossible balancing act in January. Each year, though, there are those who try because that downhill rush careening down a slippery dune is worth all the work.

CAMPING & PICNICKING

The state park has several picnic areas with shelters, a campground, and, for youth groups, the **Nassaki Youth Tent Camp**. The Nature Center is also located in this area, just east of the park offices. Campgrounds have electricity and water, as well as a dumping station. Reservations are available (and recommended) for the campground (219/926-4520). The campground is open year round and known to be very family friendly. It includes electric hookups, showers, and flush toilets. A small store sells wood, ice, groceries, and other supplies.

LOCAL BEACHES

Local communities maintain many of the lakefront beaches. None is as expansive as the national or state parks, but they tend to be popular with people from the community.

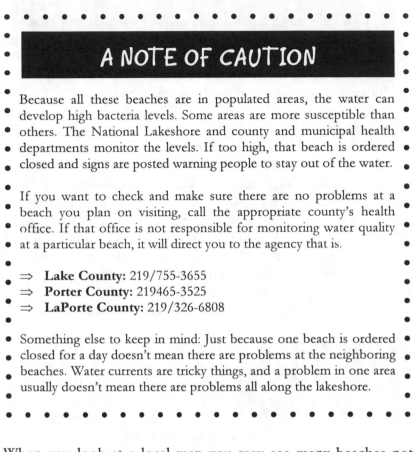

A NOTE OF CAUTION

Because all these beaches are in populated areas, the water can develop high bacteria levels. Some areas are more susceptible than others. The National Lakeshore and county and municipal health departments monitor the levels. If too high, that beach is ordered closed and signs are posted warning people to stay out of the water.

If you want to check and make sure there are no problems at a beach you plan on visiting, call the appropriate county's health office. If that office is not responsible for monitoring water quality at a particular beach, it will direct you to the agency that is.

⇒ **Lake County:** 219/755-3655
⇒ **Porter County:** 219465-3525
⇒ **LaPorte County:** 219/326-6808

Something else to keep in mind: Just because one beach is ordered closed for a day doesn't mean there are problems at the neighboring beaches. Water currents are tricky things, and a problem in one area usually doesn't mean there are problems all along the lakeshore.

When you look at a local map you may see many beaches not noted here—Long Beach and Duneland Beach among them. These communities have lakefront property, but it's all private. Venture there and you're trespassing, so it's better to stick with places in the national, state, and local park systems.

Starting with the Lakefront—the first beach in Indiana as you come from Illinois—here is a look at the community beaches:

Lakefront Park
A small beach maintained by the city of Hammond, Lakefront Park is just west of the Hammond Marina and the Horseshoe Casino riverboat. This is a good beach to watch the boat traffic in

and out of the marina on a hot day. But no swimming! Lakefront Park has "No Swimming" signs posted and no lifeguard is on duty. Located next to the marina and near Hammond's filtration plant, the water quality here is not as healthy as other places on the lakeshore.

Still, if you love bird watching you might still want to stop by. Just south of the beach is a bird sanctuary maintained by the city and state Department of Natural Resources. Sometimes called the migrant trap, it's a stopping off place for birds during migration. Prime bird-spotting time is mid-August through October. Songbirds, ducks, and Connecticut warblers are among the birds you'll spot here.

Directions: North on U.S. 41, follow the signs to the Hammond Marina. The park is just west of the marina.

Whihala Beach
1651 Park Rd.
Whiting
219/659-4015
A favorite with Hammond and Whiting residents, as well as visitors from Chicago's southeast side, this 21-acre park is maintained by the Lake County Park Department. It has restrooms, concession stands, showers, a picnic area, fishing, a boat launch, and plenty of parking. Come back in the early winter to watch for loons as they migrate to warmer climates for the season. Alcohol, glass bottles, grills, and pets are prohibited.

Whihala Beach is open 10 a.m.–7 p.m. Memorial Day–Labor Day; the boat launch opens in April and closes in November; the launch fee is $5 for Lake County residents, $8 for non-residents. Season passes are available. Parking is $2 for Lake County residents, $5 for non-residents; annual passes are available.

Whiting Park
Not the best beach for swimming. Much of the beach that fronts Whiting Park is filled with great cement boulders that were placed there to keep the lake from washing the park away. Jumping into

the water from the rocks is dangerous. The park does have a nice pier, and there is a park for children. Still, many like to come, lean back on the large rocks that cover the lakefront, and watch the water. If you've got kids, though, that's not a great idea. Those rocks can also get wet and slippery, so be careful!

Directions: From I–90 coming east, exit at Indianapolis Boulevard. Follow Indianapolis Boulevard east to 121ˢᵗ Street. Go east (left) on 121ˢᵗ to Front Avenue. North on Front Avenue to the park.

Jerose Park

Next to the **Pastrick Marina** (p. 218), in the shadow of Inland Steel is Jerose Park. Given how close industry is to this park, the water is surprisingly clean. When a lifeguard is on duty, swimming is allowed. Parking is close to the restaurants at the marina.

Directions: From I–80/94 or I–90, take Cline Avenue north to the Patrick Marina exit. Follow the marina signs. When you get to marina parking, signs will lead you to Jerose Park.

Lake Street Beach

This Gary beach is where you want to go if you've got a jet ski or want to do some water skiing. Lake Street Beach allows use of a variety of watercraft that is often restricted on other parts of the lake. As a consequence, this is not a great place to just bounce around in the water in an inner tube. Lake Street Beach is maintained by the city of Gary, and the parking lot is large enough to accommodate trailers.

Marquette Park Beach

On the northern edge of sprawling **Marquette Park**. See the section on Gary (p. 75) for more information about the park and efforts to turn the dilapidated Gary bathhouse on the beach into a museum. This beach is one of the area's most popular. The **Marquette Kids Park** is a great place for kids after they've had enough of the water. When you're ready to head for home you can stop for a burger or sandwich in Gary's Miller neighborhood.

Directions: From I–90, take U.S. 12 east. Go north at Lake Street, and follow it through Miller and into Marquette Park. Parking is available.

Northwest Indiana's local beaches offer an abundance of diversions on and near Lake Michigan.

Above: Courtesy of the LaPorte County Convention and Visitors Bureau.
Below: Courtesy of the Lake County Convention and Visitors Bureau.

Miller Beach

Popular with both local residents and visitors, this pretty stretch of lakefront is close to Gary's artsy Miller Beach section, an area with several great restaurants. Parking can be tough.

Directions: From U.S. 12, north on Grand Boulevard to Forest Avenue. Forest east to Montgomery. Montgomery north to Oak Avenue west.

Wells Street

A good-sized beach at the edge of Gary. Parking can be difficult to find, but it also means this beach is often not very crowded. Wells Street also lacks some amenities the other beaches have.

Directions: From I–90, take U.S. 20 east to County Line Road. North on County Line. Wells Street Beach is also accessible via Lake Shore Drive, which runs along the lakeshore on Gary's eastern edge.

Washington Park

The beach is part of Michigan City's large park. Washington Park's beach is beautiful, with a great view of the marina, the lighthouse (the only Lake Michigan lighthouse in Indiana), and the Lighthouse Museum. See the section on Michigan City (pp. 27–30) for more about what this park has to offer. The beach has restrooms, concession areas, and is wheelchair accessible.

Directions: From I–94, exit U.S. 421 north. This becomes Franklin Street in Michigan City. Follow Franklin through the city and into the park. From U.S. 12, at Franklin go north.

SHIPWRECKS

Tours of shipwrecks aren't on most sightseeing excursions in Northwest Indiana. Wrecks are down there, in the waters of Lake Michigan, including a barge off the coast of Gary's Buffington Harbor that went down in 1936.

Visiting these places isn't for amateurs. **The Scuba Tank** (55 S. Franklin St., Valparaiso, 219/477-4454, info@scubatank.com), offers classes and charter trips out to some of wreck sites. The federal Abandoned Shipwreck Act of 1987 makes it illegal to take "souvenirs" from a wreck site.

The next time you're sitting at the beach, trying to think of a good story to entertain the kids with, tell them the stories of the *Muskegon* and the *J.D. Marshall* and the mysterious link between the two. The steamers were built two decades apart, but they reached the bottom of Lake Michigan within hours—and within a few thousands yards—of each other.

The *Muskegon*

This steamer was called the *Peerless* when it was built in 1872, and was renamed the *Muskegon* in 1908. It had several uses over the years—passenger liner, casino boat, lumber hauler, and, finally with its purchase in 1909 by the Independent Sand and Gravel Co., a sand-hauler. Millions of tons of sand were taken from Northwest Indiana in those days to Chicago, where it was used to expand the shoreline.

The ship was in the Michigan City harbor, filled with more than 1,000 tons of sand and 10 tons of coal, when a fire broke out on the night of October 6, 1910. The coal ensured the fire burned for hours, and when it was over the *Muskegon* was a smoldering, charred, broken shell.

The ship sat there for nearly a year. On June 10, 1911, the *Muskegon* was towed out past several sandbars and sunk in 25 feet of water. She is still there, about two miles west of Michigan City and about a half-mile offshore, according to an excellent history of Lake Michigan wrecks written by Dennis R. Duncan Jr. for *Traces*, the magazine of Indiana history.

Keep in mind the date the Muskegon was sunk. It's important in the history of the *J.D. Marshall*, too.

The *J.D. Marshall*

The *J.D. Marshall*, named after a Chicago businessman, was built in 1891. For the next two decades it was used to haul lumber. In 1911 it was purchased by the Independent Sand and Gravel Co., the same company that purchased the Muskegon two years earlier. At one point, the *J.D. Marshall* was sent to try and pump sand and water from the wreckage of the *Muskegon* before that ship could be towed out and sunk.

On June 10, 1911, the *J.D. Marshall* took on a load of 500-plus tons of sand near what is now the Indiana Dunes State Park. As it prepared to leave for Chicago the hull sprung a leak and had to be patched. About 1:30 a.m. a storm kicked up, rocking the *J.D. Marshall*, which was still anchored offshore. The boat was outfitted with pumps salvaged from the *Muskegon*, but they weren't able to pump out water as fast as the ship was taking it. Soon, the boat rolled over, trapping three men below deck where they drowned. Another crewman died when he was thrown from the ship by winds and waves that buffeted the ship.

The *J.D. Marshall* is about 2,000 feet offshore in about 40 feet of water, according to information at the Old Lighthouse Museum.

• • • • • • • • • • • • • • • • •

DIANA OF THE DUNES

Some think the story of Diana of the Dunes is a legend, a ghost story about an elusive woodland spirit haunting the lakeshore.

Diana was real, although her name wasn't Diana. She was Alice Gray, a University of Chicago graduate who abandoned city life to live in the dunes in 1915. She was looking for a simpler existence, but she wound up attracting national attention.

Less than a year after arriving, Gray gave an interview to a reporter from the Chicago *Examiner* about her decision to live in the solitude of the dunes. Prompted by the article, stories circulated that she bathed nude in the lake, ran along the beach to dry off, and lived in a shack she called Driftwood.

"Alice Gray was about to become 'Diana of the Dunes,'" David Hoppe wrote in *Traces: the Magazine of Indiana History.*

Gray was 34 years old when she came to the dunes, and she wasn't a beautiful woman. A 1916 story in the *Chesterton Tribune* described her as "brown as a berry and tolerably husky."

Many mysteries endure about Gray. Around 1920 she met Paul Wilson. Some accounts say they were married, although there is also evidence that they simply lived together; some say Wilson sometimes beat her; others say they had children. There is no tangible evidence supporting any of it.

The couple lived in a shack they called the Wren's Nest. They had several brushes with the law over the next few years, and at one point Wilson was suspected of a murder. Still, the couple stayed together. Although they reportedly left several times, the pair always returned to the dunes.

Gray loved the area. "So the Indiana Dune country, like Chicago herself, is the child of Lake Michigan and the Northwest Wind," Hoppe quotes her as writing. "Besides its nearness to Chicago and its beauty, its spiritual power, there is between the Dune country and the city more than a sentimental bond—a family tie. To see the Dunes destroyed would be for Chicago the sacrilegious sin which is not forgiven."

Gray died in 1925 in the shack in her beloved dunes that she shared with her lover.

And those ghost stories? Visitors to the State Park have reported seeing her ghostly image wandering the dunes. Some also say that at night you can hear Diana's cries mixed with the sound of the wind as it whips through the trees and rustles the dune grass.

• • • • • • • • • • • • • • •

Residents in Gary's Miller Beach area called Octave Chanute the "crazy old man of the dunes." You can't blame the local residents for thinking there was something odd about the elderly Frenchman. Chanute built gliders,  climbed the area's highest sand dunes, and then tried to fly make his creations fly. They didn't realize how successful he was. Chanute's work influenced two Dayton, Ohio, brothers who had some success with flight a few years later.

Courtesy of the Calumet Regional Archives.

Octave Chanute.

Chanute conducted his experiments in the summer of 1896, and during one he tested the Chanute–Herring glider, a model developed with Augustus M. Herring. The trussed-wing design of this glider was the one used by Orville and Wilbur Wright in their first successful flight in 1903. The design gave the wings stability and strength, just as a truss design makes a bridge stable.

Chanute's most successful flight was on September 11, 1896, when one of the gliders sailed 359 feet. Herring made the flight, according to Moore, and reached speeds of more than 17 miles an hour.

Chanute died in his Chicago home on November 23, 1910. Replicas of his gliders hang at the Smithsonian Air and Space Museum in Washington, D.C., Chanute Air Force Base in Rantoul, Illinois, and the Door Prairie Auto Museum in LaPorte.

And at the Aquatorium at Miller Beach, near where Chanute conducted his experiments, a plaque now hangs to honor the "crazy old man" who was one of the nation's aviation pioneers.

• • • • • • • • • • • • • • • •

SHOPPING

Northwest Indiana has a branch of nearly every major department store established in the Midwest. For those who enjoy the mall experience, the opportunity to visit store after store tucked into one location, here is a listing of the best of what's available in the three-county area.

Highland Grove
10143 Indianapolis Blvd. (U.S. 41 and Main St.)
Highland
This open shopping center transformed the southern half of Highland from a series of farm fields into a shopping destination. Stores include Kohl's, Target, and Border's Books and Music. Nearby is an Old Navy and the Meijer shopping center across the street.
Directions: From I–80/94, south on U.S. 41.

Lighthouse Place Premium Outlets
601 Wabash St.
Michigan City
219/879-6506
www.outletsonline.com/nelpin.htm
Looking for a Brooks Brothers suit, new Reeboks for the kids, jeans from the Gap, dishes from Crate & Barrel, Lennox, or Mikasa? Try the nearly 120 stores at Lighthouse Place, Michigan City's sprawling outlet mall that attracts more than three million visitors annually. Unlike many shopping centers, Lighthouse Place is not all under one roof. The stores are in a park-like setting, with wide courtyards and plenty of open space.

On weekends, trolley service is available from the South Shore

Line station.
Open Mon.–Sat. 9 a.m.–6 p.m., Sun. 10 a.m.–6 p.m. Directions: From I-94, take 421 north (exit 34B) to Sixth Street. Make a left.

Maple Lane Mall
1450 W. Indiana 2
LaPorte
219/326-1945
A small enclosed mall with about 30 stores, it includes K-Mart and Sam Goody.
Open Mon.–Fri. 10 a.m.–8 p.m., Sat. 10 a.m.–7 p.m., Sun. 11 a.m.–5 p.m. Directions: From I–94 exit U.S. 421 south. At Indiana 2, go east to LaPorte.

Marquette Mall
U.S. 20 and U.S. 421
Michigan City
219/879-8375
www.marquettemall.com
Department stores include Sears, JC Penney, and Carson Pirie Scott. The multiplex Marquette Theatre is also inside.
Open Mon.–Sat. 10 a.m.–9 p.m., Sun. 11 a.m.–5 p.m. Hours vary during holidays. Directions: From I–94, exit 421 north.

Westfield Shoppingtown Southlake
2109 Southlake Mall
Merrillville
219/738-2260
www.westfield.com/us/centres/indiana/southlake
One of Northwest Indiana's most popular malls, Southlake turned Merrillville and Hobart into retail centers in the 1970s. Today, Westfield Shoppingtown Southlake is the state's largest indoor mall with four department stores: Sears, Carson Pirie Scott, JC Penney, and L.S. Ayres. Other stores include The Gap, The Disney Store, Abercrombie & Fitch, and Eddie Bauer.

In a separate building on the eastern edge of the mall parking lot is the **AMC Southlake 9** cineplex (219/738-2652), and across the street is the **Loews Merrillville 10** movie theater complex (219/947-4072).

Near the mall you'll find a series of large strip malls, including the popular Hobart Crossings, which includes a Barnes and Noble bookstore, in Hobart, just past I-65 and the Merrillville border.
Open Mon.–Sat. 10 a.m.–9 p.m., Sun. 11 a.m.–6 p.m. Hours are extended during the holidays. Directions: From I–65 exit U.S. 30 east. The mall is located on the right.

Woodmar Mall
6508 Indianapolis Blvd.
Hammond
219/844-7843
Woodmar Mall is the largest indoor shopping center in Hammond. While not as large as some of the area's other malls, Woodmar's layout makes it easy to navigate. All the mall shops are on the first floor, with only Carson Pirie Scott (the mall's largest tenant) having a second story.
Open Mon.–Fri. 10 a.m.–9 p.m., Sat. 10 a.m.–5:30 p.m., Sun. noon–5 p.m. Directions: From I–80/94 take Indianapolis Boulevard north. Woodmar is at Indianapolis Boulevard and 165th Street

Above: Courtesy of LaPorte Little Theatre.
Below: Courtesy of the Festival Players Guild.

LaPorte Little Theatre's *The Passion of Dracula* and
the Festival Players Guild's *Man of La Mancha*.

THEATER

Northwest Indiana has myriad theater choices for musicals, comedies, and dramas ranging from professional productions to first-rate community companies. Call for information on upcoming shows, ticket prices, subscription rates, and other details.

If you've got the acting bug or want to show off your musical talent, get in touch with one of the community-based groups who are always looking for new talent.

Acting Theatre of Michigan City
215 W. 10th St.
Michigan City
219/872-4221
The Acting Theatre mounts four productions a year (musicals, dramas, and comedies) in its 75-seat theater. Everything is locally generated, from the script, direction, and, of course, the acting and singing talent.

Community Showcase Theatre
Whiting
219/659-8709
This Whiting-based group has performed in several venues in recent years, including the stage at **Whiting High School** (1751 Oliver St.). Recent performances have included Noel Coward's *Blithe Spirit* and the musical *Grease*.

Community Theatre Guild
Chicago Street Theatre
154 W. Chicago St.
Valparaiso
219/464-1636
Founded in 1955 by parents trying to raise money for school band uniforms, the Community Theatre Guild has grown over the years and has garnered a reputation as among the best theater groups in the area. The Guild performed for decades in Valparaiso's Memorial Opera House. In the late 1990s the Guild left the Opera House because of remodeling and purchased a church from the Valparaiso Assembly of God, remodeled the three-story building, and renamed it the Chicago Street Theatre. It seats about 150. Shows are often original productions. Recent productions have included *The Memory of Water*, *Never the Sinner*, *The Seventh Monarch*, *Nunsense*, and *A Christmas Story*. CTG also sponsors theater classes.

Dunes Summer Theatre
288 Shady Oak Dr.
Michiana Shores
219/879-7509
Every summer the stage lights go up at this aptly-named theater in tiny Michiana Shores sponsored by The Dunes Arts Foundation. Recent shows: *Jesus Christ Superstar*, *The Miracle Worker*, and *Cabaret*. The arts foundation also sponsors youth and children's theaters, each of which puts on its own show every summer.

Festival Players Guild
Mainstreet Theatre
807 Franklin St.
Michigan City
219/874-4269
www.festivalplayersguild.org
Founded in 1969 at St. John's Church in Michigan City, the Guild players now take the stage at the Mainstreet Theatre,

which boasts that no one sits more than 12 rows from the stage. Recent shows have included *Play It Again Sam*, *Mame*, *Man of LaMancha*, and *Summer Stock Murder*. Each summer the Guild hosts **Canterbury Summer Theatre**, bringing a variety of performers to town.

Footlight Players

1705 Franklin St.
Michigan City
219/874-4035
www.footlightplayers.org
The Footlight Players opened in 1950, making it one of the area's oldest community theater groups. Shows are staged on the group's own theater in downtown Michigan City. Recent performances have included *The Shadow Box*, *Monkey Business*, and *The Farndale Avenue Housing Estate Townswomen's Guild Dramatic Society's Production of "A Christmas Carol."*

Genesius Guild

First United Methodist Church
6635 Hohman Ave.
Hammond
877/724-7715
Founded in 1984 by the Rev. James H. Evans, Jr., a former actor, the Guild is named for St. Genesius, the patron saint of actors. The performers and technicians are not all members of the church, but they come together to put on a variety of works, including musicals, children's theater, and dramas, which have included *Charlotte's Web*, *Once on This Island*, *Inherit the Wind*, and *City of Angels*. Most performances are held in the church's Fellowship Hall; other venues include **Phil Smidt's** restaurant (p. 104) in Hammond.

Hammond Community Theatre

219/853-6378
The Hammond Parks and Recreation Department organized

the community group. Its productions have been done in city parks and the **Hammond Civic Center** (5825 Sohl Ave.). A move to a permanent indoor venue in downtown Hammond is planned.

Highland Performing Arts Group
219/838-0114
Sponsored by the Highland Parks Department, the group puts on outdoor performances in **Main Square Park** (downtown at Fourth and Ridge Road) and indoors at **Lincoln Center** (2450 Lincoln St.). Auditions draw aspiring actors from the area for shows such as *You're a Good Man, Charlie Brown* and *Prometheus Bound.*

LaPorte Little Theatre Guild
218 A St.
LaPorte
219/362-5113
The Little Theatre Guild put on its first performance on Jan. 13, 1926, when members did three one-act plays in the LaPorte High School auditorium. In the decades since, the Guild has become an institution, offering a series of performances each year. In 1954, the Guild bought St. John's Lutheran Church and for the next few years audiences sat in the old church pews, until the Guild obtained regular theater seats. Recent productions have included *Bye, Bye Birdie, The Sound of Music, You Can't Take It With You,* and *The Nutcracker.* The Little Theatre also sponsors a children's workshop each summer for local youth. *Several ticket plans offering discounts are available.*

Lake Central Theatre Guild
Lake Central High School
8400 Wicker Ave.
St. John
219/365-8551
While based at Lake Central High School, the Guild draws

performers from throughout the area. Recent shows have included *Annie, Twelve Angry Men, Lost in Yonkers,* and *One Flew Over the Cuckoo's Nest.*
Discounts are available for tickets purchased in advance.

Marian Theatre Guild
1849 Lincoln Ave.
Whiting
219/473-7555
One of the area's oldest community theaters, the Marian Theatre Guild traces its history to a group that originally performed at St. John the Baptist Church.

Memorial Theatre Company
Memorial Opera House
104 Indiana Ave.
Valparaiso
219/548-9137
The Memorial Theatre Company performs musicals, comedies, and dramas in Valpo's historic **Memorial Opera House** (p. 193). Recent performances have been *Sweeney Todd: the Demon Barber of Fleet Street, Lend Me a Tenor,* and *The Sound of Music.*

Morning Bishop Theater
487 Broadway
Gary
219/882-5354
Morning Bishop Theatre provides a variety of local productions, puppet shows, and children's programs.

Portage Community Theatre
219/759-1408
A newcomer to the theater scene in Northwest Indiana, the Portage troupe's first show was *Fame,* in the summer of 2001. Performances are in the **Portage High School West Auditorium** (6450 Hwy. 6).

Purdue Theatre Company
Purdue University Calumet
Alumni Hall
Hammond
219/989-2357
The theater company at Purdue University Calumet, recent shows have included *Nuts.*

Ross Music Theatre
Reinhart Auditorium
Merrillville High School
276 E. 68th Pl.
Merrillville
219/947-4922
A community theater that began in 1964, the company presents several shows each year on the high school's stage.

Star Plaza Theatre
U.S. 30 and Interstate 65
Merrillville
219/769-6600
www.starplazatheatre.com
The Star Plaza is known for big musical acts, but the theater is also home to the occasional theatrical production. Call for details.

Theatre Northwest
Indiana University Northwest
Gary
219/980-6808
Theatre Northwest draws on the talent of drama students at IU's Gary campus. While students and faculty produce the shows, there are open casting calls for performers who are not enrolled at the school. Theatre Northwest also has a visiting artist program that brings in professionals from Greater Chicago. Shows performed include Sam Shepard's *A Lie of the*

Mind, Working, Hot L Baltimore, and *Kiss Me, Kate*.

Teatro Del Sol
219/838-1505
Teatro Del Sol performs in Spanish. It lacks a permanent home and has performed on several area stages, including **Purdue Calumet's Alumni Hall** (p. 99).

Theatre at the Center
The Center for Visual and Performing Arts
1040 Ridge Rd.
Munster
219/836-3255
www.theatreatthecenter.com
Theatre at the Center is the professional theater series at the **Center for Visual and Performing Arts** (p. 128). The 450-seat theater is configured so no one sits more than seven rows from the stage. The theater hosted the Chicago-area premiere of a new production of *High Society*. A seven-piece band brought the music of Indiana-native Cole Porter to life, and the show, directed by Chicagoan Michael Weber, garnered great reviews. Other recent shows include *42nd Street* and *Nunsense II*.

The VPA is also home to the **Northwest Indiana Symphony's chamber performances** and **Theatre for Young Audiences**, a program designed to introduce children to different types of performances. The center sponsors the On Stage Series that brings nationally-known musicians, comedians, and other artists to Munster such as actor William Windom, country stars The Dixie Chicks, and political humorist Mark Russell. *Ticket prices vary, and season packages are available.*

Valparaiso University
VU Center for the Arts
219/464-5445
Student productions at Valparaiso can often be ambitious. And,

with a student body from around the world, the talent level can be very high. Recent productions have included *The Yellow Boat*, *Twelfth Night*, and *Medea*.

OTHER GOOD STUFF TO KNOW

Media 289
Transportation 297
Miscellaneous 305

Courtesy of the Porter County Convention, Recreation & Visitors Commission.

Consult the local media to discover what's
going on in Northwest Indiana.

MEDIA

If you're planning a visit to Northwest Indiana, check out some of the local media for information. Chicago TV newscasts and newspapers are prevalent in much of the area, but there are plenty of homegrown news outlets, too.

NEWSPAPERS

Post-Tribune
1433 E. 83rd Ave.
Merrillville
219/648-3000
www.post-trib.com
Below the masthead on the front page, the phrase "Northwest Indiana's Leading Newspaper" has appeared for decades. The paper is one of two (*The Times* is the other) that aggressively covers Lake and Porter Counties.

Friday's Weekend section covers what there's to do on Saturday and Sunday. Jim Gordon, who writes a column in the news section, contributes movie reviews; the Eats column tells which restaurants are worth visiting; and there is comprehensive coverage of theater.

The *Gary Weekly Tribune* was first published in June 1907 by two former *Chicago Tribune* reporters. It became a daily paper on Sept. 7, 1908. On August 2, 1909, a rival, the *Gary Evening Post,* appeared. After more than a decade of intense competition, the two merged and the *Gary Evening Post and Daily Tribune* hit the stands on July 11, 1921. The more simply-named *Gary Post-Tribune* debuted on Aug. 26, 1922. Today, the "Gary" designation appears only on editions for northern Lake County.

The *Post-Tribune* is printed in Gary, but the main business offices are in Merrillville.

The Times
601 W. 45th Ave.
Munster
219/933-3200
800/589-3331
www.thetimesonline.com
Some still call it *The Hammond Times,* although it hasn't gone by that name for decades. Today, The *"Hammond" Times* is just one of more than a half-dozen different editions *The Times* publishes, each tailored to specific parts of the region.

It's the largest paper in Northwest Indiana, focused mostly on Lake and Porter Counties and Chicago suburbs bordering Lake County. In addition to local news, it provides extensive coverage of area high school sports and most of Chicago's professional teams. It is also the only Northwest Indiana newspaper with a full-time statehouse reporter in Indianapolis.

Movies, local theatre, and music are covered in the Friday On the Go section, which also carries restaurant reviews by Jane and Phillip Dunne. More entertainment options are often listed in the weekly Your Saturday section, including a popular feature, One Tank Trips, that often suggests outings in Indiana and surrounding states. Arch McKinlay writes regularly about local history.

The Times was first published in Hammond on June 18, 1906, as the *Lake County Times.* The Lake County designation was dropped on Aug. 28, 1933 when the paper became *The Ham-*

mond Times. The paper actually began life as the weekly *Western Indiana Tribune* founded in 1880.

The Times is based in Munster, although it has several regional offices in Lake and Porter Counties.

Chesterton Tribune
193 S. Calumet
Chesterton
219/926-1131
www.chestertontribune.com
The Chesterton Tribune, founded Oct. 28, 1882, is the source for news in northern Porter County.

LaPorte Herald-Argus
701 State St.
LaPorte
219/362-2161
www.heraldargus.com
LaPorte's daily newspaper covers southern LaPorte County. Among the paper's claims to fame: Ernie Pyle, the Pulitzer Prize-winning World War II correspondent who was killed by a sniper while covering the war, once worked at the Herald.

Michigan City News-Dispatch
911 Franklin St.
Michigan City
219/874-7211
www.michigancityin.com/news-dispatch
Michigan City's daily newspaper has aggressive local coverage of LaPorte County and is an excellent source for entertainment options along the lakeshore.

The paper traces its history to the *Michigan City News,* which first published in 1847, and *The Evening Dispatch,* which appeared in 1887. The two merged on June 4, 1938.

South Bend Tribune
225 W. Colfax Ave.
South Bend
219/235-6161
www.southbendtribune.com
Located in north central Indiana, the *South Bend Tribune* was founded in 1872. Today it is one of the dominant papers in northern Indiana, and its coverage often includes news of LaPorte County and its entertainment options.

Chicago Sun-Times
401 N. Wabash Ave.
Chicago
312/321-2522
www.suntimes.com
The Weekend Plus section, published on Friday, often contains entertainment options in Northwest Indiana. Restaurant critic Pat Bruno has rated many of the area's restaurants, and John Grochowski's gaming column on Friday and Sunday always has the first word on what's new at Northwest Indiana's five gambling boats.

The *Daily Illustrated Times* (which soon became simply the *Chicago Times*) debuted on Sept. 3, 1929. The Chicago Sun was founded on Dec. 4, 1941. In 1948, the *Sun* absorbed the *Times* and adopted that paper's tabloid format. The paper has developed a reputation for aggressive coverage of local news and sports.

Chicago Tribune
435 N. Michigan Ave.
Chicago
312/222-3232
www.chicagotribune.com
The *Tribune* is the largest paper in the Midwest and provides extensive coverage of the greater Chicago area. The Friday

entertainment section—named, appropriately enough, Friday—often includes items about Northwest Indiana. Restaurant critic Phil Vettel has reviewed many of Northwest Indiana's best eating spots.

The *Tribune* was founded on June 10, 1847. It has grown to become one of the nation's largest and most influential papers.

MAGAZINES

Lake Magazine
701 State St.
LaPorte 46350
219/362-8592
877/362-8592
www.lakemagazine.com
A terrific source for what's happening along the lakeshore, from Chicago, through Indiana and into southwestern Michigan. *Lake Magazine* does a great job of finding the newest restaurants and trendiest shops just as soon as they open.

Editor and publisher Pat Colander is a former *Chicago Tribune* reporter who did stints in the newsroom and with the business side at *The Times* in Munster.

She's does a great job of attracting some of the area's top writers, including some whose work appears in Chicago's two dailies, and turning them loose on undiscovered corners of Northwest Indiana.

TELEVISION

WYIN-TV
8625 Indiana
Merrillville
219/756-5656
www.wyin.tv
WYIN-Channel 56 is the area's only truly local station. A Public Broadcasting System station, it produces a nightly newscast. In addition to the usual documentaries and high-end offerings, WYIN also broadcasts college basketball games, features on local high school athletes, and shows like *Indiana Week in Review*, which is produced by a TV station in Indianapolis.

RADIO

Chicago radio stations are most prevalent in northwest Indiana cars, but the area does have many local stations. And while a Chicago station isn't going to carry Indiana University basketball or Purdue University football games, some of these Hoosier stations will:

WAKE–1500 AM (Valparaiso)
Standards, IU basketball and football.

WCOE–96.7 FM (LaPorte)
Country music, NASCAR, Chicago Bulls.

WDSO–88.3 FM (Chesterton)
Operated by Chesterton High School.

WEFM–95.9 FM (Michigan City)
Adult contemporary, Notre Dame and IU basketball and foot-

ball games, Indianapolis Colts games.

WGVE–88.7 FM (Gary)
Educational, R&B, Gary Steelheads basketball games. Owned
by the Gary public schools.

WIMS–1420 AM (Michigan City)
www.wimstalk.com
Talk, IU sports, One-On-One sports network.

WJOB–1230 AM (Hammond)
www.wjobtalk.com
Talk, One-On-One sports network, Purdue and IU football,
IU basketball.

WLJE–105.5 FM (Valparaiso)
www.indiana105.com
Country music.

WLOI–1540 AM (LaPorte)
Adult standards, Purdue sports.

WLTH–1370 AM (Gary)
R&B, talk radio, IU basketball.

WNDZ–750 AM (Portage)
Gospel, ethnic programming.

WPWX–92.3 FM (Hammond)
Rap/hip-hop.

WVUR–95.1 FM (Valparaiso)
www.valpo.edu/student/wvur
Variety, Valparaiso University sports. Owned by VU.

WXRD–103.9 FM (Crown Point)
Country music, IU sports.

WYCA–92.3 FM (Hammond)
Religious broadcasting.

WZVN–107 FM (Merrillville)
Oldies, contemporary music.

TRANSPORTATION

• • • • • • • • • • • • • • •

To the newcomer, getting to and around Northwest Indiana can seem daunting. The expressways turn into giant parking lots, side streets seem impossible to navigate, and—short of swimming—is there any quick way into Chicago?

Take heart. Getting around isn't nearly as tough as you might think. Here's a quick lesson in navigating Northwest Indiana.

AIR

Gary/Chicago Airport
6001 W. Industrial Hwy.
Gary
219/949-9722
www.garychicagoairport.com
The Gary/Chicago Airport is located on the north side of Gary with a large, free parking lot next to the terminal.

Although the airport is run by the city of Gary, it's part of a bi-state compact so it shares resources with Chicago (hence the name Gary/Chicago). If you fly into Gary and need to get to downtown Chicago, the drive will take you about 35 to 45 minutes. At the height of rush hour you can add half an hour to that travel time. Limousine service to Chicago is available

Because the airport is small, you won't find the rows of restaurants and gift shops that fill Chicago–O'Hare International. But you can get from the ticket counter to the gate in less

Photo by John J. Watkins.

A flight from Gary Airport.

than a minute.

Directions: From I–90 or I–80/94 take Cline Avenue north. The airport exit is clearly marked. Park right out front. The lot is patrolled around the clock by security.

Chicago's two major airports are well-served by Coach USA airport bus and shuttle services that operate from Northwest Indiana.

Coach USA/Tri-State Coach (800/248-8747) stops in Portage, Merrillville, Gary, and Hammond/Highland. **Coach USA/United Limo** (800/833-5555) stops at a terminal in Michigan City, as well as serving areas further east such as South Bend. The buses are comfortable, and drop passengers right at their terminal. Schedules and fares are available at www.busville.com.

Chicago–O'Hare International
Chicago
773/686-2200
http://www.ohare.com
Named for Medal of Honor recipient Navy Lt. Edward
"Butch" O'Hare, it is currently the nation's busiest airport.
Depending on the time of day and where you leave from, travel
to O'Hare, on Chicago's northwestern perimeter, from Northwest Indiana can take from one to two-plus hours.

Midway Airport
5700 S. Cicero Ave.
Chicago
773/838-0600
http://www.ohare.com/midway/home.cfm
Dedicated in 1927, Midway Airport, on Chicago's southwest
side, has been expanded and rehabbed in recent years. From
Northwest Indiana, it's easy to reach via I-294, then north on
Cicero. Depending on the time of day, the trip can take from 30
minutes to an hour.

INTERSTATES AND HIGHWAYS

Negotiating the interstate and highway systems isn't that tough,
but it helps to remember that the major roadways to Chicago
and to the steel mills can get jammed in the early morning and
late afternoon rushes. A trip that would take you 20 minutes at
1 P.M. can take three times as long a few hours later.

Indiana's Travel Hotline (800/261-7623) provides information about trouble on major roads. If you experience problems
and need police help, call the **Indiana State Police** (800/552-
8917–this number only works in state; 219/696-6242) in Lowell, which is responsible for the northwest corner of the state.

Interstates

I–80/94 is known locally as the **Frank Borman Highway,** or simply the Borman. Gary native Borman was the astronaut who commanded the Apollo 8 when it made the first manned voyage around the moon. The Borman is a major east–west highway through Lake County, and it's also among the nation's five busiest highways.

I–90 is the **Indiana Toll Road.** It starts right where the Chicago Skyway leaves off at the Indiana line and continues east across the northern edge of the state. Toll fares vary. The first one as you enter Chicago from Indiana is 50 cents. To go all the way across the state—from the Illinois line to Ohio—will set you back $4.15.

Things get a little tricky as these interstates head east. Just before Lake County ends and Porter County begins, the two interstates cross, and I–94 continues northeast toward Michigan. I–80 is now joined with I–90 and continues on through LaPorte, to South Bend, and on to Ohio.

I–65 is the major north–south expressway. Its northern edge begins at I–90 and continues south through Lake County. Stay on I–65 long enough and you'll get to Indianapolis. Stay on it longer, and you'll find yourself in Kentucky.

Highways

There are several U.S. highways running through northwest Indiana. A couple things to keep in mind: The speed limit is 65 MPH on interstates and 55 MPH on highways, unless posted speeds are lower. And they often are lower through the residential and business districts.

U.S. 41 is **Lake Shore Drive** in Chicago. By the time it winds its way south and into Indiana it's known as **Indianapolis Boulevard.** That doesn't mean you can take it to Indianapolis, although if you stay on U.S. 41 long enough you'll wind up in

Terre Haute. This highway is a good north–south route through western Lake County.

U.S. 6 runs with I–80/94 from the Illinois line east to the western part of Lake County, cuts south for a few miles, and veers east again through Porter County and into LaPorte County

U.S. 12 is the **Dunes Highway**. It's a good east–west route through much of the lakeshore, through Michigan City, and into Michigan.

U.S. 20 joins U.S. 12 in Lake County, breaks off just south of Gary's eastern edge and runs parallel to U.S. 12 into Porter County. It's a good east–west route, especially if U.S. 12 is congested.

U.S. 30 is the **Lincoln Highway**. It's a good east–west alterna tive to the expressways and will take you through the prime shopping areas in Merrillville and Hobart and into Porter County, where it passes the campus of Valparaiso University.

U.S. 35 begins in Michigan City at I–94 and wends south through the central part of the state.

U.S. 231 begins at U.S. 41, just south of St. John in Lake County, runs southeast into Porter County, and then heads south at Hebron.

U.S. 421 begins in Michigan City at I–94 and continues south.

RAIL

South Shore Line

800/356-2079
219/926-5744
www.nictd.com

Rail lovers come to Northwest Indiana for the chance to ride the nation's last electric inter-urban railway. The South Shore Line carries 3.5 million passengers annually on the 90-mile journey from South Bend to downtown Chicago.

Operated by the **Northern Indiana Commuter Transportation District (NICTD)**, the South Shore has a notable history. It began as The Chicago & Indiana Air Line Railway in 1903 with a streetcar in East Chicago. Six years and several expansions later, the rail line provided service from Indiana to Illinois. Limited service to Chicago began in 1912. Samuel Insull, a protégé of Thomas Edison and an electric utilities magnate, purchased the South Shore in 1925 and invested the money necessary for the line to grow.

The line serves a dozen stops in Indiana, beginning with Hammond. The cost of a one-way ticket to Chicago ranges from $4.55 from Hammond or East Chicago, and $5.30 from Gary, to $10.35 from South Bend, the last Indiana stop. Up to two children age 13 or younger ride free with an adult at off-peak weekday times and on weekends.

In Illinois, the South Shore serves Chicago's Hegewisch neighborhood on the southeast side, then makes several more stops to the Loop. It takes about 45 minutes to get from Gary to the Randolph Street station in downtown Chicago.

The quality of the stations varies. Some are covered platforms with large parking lots next to the train tracks. **Hammond,**

East Chicago, **Gary's Adam Benjamin Metro Center** (named for a former congressman), and **Dunes Park** in Chesterton are large and have room to wait inside during cold weather. The **Beverly Shores** stop is among the most stunning—the historic train station is also used as a museum (pp. 165–166)!

Here's a tip for Notre Dame football fans—taking the train is a great way to get to South Bend on a Saturday, and you can avoid the crush of people trying to get home on the toll road afterward.

Fare and schedule information is available by calling NICTD or on the organization's website. During the week, the first train to Chicago leaves Michigan City at 4:02 a.m. The first train from South Bend leaves a bit later, at 5:42 a.m. Trains start running from Chicago to Indiana at 6:10 a.m. from the Randolph Street station.

Amtrak
800/USA-RAIL
800/872-7245
Amtrak makes three stops in Northwest Indiana, **Hammond** (1135 Calumet Ave.), **Dyer** (Sheffield Road, near Matteson Street), and **Michigan City** (100 Washington St.). These are served by trains including the *Capitol Limited* en route to Washington, D.C., and the *Kentucky Cardinal* on its way from Chicago to Louisville, Kentucky.

The largest local station is in Hammond, just south of the Hammond Marina. Of the three, this is the only one that offers ticket sales and baggage check. For the other two, passengers must already have tickets or make arrangements to buy them on the train.

BUS

Hammond, **Gary**, and **East Chicago** all have transit systems that run buses through their communities and neighboring cities and towns. In addition, **PACE**, the bus system in Chicago's suburbs, stops in downtown Hammond at the **Dan Rabin Transit Plaza**.

For schedules, call one of the following:

⇒ **East Chicago Transit:** 219/391-8465
⇒ **Gary Public Transportation Corp.:** 219/884-6100
⇒ **Hammond Transit System:** 219/853-6513
⇒ **PACE:** 312/836-7000

MISCELLANEOUS

All right, now you know where to go and what to do. But, there were a few things not addressed in the preceding chapters that you might want to know before planning that weekend trip to the Dunes.

Alcoholic Beverages
Need some beer or wine for a Sunday picnic? You had better plan ahead. Retailers can't sell beer, wine, or any type of alcoholic beverage on Sunday in Indiana. Any other day liquor stores can sell beverages between 7 a.m. and 3 a.m. The Sunday rule doesn't apply to restaurants, bars, or wineries.

Area Codes
In 2002, the Indiana Regulatory Commission split northern Indiana into three different area codes. Lake and Porter Counties kept the 219 area code.

LaPorte County was split. Michigan City and LaPorte kept 219, but much of that county now has a 574 area code. The northeast corner of the state switched to 260.

Camping
www.campindiana.com
A few campgrounds are noted in this book, but for a comprehensive list contact the **Recreational Vehicle Indiana Council** (317/247-6258) in Indianapolis.

Fishing
Anglers have mapped out thousands of spots on Lake Michigan and the inland lakes for bluegill, perch, catfish, and bass. But

before you head out, you need to get a fishing license.

Indiana residents can get a season-long license for $14.25, or $7 for a one-day license. If you're from out of state, it's going to cost you more: $24.75 for an annual license, $7 for a one-day permit or $12.75 for a seven-day license. Lifetime licenses are also available for $285. For information, contact the **Indiana Department of Natural Resources** at 317/233-4976 or www.in.gov/dnr.

A copy of Indiana's fishing regulations is available from the Indiana DNR's **Division of Fish and Wildlife** (317/232-4080). Also ask them to put you on the list to receive *Focus*, their free newsletter on the state's fish and wildlife programs.

Biologists, researchers, and others have sometimes put special tags on fish in Lake Michigan and its tributaries to study migration patterns and other elements of local aquatic life. If you catch one of these fish, don't worry—but don't throw away the tag either! In some places you'll see tag-return boxes. If not, save information on what type of fish it was, its size, weight, the date, and where you caught it. Questions? Call the **Division of Fish and Wildlife**.

Finally, keep current on where the best fishing is with the **state's fishing hotline** (219/874-0009). It's updated weekly March through December and includes information on Lake Michigan.

Time Zones
There never seems to be enough of it when you're having fun. But if you're not careful, you could find yourself literally losing an hour by accident. Here's a quick lesson on one of the quirkier things about Indiana: most of the state doesn't observe the change from Central Daylight Time to Central Standard Time. But Lake, Porter, and LaPorte Counties are among a

handful that does make the switch

What does this mean? In the summer, nothing—because most of the state is on the same time as its northwest corner. But in the fall, when Northwest Indiana and most of the country turns its clocks back an hour, most of Indiana does not. So if you're visiting from downstate Indiana or an eastern state in the winter, remember that Northwest Indiana's clocks are the same as Chicago. That's an hour *behind* Indianapolis.

Traffic Laws

Laws vary from state to state. Keeps these in mind when traveling in Indiana:

⇒ People in the front seat have to wear a seatbelt.
⇒ Children have to be placed in a safety seat until age 5.
⇒ The legal blood–alcohol limit is .08 percent.

Photo by John J. Watkins.

Red Baron planes at the Gary Airport.

Above: Photo by John J. Watkins., Below: Photo by the author.

The Gary Steelheads play at the Genesis Convention Center (above).
The new stadium of Gary's minor league Southshore RailCats (below).

BIBLIOGRAPHY

• • • • • • • • • • • • • • • • •

Some may disagree with the incorporation dates listed in this guide, especially those given for the oldest communities. Unfortunately, there is often discrepancy here, even in the official records. It was also often decades between when a community was founded and when it was officially incorporated. Then, even with an incorporation date, there is uncertainty, because there are often differences between when a community voted on incorporation, when it became effective, and when it was recognized by the state. I have tried to use the date the state recognized the incorporation whenever possible.

The population figures and community sizes given here both come from the U.S. Census Bureau. The populations are from Census 2000. The community sizes come from the *Census Gazetteer of Counties, Places and Zip Codes.*

Anderson, Christopher. *Michael Jackson Unauthorized.* New York: Pocket Books. 1995.

Ball, T.H. *Northwest Indiana From 1800 to 1900.* Chicago: Donohue & Henneberry. 1900.

Cohen, Ronald D. and Stephen G. McShane. *Moonlight in Duneland: The Illustrated Story of the Chicago South Shore and South Bend Railroad.* Bloomington: Indiana University Press. 1998.

Drury, John. *This is Lake County, Indiana.* Chicago: Inland Photo Co. 1956.

Duncan, Dennis R. Jr. "Lost In Lake Michigan." *Traces of Indiana and Midwestern History,* Vol. 10, No. 3 (Summer 1998).

Engel, J. Ronald. *Sacred Sands: The Struggle for Community in the Indiana Dunes.* Middletown, Conn.: Wesleyan University Press. 1983.

Gray, Ralph D. *Public Ports For Indiana: A History of the Indiana Port Commission.* Indianapolis: Indiana Historical Bureau. 1998.

Hoppe, David. "Child of the Northwest Wind: Alice Gray and `Diana of the Dunes.'" *Traces of Indiana and Midwestern History,* (Spring 1997).

Jackson, Michael. *Moonwalk.* New York: Doubleday. 1988.

Lane, James B. *City of the Century: A History of Gary, Indiana.* Bloomington: Indiana University Press. 1978.

McPherson, Alan. *Nature Walks in Northern Indiana.* Indianapolis: Hoosier Chapter/Sierra Club, 1996.

Miller, Donald L. *City of the Century: The Epic of Chicago and the Making of American.* New York: Simon & Schuster. 1996.

Moore, Powell A. *The Calumet Region: Indiana's Last Frontier.* Indianapolis: Indiana Historical Bureau. 1959.

Shepherd, Jean. *In God We Trust, All Others Pay Cash.* Garden City, New York: Dolphin Books. 1972.

Smith, Polly and Dennis Varney, eds. *Times Capsule.* Munster, Ind.: Northwest Indiana Newspapers, 1999.

Strietelmeier, John. *Valparaiso's First Century: A Centennial History of Valparaiso University.* Valparaiso, Ind.: Valparaiso University. 1959.

Taylor, Robert M., Jr. and Connie A. McBirney. *Peopling Indiana: The Ethnic Experience.* Indianapolis: Indiana Historical Society. 1996

Thomas, Phyllis. *Indiana Off the Beaten Path.* Old Saybrook, Conn.: Globe Pequot Press, Inc. 1995.

Vass, George. *George Halas and the Chicago Bears.* Chicago: Henry Regnery Co. 1971.

INDEX

Italicized page numbers indicate photos.

49er Drive-In Theatre, 199

Aberdeen Brewing Co., 203
Acting Theatre of Michigan City, 279
Ahlgrim, Fred, 28
alcoholic beverages, 305
Amtrak, 303
Anderson's Orchard & Vineyards, 195–196
Antique Junction Mall, 211
Antique Market, The, 214
Antique Shoppe, 209
antiques, 207–216
Antiques 102, 207–208
Aquatorium, The, 75
area codes, 305
Armour Bros., 48
Art Barn, 196–197

Back Road Brewery, 20
Bailly Homestead and Chellberg Farmhouse, 252–253
Barker, John H., 30–31
Barker Mansion, 30–31
Bartlett Frederick and Robert, 163–164
Baxter, Anne, 27
beaches, 256–259, 263–268. *See also* names of individual beaches
Beachwood Golf Course, 235
Beacon Hills Country Club, 235
Beaver Lake Ditch, 147
Bettenhausen Memorial, Tony, 143
Beverly Shores, *1*, 33, 163–166, 169, 207

Beverly Shores Depot Museum and Gallery, 165–166
Biedron, Fred P. and Fred W., 100–101
Bieker Woods, 135–136
Bistro 157, 202
Black, David, 96
Blank Center for the Arts, John G., 31
Blue Chip Casino, 220, 225–227
Blue Herron Inn, 22
Blue Top Drive-In, 112
Bluegrass Festival, 55
Blues Fest, 81
Blues, Jazz, and Arts on the Ridge, 138
boating, 217–221
Bramletts Pond, 55
Brickie Bowl, 118
Bright Spot Diner, 120
Brassie Golf Club, 235–236
Briar Leaf Golf Club, 236
Buckley Homestead, 123–124
Buell Memorial Visitor Center, Dorothy, 250–*252*
Buffington Harbor, 230–233, 268
Burns, Randall W., 181–182

Cady Marsh, 133
Cafe Fondue, 131
Café 444, 84
Café Elise, 139
Café L'Amour, 21
Café Venezia, 131–132
Calumet Bakery, 153
Calumet Golf Course, 236
Calumet Region, The, 63, 156, 193
Calumet Trail, 262–263

camping, 305
Canadian National railroad, 89
Capone, Al, 23
Carmelite Monastery Shrines, 135
Carnegie, Andrew, 19, 40, 56, 65, 155, 174
Carol's Antique Mall & Howard's Militaria, 210
Carol's Antiques, 208
Carriage House, 213
Casa Blanca, 68
casinos, 225–233
Cedar Creek Golf Center, 236
Cedar Lake, *46*, 47–50
Cedar Lake Golf Course, 237
Center for the Visual and Performing Arts, 128, 134
Central Avenue Beach, 258
Chanute, Octave, 18, 272–273
Chapel of the Resurrection, *190*, 193
charter services (boats), 221
Chesterton, 167–172, 185, 207–209, 254, 291
Chesterton Art Fair, 170
Chesterton Tribune, 271, 291
Chicago Sun–Times, 107, 292
Chicago Tribune, 140, 292–293
Christmas Open Houses, 178
Christmas trees, 223–224
Civil War Memorial (Lowell), *122*
Clarkson, John M., 29
Coachman Antique Mall, 212
Cobe Cup, 55
Cochran, J.C., 54
Colfax, Harriet, 29–30
Col. Murray Memorial Kite Festival, 201
Columbia yacht race, 27
Community Showcase Theatre, 279
Community Theatre Guild, 280
Community Veterans Memorial, 136–137
Corn Roast, 144
Corner Cafe, 93

Corner Cupboard, 212
Cornerstone Art Center, 155
Countryside Museum, 183
Course at Aberdeen, The, 237
Cowles Bog, 255
Crawfordsville, 25
Creekside Golf Course and Training Center, 237–238
Creekwood Inn, 34
Cressmoor Country Club, 238
Crown Point, 45, 51–58, 67, 209, 223, 224
Crown Point Community Library, 56
Crown Point Motor Speedway, 57

Deep River, 115
Deep River Grinders, *114*, 117–118
Deep River Park, *114*, 116–117
Deep River Waterpark, 129–130
Detroit, MI, 191
Devil's Slide, 263
Diana of the Dunes, 270–272
Dillinger, John, 44, 54–55, 66–67, 123
Dillinger Museum, John, 44
Dimitri's Cake and Steak, 157
Door Prairie Auto Museum, 18
Douglas Center for Environmental Education, Paul H., 253–254
Douglas, Paul H., 250, 253
Duck Creek Golf Club, 238
Duncan, Dennis R. Jr., 269
Dune Acres, 257
Dune Antiques & Interiors, 207
Dune Ridge Trail, 257
Dune Ridge Winery, 185–186
Duneland Beach, 264
Duneland Woodcarving Show, 201
dunes. *See* lakeshore
Dunes Summer Theatre, 280
Dunewood Campground, 254
Dunn's Bridge, 14, *176*, 177–178
Dyer, 59–61, 303
Dyer Historical Society Museum, 60–61

Earl, George, 115
East Chicago, 62, 63–69, 218–219, 227
East Chicago Public Library, viii, 66, 67
East Chicago Room, viii, 66
Edison Homes, Thomas, 77–78
Egolf Christmas Trees, 223
El Ranchero, 69
El Taco Real, 105
Elgin, Joliet & Eastern railroad (EJ&E), 89
Elston, Major Issac C., 25
Elzinga Farm Market, 144
Environmental Learning Center and Camp Good Fellow, 254
Estate Liquidators, 208
Experimental Highway, 60

Fall Fest, 111
Fancher Lake, 45
Felicia's, 213
Ferns at Creekwood Inn, The, 34–35
Festival of Lights, 28
Festival Park, 119
Festival Players Guild, 278, 280–281
Firefighter Memorial, 100–101
First National Bank Building
East Chicago, 66–67
LaPorte, 21
Fisher, Carl, 60
fishing, 305–306
Footlight Players, 281
Forest Park, 198
Golf Course, 238
Frank Lloyd Wright Homes, 75–78
Friends of the Indiana Dunes, 251
Front Porch Music, 200

Galveston Steakhouse, 34
gaming, 225–233
Gary, 53, 70, 71–87, 181, 230–233, 249, 253, 266, 268, 272, 283, 284, 297–298

City Hall, 70
Gary Air Show, 72, 79, 80–81
Gary, Elbert, 70, 71
Gary Southshore RailCats, 73–74
Gary Steelheads, 72–73
Gary/Chicago Airport, 297–298
Genesius Guild, 281
Genesis Convention Center, 72–73, 308
Gerber, Arthur, 165
Gibson Woods Nature Preserve, 98
Giovanni's, 140
golf courses, 235–245. See also names of individual courses
Goods, The, 212
Grand Kankakee Marsh County Park, 15, 174
Grand Trunk Railroad, 89, 91
Gray, Alice. See Diana of the Dunes
Great Lakes, 29
Great Lakes Museum of Military History, 32
Griffith, 88, 89–93, 210
Griffith Golf Center, 239
Griffith Historical Park and Depot Museum, 91–92
Griffith Historical Society, 89, 91
Griffith Railroad Fair, 92
Gunness, Belle, 19, 20
Guse Tree Farm, 223

Hack, John, 149, 150
Halas, George, 96
Halsted, Melvin A., 123
Hammond, vii, 43, 94, 95–107, 151, 154, 177, 217–218, 228, 265, 277, 281–282, 284, 303
City Hall, 94
Hammond Community Theatre, 281–282
Hammond, George, 95
Hammond Marina, 95, 217–218, 265
Hammond Public Library, 102–103
Hammond Rotunda, 96

Harrah's Casino, 218, 227–228
Hart, Aaron & Martha, 59, 143
Hart Ditch, 59
Haskell & Barker Railroad Car Co., 30
Hatcher, Richard G., 76
Haunted Trail, 21
Hawkeye's Restaurant, 125
Hebron, 15, 173–175, 210
Hebron Historical Society, 174–175
Hebron Public Library, 174–175
Heritage Galleries, 209
Heron Rookery, 39
Hesston Steam and Power Show, 17
Hesston Steam Museum, 17–18
Hessville Historical Society, 98–99
Heston Bar, 21–22
Highland, 59, 109–113, 234, 275, 282
Highland Grove, 275
Highland Historical Society, 111
Highland Performing Arts Group, 282
Highway of Flags, 109
hiking, 261–263
Historical Society of Porter County, 194
Hobart, 114, 115–121, 211
Hobart Historical Society Museum, 118
Hog Creek, 37
Hohman, Ernest & Caroline, 95
Holley, Lillian, 54
Hometown Festival Days, 57
Hoosier Bat Co., 197
Hoosier Chapter of the Sierra Club, 251
Hoosier Prairie Nature Preserve, 90
Hoosier Slide, 25
Hoosier Theatre, 153–154
horse racing, 233
Horseshoe Casino, 95, 217, 228–230
Hot or Not, 183–184
House of Kobe, 144–145

Iannelli, Alfonso, 94
Ice Carving Competition, 139

Illiana Motor Speedway, 143–144
Imagination Glen Park, 182–183
Indian Oak Resort, 169–170
Indian Ridge, 239
Indiana Aviation Museum, 196
Indiana Dunes National
   Lakeshore, 1, 39–40, 90, 161, 163,
   165, 179, 185, 250–259
Indiana Dunes State Park, 161, 170,
   256, 257, 260–263, 270
Indiana Harbor, 63
Indiana Historical Society, 180
Indiana University Northwest, 78–80
Inland Steel, 218, 266
International Culture Festival, 103
International Friendship Gardens, 33
In-Water Sail and Power Boat Show,
   33–34
It's a Wonderful Life Antique Mall,
   212

J. Ginger's American Grille, 128
Jackson, Michael, 84–85
Jackson Park (Chicago), 25
Jalapeños, 145
J.D. Marshall, The, 270
Jerose Park, 218, 266
Just Little Things, 216

Kankakee Marsh, 13, 147
Kankakee River, 14, 147–148, 174,
   177–178
Kankakee State Fish and Wildlife
   Area, 14
Kasas, Ernest, 65–66
Kathy's Antiques, 208
Keith's, 158
Kemil Beach, 256, 257–258, 259
Kingsbury, 13–15
Kingsbury State Fish and Wildlife
   Area, 13–14
Klen, Joseph, vii
Knotts, Mayor Thomas E., 86–87
Kouts, 14, 176, 177–178, 211

Kouts Antique Market, 211

Labor Day Parade (Lowell), 125
Lake Central Theatre Guild, 282
Lake Chubb, 169
Lake County, vii, 2, 41–158, 42, 207
Lake County Convention and Visitors
  Bureau, 43–45, 44, 67
Lake County Fair, 45, 55
Lake County Government Center, 52
Lake County Historical Museum, 53
Lake County Jail (Old Jail), 54–55, 67
Lake County Vietnam Veterans
  Memorial, 56
Lake Etta County Park, 78
Lake George, 115
Lake Hills Golf Course and Country
  Club, 239
Lake Magazine, 293
Lake Michigan, 11
Lake Michigan Winery, 154
Lake of the Red Cedars Museum,
  47–48
Lake Region Christian Assembly, 48
Lake Station, 51
Lake Street Beach, 266
Lake Street Gallery, 80
Lake View Beach, 258
Lakefront Art Festival, 27
Lakefront Park, 217–218,
  Beach, 264–265
lakeshore, 246, 247–273
LaPorte, 13, 17–22, 211–212, 224,
  273, 276, 282, 291, 293
LaPorte County, vii, 9, 10, 11–40, 207
LaPorte County Antique Show, 20
LaPorte County Convention and
  Visitors Bureau, 11–12
LaPorte County Courthouse, 19
LaPorte County Fairgrounds, 12
LaPorte County Historical Museum,
  19
LaPorte County Historical Steam
  Society, 17

LaPorte County Public Library, 19
LaPorte Herald–Argus, 291
LaPorte Little Theatre Guild, 278, 282
LaSalle Fish & Wildlife Area, 15, 147–
  148
Lassen, Christopher, 48
Lembke, Charles, 194
Lemon Lake, 49
Leroy, 55
Lighthouse Place Premium Outlets,
  275
Lincoln Center, 111
Lincoln Highway, 60
Little Calumet River, 59, 133, 219
Little Red Schoolhouse, 98–99
Little Symphony Theater, 33
Liverpool, 51
Long Beach, 23–24, 264
Long Beach Town Hall, 24
Long Lake, 257
Lost Marsh, 240
Louis' Bon Appetit, 58
Lowell, 55, 122, 123–126, 213
Lubeznik Center for the Arts, The
  Jack & Shirley, 31–32
Lubeznik, Jack and Shirley, 31–32
Lucrezia Cafe, 171
Ludwig's Club Café, 105–106
Luers Christmas Tree Farm, 223–224
Luhr County Park and Nature Center,
  20
Lustron Home, 169
Ly-co-ki-we Trail, 255

MacArthur Golf Course, 240
Maher, George, 75
Majestic Star, 230–231
Malden, Karl, 76
Manhattan Project, 151–152
Maple Lane Mall, 276
Marian Theatre Guild, 283
marinas, 217–220. *See also* names of
  individual marinas
Mark, Clayton, Sr., 62, 64

Marktown, viii, 4, *62*, 64–65
Marquette Mall, 276
Marquette Park, 74, 80
  Aquatorium & Aviation Museum,
  75
  Beach, 266
Marquette Yacht Club, 219
McGee's Restaurant and Speakeasy,
  104–105
McPhearson, Alan, 174, 251
Memorial Opera House, 193–194
Memorial Theatre Company, 283
Merrillville, 127–132, 144, 213, 233,
  276, 284, 290–291, 294
Merrillville/Ross Township
  Historical Museum, 129
Mexican Independence Celebration,
  68
Meyer, Joseph Ernest, 59–60
Meyer's Castle, 59–60, 61
Michiana Shores, 280
Michigan Central Railroad, 25, 185
Michigan City, 25–35, 214, 220, 225,
  247, 249, 268, 269, 275, 276, 279,
  280, 281, 291, 303
  Marina, *26*
Michigan City Center for the Arts, 32
Michigan City Historical Society, 30
Michigan City Lighthouse, *12*, 259
Michigan City Municipal Golf Center,
  240
Michigan City News–Dispatch, 291
Midnight Parade (Porter), 187
Midway Airport, 299
Midwest Waterfowl Expo, 57
Miller Bakery Café, 81–82
Miller Beach, 272
Miller Beach Café, 83
Miller Pizza Station, 82–83
Miller Woods, 253
Miner–Dunn Restaurant, 112
Mink Lake Golf Course, 241
Mixsawbah Fish Hatchery, 14
Monastery Golf Course, 241

Moore, Powell A., 63, 193
Moratz, Paul, 155
Morning Bishop Theatre, 283
Mount Baldy, 189, 258, 259
Mount Tom, 261, 262
Mozoliauskas, Ramojus "Ray", 101
Munster, 59, 133–141, 285, 290–291
Munster, Eldert, 133
Munster Historical Society, 135
Murad, Ferid, 152
Muskegon, The, 269
Myers, Paul, 64

National Park (Indiana Dunes),
  250–259
Nature Walks in Northern Indiana, 174,
  251
Naval Armory Building, 27
Nelson, Jean, 167–168
newspapers, 289–293. *See also* names
  of individual newspapers
Newton County, 147
Neiman Mural, LeRoy, 101–102
Northwest Indiana Arts Association,
  134
Northwest Indiana Festival of Lights,
  130
Northwest Indiana Pipes and Drums,
  125
Northwest Indiana Storytelling
  Festival, 170–171
Northwest Indiana Symphony, 128,
  134

Oak Knoll Golf Course, 241
Oak Ridge Prairie, *88*, 90–91
Ogden Dunes, 179–180, 219
Ogden, Francis A., 179
O'Hare International Airport, 299
Old County Jail Museum, 194–195
Old Farmhouse Antiques, 210
Old Lake County Courthouse, 52–54,
  53

Old Lighthouse Museum, 29–30, 220, 270
Old Town Hall, 141
Old Town Square, 124
Old Town Square Antique Mall, 209
O'Malley, Walter Patrick, 67
Ores, Holley, 137

Palmira Golf Course, 241–242
Panhandle Depot, 173
Park Full of Art, 92
parks. *See* names of individual parks
Pastrick Library, 65–66
Pastrick Marina, 218–219, 266
Pastrick, Mayor Robert, 65, 218
Perkins, Frederick, 30
Pheasant Valley Country Club, 242
Phil Smidt's, 104, 217
Pierogi Festival, 156–*157*
Pine Lake, 22
Pines Peak Family Ski Area, 197–198
Pinhook Bog, 39–40
Popcorn Festival, 200–201
Pork Fest, 178
Port of Indiana–Burns Harbor, 181–*182*, 249
Portage, 181–184, 219, 283
Portage Community Historical Society, 183
Portage Community Theatre, 283
Portage Public Marina, 219
Porter, 185–188, 214
Porter Beach, 256
Porter, Commander David, 161, 191, 195
Porter County, vii, 14, 159–204, *160*, 207, 249
Porter County Convention, Recreation, and Visitor Commission, 161, 164
Porter County Fair, 161
Porter County Home & Garden Show, 201–202
Post–Tribune, viii, 289–290

Potawatomi, 47, 115, 127, 161, 191
Prohibition, 47, 125
Public Works Arts Project, 65–66
Puerto Rican Festival, 67–68
Pullman, George, 30
Pullman neighborhood, 64
Pullman–Standard, 30, 91
Pumps on 12, 189
Purdue Theatre Company, 284
Purdue University, 31, 39
   Calumet, 94, 99–100

radio stations, 294–296
Radisson Hotel at Star Plaza, 128
Rainboutique, 214
recreation, 205–286
Red Rooster Restaurant, 121
Redenbacher, Orville, 199, 200
Reed, James, 196
Restaurante Don Quijote, 202
Retailleau, Louis, 58
Ridgewood Arts Foundation, 134
Roadhouse Antiques and Collectibles, 215
Robbinhurst Golf Club, 242
Robertsdale, 97, 154
Robinson, Glen "Big Dog", 76
Robinson, Solon, 51
Rockefeller, John D., 156
Rodizio's, 61
Rogers–Lakewood Park, 198
Rosebud Antique Gallery, 215
Roskoe's, 22
Ross, Lt. Col. Jerry, 54
Ross Music Theatre, 284
Rugh, Billy, 86–87
Russ & Barb's Antiques, 208

Salt Creek, 182
Sampler Square Antiques, 210
Samuelson, Paul A., 76
Sandburg, Carl, 1, 247
Sandy Pines Golf Course, 243
Save the Dunes Council, Inc., 251

Scarecrow Festival, 37
Scherer, Nicholas, 143
Schererville, 143–146
Schererville Lounge, 145
Scherwood Golf Course, 243
Schmal, Richard, 123
Schneider, 147–148
Scholl, Dr., 47
Schoolhouse Shop & Antiques, 208
Schoop's, 141
Scuba Tank, The, 268–269
Serb Fest, 120
Shaw, Howard Van Doren, 64
Shedd, John G., 48
Shepherd, Jean, 106–107
shipwrecks, 268–270
    J.D. Marshall, The, 270
    Muskegon, The, 269
shopping malls, 275–277
Skystone N' Silver, 119
sledding, 198
Soldiers Memorial Park, 18–19
South Bend, 11, 227, 292
South Bend Tribune, 292
South Gleason Golf Course, 243
South Shore Golf Course, 244
South Shore Line, 165, 258, 302–303
Southard's Christmas Tree Farm, 224
Splash Down Dunes, 186–187
SS. Constantine and Helen Greek
    Orthodox Cathedral, 130
St. James the Less Catholic Church,
    110
St. John, 149–150, 215, 282
St. John Evangelist Church, 149, *150*
St. Joseph County, 11
St. Sava Serbian Orthodox Church,
    120
Stagecoach Inn Museum, 173–174
Standard Oil, 151, 152, 155, 156
Standard Steel and Iron Co., 63
Star Plaza Theatre, 127–128, 284
State Park and Beach (Indiana
    Dunes), 260–263

Station House Pottery, 170
Statue in a Field, 149–150
Stauffer brothers, 33
Steeltown Records, 85
Stocking Bale Antiques, 214
Stone Lake, 18
Stoney Run Park, 55–56
Strongbow Inn, 203
Substation No. 9, 100
Summerfest (Cedar Lake), 50
Summertree Golf Club, 244
Sunset Hill Farm County Park,
    198–199

Tamarack Lake, 14
Tandoor, 146
Teatro Del Sol, 285
Teibel's, 145–146
television
    WYIN–TV, 294
theater, 279–286. *See also* names of
    individual theaters
Theater at the Center, 285
Theater of Nations, 33
Theatre Northwest, 284–285
Thomas Centennial Park, 167
Thomas Edison Homes, 77–78
Three Creeks Monument, 124
Three Floyds Brewery, 136
time zones, 306–307
Times, The, viii, 290–291
Tobe's Restaurant, 50
Tom's Old Country Barn, 215
Town Club, The, 113
Town of Pines, 189, 215
Town Theater, The, 110
Traces: The Magazine of Indiana History,
    269, 271
Trackside OTB, 233
traffic laws, 307
Trail Creek, 25
    Marina, 220, *226–227*
transportation
    air, 297–299

transportation (*continued*)
  bus, 304
  interstates and highways, 299–301
  rail, 302–303
Treasure House Antiques, 211
Treasurer Hunt Mall, The, 213
Trump Casino, 230, 232–233
Turkey Creek Golf Course, 244
Twiggy (the water-skiing squirrel), 34

University of Notre Dame, 11
U.S. Steel, 70, 71
U.S. Steel Yard, 73–74

Valparaiso, 162, 191–204, 215, 280, 283, 285–286
Valparaiso Antique Mall, 215
Valparaiso Moraine, 191, 198
Valparaiso University, 161, *190*, 191, 192–193
  Chapel of the Resurrection, *190*, 193
  Theater (VU Center for the Arts), 285–286
Valpo Velvet Shoppe, 204
Vanzant's Ribs on the Run, 83–84
Vault, The, 213
Vee-Jay Records, 72

Wagner's Ribs, 187–188
Wanatah, 37, 223
Warren, Frank, 33
Washintgon Park and Beach, 27–28, 268
Washington Park Marina, 220
Washington Park Zoo, 28–29, 220
Wells Street Beach, 268
West Beach, 256
Westchester Public Library, 167
Westfield Shoppingtown Southlake, 115, 276–277
Westville, 39–40
Westville–New Durham Township Library, 40

Whihala Beach, 265
Whistle Stop Days festival, 17
White Hawk Country Club, 244–245
White's Tree Farm, 224
Whiting, 97, 151–158, 216, 265, 279, 283
  City Hall, 152–153
Whiting Community Center, 155
Whiting, Herbert L. "Pop", 151
Whiting Lakefront Park, 151, 152, 265–266
Wicker Memorial Park, 110
Wicker Park Memorial Golf Course, *234*, 245
Wingfield's, 171–172
Winterbotham Monument, 27
Wisecracker's Comedy Club, 128
Wizard of Oz Fantasy Parade and Festival, 167–169
Wolf Lake Park, 95, 97–98
Wolfe Musical Instruments and Antiques, 212
Wood, John, (Wood's Mill), 116
Woodmar Mall, 277
Worker's Sculpture, *137*
Works Progress Administration, 28
World's Fair (Chicago 1933), 33
  Homes, 164, 169
  Columbian Expo 1893, 177–178
Wright, Frank Lloyd, 23, 27
  Homes, 75–78
Wright, John Lloyd, 23–24

Yellow Brick Road Shop, 168–169
Yesterday's Treasures, 209

Zale, Tony, 76
Zuni's Restaurant and Lounge, 126

Lake Claremont Press is . . .

• • • • • • • • • • • • • • • •

Midwest Travel

Ticket to Everywhere: The Best of *Detours* Travel Column
by Dave Hoekstra, foreword by Studs Terkel
Chicago Sun-Times columnist Dave Hoekstra has compiled over 50 of his best
road trip explorations into the offbeat people, places, events, and history of
the greater Midwest and Route 66 areas. Whether covering the hair museum
in Independence, Missouri, Wisconsin's "Magical Mustard Tour," the Ohio
Tiki bar on the National Register of Historic Places, Detroit's polka-dot
house, or Bloomington, Illinois—home to beer nuts, Hoekstra's writings will
delight readers and instruct tourists.
1-893121-11-9, November 2000, softcover, photos, maps, $15.95

A Native's Guide to Chicago, 4th Edition
by Lake Claremont Press
Venture into the nooks and crannies of everyday Chicago with this comprehensive budget guide that picks up where other guidebooks leave off. Over
400 pages of free, inexpensive, and unusual things to do in the Windy City
make this the perfect resource for tourists, business travelers, visiting
suburbanites, and resident Chicagoans. Called the "best guidebook for
locals" in *New City*'s 1999 "Best of Chicago" issue!
1-893121-23-2, September 2003, softcover, 450 pages, photos, maps, $15.95

Ghosts and Graveyards

Chicago Haunts: Ghostlore of the Windy City
by Ursula Bielski
From ruthless gangsters to restless mail order kings, from the Fort Dearborn
Massacre to the St. Valentine's Day Massacre, the phantom remains of the
passionate people and volatile events of Chicago history have made the
Second City second to none in the annals of American ghostlore. Bielski
captures over 160 years of this haunted history with her distinctive blend of
lively storytelling, in-depth historical research, exclusive interviews, and
insights from parapsychology. Called "a masterpiece of the genre," "a
must-read," and "an absolutely first-rate-book" by reviewers, *Chicago Haunts*
continues to earn the praise of critics and readers alike.
0-9642426-7-2, October 1998, softcover, 277 pages, 29 photos, $15

More Chicago Haunts: Scenes from Myth and Memory
by Ursula Bielski
1-893121-04-6, October 2000, 312 pages, 50 photos, $15
50 new stories! Step back inside "the biggest ghost town in America."

Haunted Michigan: Recent Encounters with Active Spirits
by Rev. Gerald S. Hunter
Within these pages you will not find ancient ghost stories or legendary accounts of spooky events of long ago. Instead, Rev. Hunter shares his investigations into modern ghost stories—active hauntings that continue to this day. Wherever you may dwell, these tales of Michigan's ethereal residents are sure to make you think about the possibility, as Hunter suggests, that we are not always alone within the confines of our happy homes.
1-893121-10-0, October 2000, 207 pages, 20 photos, $12.95

More Haunted Michigan:
New Encounters with Ghosts of the Great Lakes State
by Rev. Gerald S. Hunter
1-893121-29-1, February 2003, 260 pages, 22 photos, $15

Regional History

Hollywood on Lake Michigan: 100 Years of Chicago and the Movies
by Arnie Bernstein, foreword by *Soul Food* director George Tillman, Jr.
This engaging history and street guide finally gives Chicago and Chicagoans due credit for their prominent role in moviemaking history, from the silent era to the present. With trivia, special articles, historic and contemporary photos, film profiles, anecdotes, and exclusive interviews with dozens of personalities, including Studs Terkel, Roger Ebert, Gene Siskel, Dennis Franz, Harold Ramis, Joe Mantegna, Bill Kurtis, Irma Hall, and Tim Kazurinsky. **Winner of an American Regional History Publishing Award: 1st Place—Midwest!**
0-9642426-2-1, December 1998, softcover, 364 pages, 80 photos, $15

Chicago's Midway Airport: The First Seventy-Five Years
By Christopher Lynch
Midway was Chicago's first official airport, and for decades it was the busiest airport in the nation, and then the world. Lynch captures the spirit of adventure of the dawn of flight, combining narrative, essays, and oral histories to tell the engrossing tale of Midway Airport and the evolution of aviation right along with it. Recommended by the *Chicago Sun-Times*.
1-893121-18-6, January 2003, softcover, 10" x 8", 201 pages, 205 historic and contemporary photos, $19.95

Order Form

A Native's Guide to Northwest Indiana	_____ @ $15.00 =	_____
Ticket to Everywhere	_____ @ $15.95 =	_____
A Native's Guide to Chicago	_____ @ $15.95 =	_____
Hollywood on Lake Michigan	_____ @ $15.00 =	_____
Chicago's Midway Airport	_____ @ $19.95 =	_____
Chicago Haunts	_____ @ $15.00 =	_____
More Chicago Haunts	_____ @ $15.00 =	_____
Graveyards of Chicago	_____ @ $15.00 =	_____
Haunted Michigan	_____ @ $12.95 =	_____
More Haunted Michigan	_____ @ $15.00 =	_____
_____	_____ @ $_____ =	_____
_____	_____ @ $_____ =	_____

Subtotal: _____

Less Discount: _____

New Subtotal: _____

8.75% Sales Tax for Illinois Residents: _____

Shipping: _____

TOTAL: _____

Name_____

Address_____

City_____State_____Zip_____

Please enclose check, money order, or credit card information.

Visa/Mastercard#_____Exp. _____

Signature_____

Discounts when you order multiple copies!
2 books—10% off total, 3–4 books—20% off,
5–9 books—25% off, 10+ books—40% off

—Low shipping fees—
$2.50 for the first book and $.50 for each additional book, with a maximum charge of $8.

Order by mail, phone, fax, or e-mail.
All of our books have a no-hassle, 100% money back guarantee.

LAKE CLAREMONT PRESS

4650 N. Rockwell St.
Chicago, IL 60625
773/583-7800
773/583-7877 (fax)
lcp@lakeclaremont.com
www.lakeclaremont.com

 **Mark Skertic** was born in East Chicago, Indiana, and raised in Hammond. A reporter for the *Chicago Tribune*, formerly with the *Chicago Sun-Times*, he makes his home in Northwest Indiana. His roots in the area run deep. His late grandfather, Joseph Klen, was a longtime area politician, serving two terms as mayor of Hammond. In his free time, Mark and his wife and two daughters enjoy exploring the dunes, hiking the trails, and spending time on the beach.